THE PREACHER LADY'S COOKBOOK FOR THE HUNGRY HEART

500 Recipes, Scriptures and Prayers
From People of Faith for the Family of God

A pastor's collection from decades
of church suppers, picnics and potlucks

Susan Spencer-Smith, M.S., M.Div., D.Min.

HOOPIE GIRL PRESS

HOOPIE GIRL PRESS, INC.
Westerville, Ohio 43081
Weirton, West Virginia 26062
www.askpastorannie.com

Copyright © 2010 Susan Spencer-Smith

All rights reserved. Permission is granted to copy or repriint portions for any noncommercial use, although they may not be posted online without permission.

Cover art by Brion Sausser at Book Creatives

ISBN-13   978-0-692-00835-5
ISBN-10   0-692-00835-7

All cooking temperatures herein are stated in degrees Fahrenheit.

Ingredients, in many cases, are approximated herein to reflect the recessionary downsizing of packaging in the United States.

THANKS

I thank our God for churches, where the Bread of Life is celebrated and the fruit of the earth served.

I remember fondly the congregations of the body of Christ with whom I have been privileged to journey for a season, particularly the cooks—men and women—who turned groceries and recipes into ministries.

I thank these friends and family members for personal contributions to *The Preacher Lady's Cookbook for the Hungry Heart:* Bryan Beamer, Mary Louise Danek, Becky Jarvi, Kate Jarvi, Rhonda Long, Martha Matteson, Barbara Parr, Kathern Taylor and Roberta Taylor.

I honor the memory of these magnificent cooks, whose good culinary deeds have surely gone before them: Mary Jo Scovill Beamer, Mari Egerdahl, Fay Smith Kearns, Mary Susan Spencer Kearns, Edith Stealey Smith and Annie Ido Stealey.

I appreciate the professional courtesies of literary agent Christine Witthohn, who graciously helped me see the path forward.

Most especially, I thank my husband, Grant Beamer, and my sister, Roberta Taylor, whose unfailing optimism, material support, technical skill and confidence in me made it impossible to say, "Impossible."

With peace and joy,

Susan Spencer-Smith

Summer 2010

ABBREVIATIONS

Eleven translations of God's Holy Word, designated by the following abbreviations, are quoted herein:

Amplified Bible—AB

King James Version—KJV

Living Bible—LB

New American Standard—NASB

New English Bible—NEB

New International Version—NIV

New Jerusalem Bible—NJB

New Revised Standard Version—NRSV

Tanakh The Holy Scriptures (Jewish Publication Society)—JPS

The Message—TM

Today's English Version—TEV

CONTENTS

Appetizers and Dips	1
Beef and Pork	17
Beverages	39
Bread, Rolls and Biscuits	53
Brownies and Bars	73
Cakes and Frostings	97
Candy	125
Casseroles	145
Chicken and Turkey	165
Cookies	185
Eggs and Quiches	207
Fish and Seafood	227
Frozen Treats and Toppings	249
Pasta and Rice	265
Pies, Cobblers and Dumplings	287
Potatoes	313
Salads and Dressings	333
Soups and Stews	351
Sweet Breads and Muffins	371
Veggies and Beans	391
Index	413

COMING WINTER 2010

Death in the Parsonage

A Christian mystery novel by
Susan Spencer-Smith

A parsonage with a secret and a town that covered it up await Pastor Annie Ido Scovill in Biddlebourne, West Virginia.

Order online at Amazon.com

APPETIZERS AND DIPS

In the beginning God created the heaven and the earth.
Genesis 1:1 KJV

ABC Dip
⅓ c. almonds, coarsely chopped
3 strips bacon, fried crisp, drained, crumbled
1½ c. sharp cheddar cheese, shredded
1 T. plus 1 tsp. finely grated onion
¾ c. zesty creamy salad dressing
Paprika

In small bowl combine almonds, bacon, cheese, onion and salad dressing. Stir lightly. Turn into serving bowl or plate. Sprinkle with paprika. Refrigerate unused portion in airtight container.

O God, let me start everything with you. Amen.

And the spirit of God moved upon the face of the waters.
Genesis 1:2b KJV

Bagelettes
8 oz. cream cheese, softened
½ c. mayonnaise
5 strips bacon, crumbled (optional)
1 T. chopped green onion
½ tsp. dill weed
⅛ tsp. pepper
12 mini-bagels, separated and toasted
1 c. chopped pecans

In medium bowl combine cream cheese, mayonnaise, bacon, onion, dill weed and pepper. Mix until creamy. Spread mixture on bagels. Top with chopped pecans. Refrigerate until serving.

The seven seas flow with your spirit, O Great I Am. Amen.

~~~

And God said, "Let there be light"; and there was light.
Genesis 1:3 KJV

Barbecued Mini Franks
4 lbs. miniature hot dogs
1 c. finely chopped onion
1 c. ketchup
⅓ c. Worcestershire sauce
¼ c. sugar
¼ c. cider vinegar
4 tsp. prepared mustard
1 tsp. pepper

Preheat oven to 350 degrees. Place hot dogs in one layer in two large pans. In bowl mix remaining ingredients. Pour mixture on hot dogs. Bake 25 minutes. Serve warm on toothpicks.

God of the Universe, lead me into your light today. Amen.

And God said, "Let the earth bring forth grass, the herb yielding seed, and the fruit tree yielding fruit after his kind, whose seed is in itself, upon the earth"; and it was so.

Genesis 1:11 KJV

Cheese and Spinach Puffs

10 oz. frozen chopped spinach
½ c. chopped onion
2 eggs, beaten
½ c. grated Parmesan cheese
½ c. shredded cheese of choice
½ c. blue cheese salad dressing
¼ c. margarine, melted
⅛ tsp. garlic powder
1 pkg. corn muffin mix, about 8 oz.

In saucepan combine spinach and onion. Cook according to spinach package directions. Drain well. In large bowl combine eggs, cheeses, salad dressing, margarine and garlic powder. Combine spinach mixture, egg mixture and muffin mix. Mix well. Cover and chill. Shape dough into about 60 one-inch balls. Chill or freeze until serving time.

To serve, preheat oven to 350 degrees. Coat baking sheet. Place chilled or frozen puffs on prepared sheet. Bake until brown, 10 to 12 minutes for chilled puffs and 12 to 15 minutes for frozen puffs. Serve warm.

Thank you, God of Delight, for the smell of grass. Amen.

And God said, "Let the waters bring forth abundantly the moving creature that hath life, and fowl that may fly above the earth in the open firmament of the heaven."

Genesis 1:20 KJV

Cheese Ball
6 oz. cheddar cheese, finely grated
8 oz. cream cheese, softened
2 onion slices, minced
2 T. butter, softened
1 tsp. lemon juice
Dash celery salt
½ tsp. Worcestershire sauce
1 c. chopped pecans

In medium bowl mix cheeses. Add onion, butter, lemon juice, celery salt and Worcestershire sauce. Mix well. Shape into ball and roll in pecans. Chill several hours before serving.

Lord of Abundance, I respect your handiwork. Amen.

~~~

And God blessed the seventh day, and sanctified it; because that in it he had rested from all his work which God created and made.

<div align="right">Genesis 2:3 KJV</div>

Chip Dip
2 c. mayonnaise
1½ c. sour cream
½ tsp. onion salt
½ tsp. garlic salt
1½ tsp. dill weed
1½ tsp. parsley flakes

Mix ingredients well and refrigerate in airtight container. Serve with chips, pretzels, fresh vegetables or baked potatoes.

God Who Understands, teach me to rest, for I am weary. Amen.

Noah was a just man and perfect in his generations, and Noah walked with God. Genesis 6:9b KJV

Girlfriend Friendly Dip
2 cans fat-free refried beans, about 16 oz. each
8 oz. reduced-fat cream cheese
8 oz. light sour cream
1 clove garlic, pressed or finely minced
2 T. Southwest seasoning
12 oz. low-fat Mexican-style shredded cheese
1 jar salsa
1 bag tortilla chips

Preheat oven to 350 degrees. Spread beans in bottom of 12-inch round baking dish. In bowl mix cream cheese, sour cream, garlic and seasoning. Top with shredded cheese. Bake until cheese melts. Remove from oven and top with salsa and chips

Let me understand, Yahweh, the joy of walking with you. Amen.

~~~

Neither will I again smite any more every thing living, as I have done. Genesis 8:21c KJV

Gooey Bean Dip
1 can kidney beans, about 16 oz.
¼ c. butter, melted
¼ tsp. garlic powder
¼ tsp. chili powder or cumin
1 c. shredded cheddar cheese

Drain beans, reserving liquid. In small saucepan mash beans to smooth paste. Add butter. Cook over medium heat about 5 minutes. Stir in garlic powder and chili powder. Add bean liquid to reach dipping consistency. Stir in cheese and heat until melted. Serve warm with corn chips or tortilla chips.

You repent, Holy God, and I must do the same. Amen.

And I will make of thee a great nation, and I will bless thee, and make thy name great; and thou shalt be a blessing.
Genesis 12:2 KJV

Hanky Panky
1 lb. ground beef
1 lb. pork sausage
1 lb. boxed processed cheese, diced
1 tsp. Worcestershire sauce
1 tsp. oregano
½ tsp. garlic salt
½ tsp. salt
Dash pepper
1 loaf party rye bread, sliced

In large skillet brown meat. Drain off fat. Add cheese. Heat and stir until cheese melts. Add Worcestershire sauce, oregano, garlic salt, salt and pepper. Spread on bread slices. Place on baking sheet. Freeze until firm. Place in plastic bags in freezer until ready to use. When ready to use, place on cookie sheet under broiler until cheese bubbles, 3 to 5 minutes.

Use me to bless this world, O God My Help. Amen.

~~~

And Moses said unto the people, "Fear ye not, stand still, and see the salvation of the Lord . . . ."
<div align="right">Genesis 14:13a KJV</div>

Oriental Wings
1½ lbs. drumstick sections of chicken wings, about 16
¼ c. firmly packed light brown sugar
½ tsp. dry mustard
2 T. butter
¼ c. soy sauce

Preheat oven to 350 degrees. Butter 8 by 8-inch baking dish. Place wings in dish. In small bowl combine brown sugar and mustard. Set aside. In small saucepan melt butter over low heat. Add soy sauce and brown sugar mixture. Bring to boil over medium heat, stirring constantly. Pour over wings. Bake 45 minutes, turning once after 25 minutes. Drain briefly on paper towels before serving.

Mighty One, do you mean that you are at work even when I am still? Amen.

~~~

And God said, "Sarah thy wife shall bear thee a son indeed; and thou shalt call his name Isaac; and I will establish my covenant, and with his seed after him."

Genesis 17:19 KJV

Pizza Butter

1 lb. butter, softened
8 oz. shredded mozzarella cheese
6 oz. tomato paste
2 T. oregano
2 tsp. sugar
1 tsp. salt
Garlic salt
Italian or other bread slices

In medium bowl mix butter, cheese, tomato paste, oregano, sugar, salt and garlic salt. Spread on bread. Broil until light brown. Refrigerate unused portion.

Help me to keep my promises, God of Integrity, as reliably as you keep yours. Amen.

"Is anything too hard for the Lord?"

Genesis 18:14a KJV

Pocket Bread with Dried Tomato Topping
1 T. butter
2 c. leeks, thinly sliced, white and pale green parts only
2 c. mushrooms, sliced
¼ c. dried tomatoes packed in olive oil, drained, chopped
4 pita rounds
½ c. grated mozzarella cheese
¼ c. crumbled feta cheese (optional)

Preheat oven to 450 degrees. Lightly coat large baking sheet with olive oil. In large skillet over medium-high heat, saute leeks in butter until soft, about 10 minutes, stirring frequently. Add mushrooms and tomatoes and continue to saute for 10 minutes, stirring frequently. Place pita rounds on prepared baking sheet. Sprinkle half the mozzarella cheese on top. Spoon sauteed vegetables on cheese. Top with remaining mozzarella and feta cheese. Bake until brown and bubbly, about 8 minutes.

Lord Who Abides, my deepest trouble is within your reach. Amen.

~~~

For Sarah conceived, and bare Abraham a son in his old age, at the set time of which God had spoken to him.

Genesis 21:2 KJV

Poor Folks' Caviar
1 large eggplant
1 T. vegetable oil
1 small onion, chopped
1 clove garlic, minced
¼ c. green pepper, chopped
1½ T. lemon juice
½ c. parsley, chopped
⅛ tsp. pepper

Place whole eggplant under broiler. Broil, turning once, until skin turns brown and eggplant is soft to the touch. Cool, cut in half and scoop out pulp. Mash pulp with fork. In small skillet heal vegetable oil and saute onion and garlic. Stir in eggplant. Add green pepper, lemon juice, parsley and pepper. Saute until flavors meld. Serve with crackers.

You are our Wonderful God, full of surprise and mystery, and you make us laugh with joy. Amen.

~~~

"And in thy seed shall all the nations of the earth be blessed; because thou hast obeyed my voice."
<div align="right">Genesis 22:18 KJV</div>

Roberta's Shrimp Dip
16 oz. cream cheese, at room temperature
1 c. sour cream, divided
1 c. cocktail sauce
¾ c. salsa
8 oz. shredded cheddar or Monterey Jack cheese
16 oz. small cooked shrimp, peeled and deveined
1 can sliced black olives, about 3 oz.
Tortilla chips

In mixer bowl combine cream cheese and ½ cup of the sour cream. Beat until smooth. Add cocktail sauce. Blend well. Spread mixture in 9 by 13-inch glass bowl or platter. Spread remaining ½ cup sour cream on top. Spread salsa evenly on top. Sprinkle shredded cheese over all. Arrange shrimp evenly on cheese. Sprinkle olives on top. Serve with tortilla chips. Refrigerate unused portion in airtight container.

God of All Things, you do your most marvelous works when we obey your word. Amen.

Then Isaac sowed in that land, and received in the same year an hundredfold; and the Lord blessed him.

Genesis 26:12 KJV

Sausage Balls

1 lb. ground sausage
1 lb. boxed processed cheese, cut in small chunks
3 c. baking mix
¾ c. water

Preheat oven to 350 degrees. Coat baking sheet. In skillet, fry sausage. Drain and cool. In large bowl combine sausage, cheese, baking mix and water. Mix well. Shape into small balls. Place on prepared baking sheet. Bake 15 minutes or until sausage balls brown.

Redeemer, let me plant a seed for you today. Amen.

~~~

And Jacob was left alone; and there wrestled a man with him until the breaking of the day.

Genesis 32:24 KJV

Spicy Taco Dip

1 c. plain lowfat yogurt
3 T. tomato paste
½ tsp. dry mustard
⅛ to ¼ tsp. chili powder
1 tsp. chopped onion

In small bowl combine yogurt and tomato paste and blend well. Stir in dry mustard, chili powder and onion. Refrigerate at least 2 hours. Serve with chips or fresh vegetables.

Overpower me, Lord God, for I am full of myself. Amen.

And he said, "Thy name shall be called no more Jacob, but Israel: for as a prince hast thou power with God and with men, and hast prevailed." Genesis 32:28 KJV

Spinach Bars

1 c. all-purpose flour
1 tsp. baking powder
1 tsp. salt
2 extra-large eggs
6 T. butter, melted
2 lbs. fresh spinach, cooked, drained, finely chopped
¼ c. finely grated onion
1 lb. Monterey Jack cheese, shredded

Preheat oven to 350 degrees. Lightly coat 10 by 15-inch baking pan with vegetable oil. Onto waxed paper sift flour, baking powder and salt. Set aside. In medium mixer bowl beat eggs lightly at medium speed. Add butter. Beat at medium speed until blended. Add spinach, onion and cheese. Using mixing spoon, fold in flour mixture until evenly distributed. Spoon mixture lightly and evenly into prepared pan. Bake 40 minutes.

Remove from oven and place on wire rack. Cool 5 minutes. Using sharp, thin-bladed knife, cut into 64 bars. Remove bars from pan with small spatula and place briefly on 3 layers of paper towels before transferring to serving plate. Serve immediately.

Please change me, God Who Makes New, into the one you want me to be. Amen.

And Jacob called the name of the place where God spake with him, Bethel. Genesis 35:15 KJV

Spinach Dip
2 scant c. mayonnaise
1 pkg. frozen chopped spinach, slightly thawed, about 10 oz.
½ c. finely chopped onion
½ c. chopped fresh parsley
Salt and pepper

In medium bowl mix all ingredients thoroughly. Chill at least 6 hours. Serve with fresh vegetables or crackers.

God of the Deep Places, your words anchor me. Amen.

~~~

And God sent me before you to preserve you a posterity in the earth, and to save your lives by a great deliverance.
Genesis 45:7 KJV

Stuffed Mushrooms
24 large mushrooms, capped
1 tsp. olive oil
½ c. green onion, diced, white and light green parts
2 cloves garlic, minced
½ (10 oz.) pkg. chopped frozen spinach, cooked and drained
8 oz. fat-free cream cheese, softened
½ c. bacon bits

Preheat oven to 375 degrees. Coat baking sheet. Dice mushroom stems. In small skillet saute stems in olive oil with green onion and garlic until tender. In medium bowl combine spinach, cream cheese and bacon bits. Mix well. Fold in mushroom-onion mixture. Spoon heaping spoonful of stuffing into each mushroom cap and place on prepared baking sheet. Bake 15 minutes.

Help me, O God Who Loves, to recognize my salvation. Amen.

I have waited for thy salvation, O Lord.

Genesis 49:18 KJV

Sweet and Tangy Meatballs
1 T. olive oil
1 small red onion, cut in chunks
1 small red bell pepper, cut in chunks
1 jar pasta sauce, 26 to 28 oz.
8 oz. pineapple chunks in juice, drained (reserve 1 T. juice)
1 jar grape jelly, about 12 oz.
20 oz. fully cooked cocktail-size meatballs, unfrozen

In large skillet heat olive oil over medium-high heat. Saute onion and red pepper, stirring occasionally, 4 minutes or until crisp-tender. Remove mixture and set aside. In same skillet stir in pasta sauce, reserved 1 tablespoon pineapple juice and grape jelly. Bring to boil over medium-high heat. Add meatballs. Reduce heat and simmer, stirring occasionally, 10 minutes or until meatballs heat through and sauce thickens. Return vegetables to skillet. Stir in pineapple and heat through. May be served over hot rice.

Waiting, waiting, waiting for you am I, Lord of Hosts. Amen.

~~~

The midwives, fearing God, did not do as the king of Egypt had told them; they let the boys live.

Exodus 1:17 JPS

Swiss Cheese Spread
1 c. shredded Swiss cheese
1 c. mayonnaise
¾ c. chopped red onion

In medium bowl mix all ingredients well. Serve with crackers or fresh vegetables. Refrigerate unused portion in airtight container.

The right thing, in your name, is what I desire, Holy One. Amen.

Then said his sister to Pharaoh's daughter, "Shall I go and call to thee a nurse of the Hebrew women, that she may nurse the child for thee?"

Genesis 2:7 KJV

Taco Chips
1 package fresh or thawed tortillas
Garlic powder
Onion powder
Chili powder

Preheat oven to 400 degrees. Cut each tortilla into eight pie-shaped pieces. Sprinkle with seasonings (or leave plain for corn chips). Place on ungreased baking sheets and bake 5 minutes on each side. If desired, add more seasonings when turning chips.

I want to step up for you, God of the Ages. Amen.

~~~

And Pharaoh's daughter said to her, "Go." And the maid went and called the child's mother. Genesis 2:8 KJV

Tortilla Bean Dip
1 can refried beans, about 16 oz.
1 carton sour cream, about 8 oz.
¾ c. mayonnaise
½ c. sliced green onions
1 large tomato, diced
8 oz. shredded cheddar cheese
Tortilla chips

In 8-inch dish, layer in order: refried beans, sour cream, mayonnaise, onions, tomato and cheese. Serve with tortilla chips.

You work in ways magnificent and detailed, Lord of Beginnings. Amen.

God heard their moaning . . . . Exodus 2:24a JPS

Veggie Dip
½ c. sour cream
½ c. jarred spreadable cheese
½ c. zesty creamy salad dressing
½ tsp. Worcestershire sauce
1 T. dry onion mix

In medium bowl combine all ingredients. Mix well. Refrigerate in airtight container. Serve with fresh vegetables or crackers.

I cry out for deliverance; hear my cries, my Lord and my God. Amen.

~~~

And when you have freed the people from Egypt, you shall worship God at this mountain.
 Exodus 3:12b JPS

Water Chestnuts with Sauce
1 can whole water chestnuts, about 16 oz.
12 oz. bacon, uncooked
½ c. ketchup
3 T. brown sugar
1 tsp. lemon juice

Preheat oven to 350 degrees. Drain water chestnuts and wrap each in ½ strip bacon, fastening with toothpicks. Fry in skillet over medium heat until bacon is brown. In small bowl combine ketchup, brown sugar and lemon juice. Dip browned water chestnuts in ketchup mixture. Place sauced water chestnuts in ungreased baking pan and bake 45 minutes.

All my victories are your doing, God Who Liberates. Amen.

BEEF AND PORK

"When I see the blood I will pass over you, so that no plague will destroy you when I strike the land of Egypt."
Exodus 12:13 JPS

Barbecued Beef
3 lbs. chuck beef
4 c. tomatoes
1 can tomato sauce, about 8 oz.
¼ c. Worcestershire sauce
½ c. water
1 medium onion, chopped
½ c. cider vinegar
4 T. sugar

In large heavy pot combine all ingredients over medium-high heat. Bring to boil. Reduce heat. Cook slowly, uncovered, until meat falls apart, 4 to 5 hours. May also be cooked in slow cooker. Serve hot or cold.

Help me to do in full faith what you ask in full love, Elohim. Amen.

That very day the Lord freed the Israelites from the land of Egypt, troop by troop. Exodus 12:51 JPS

Basic Barbecue Sauce
2 cans tomato sauce, about 15 oz. each
1 c. corn syrup, light or dark
1 c. finely chopped onion
⅔ c. cider vinegar
4 cloves garlic, pressed
½ tsp. pepper

In large heavy pot combine all ingredients. Bring to boil over medium heat, stirring frequently. Boil 30 to 35 minutes until reduced to 4 cups. Add special flavorings (options below) if desired. Serve hot or cold.

Chili Barbecue Sauce: To 1 cup Basic Barbecue Sauce add 2 to 3 teaspoons minced hot green chili peppers or pickled jalapeno peppers, ¼ teaspoon dried oregano leaves and, if desired, ⅛ teaspoon ground cumin.

Ginger-Soy Barbecue Sauce: To 1 cup Basic Barbecue Sauce add 2 tablespoons soy sauce, ½ teaspoon ground ginger, ⅛ teaspoon ground cinnamon and 1 pinch ground cloves.

Orange Barbecue Sauce: To 1 cup Basic Barbecue Sauce add 2 tablespoons thawed orange juice concentrate.

O Lord our God, we are an army empowered by your might. Amen.

The angel of God, who had been going ahead of the Israelite army, now moved and followed behind them; and the pillar of cloud shifted from in front of them and took up a place behind them. Exodus 14:19 JPS

Beef Stroganoff

1½ lb. sirloin tip roast, cut into bite-size pieces
Salt
Flour
Oil
½ lb. mushrooms
2 T. ketchup
1 T. Worcestershire sauce
1 can beef bouillon, about 8 oz.
2 T. butter
1 T. dry mustard
1 c. sour cream

Season sirloin pieces with salt and dip in flour. In Dutch oven or large saucepan brown sirloin in oil. Add mushrooms, ketchup, Worcestershire sauce, bouillon, butter and dry mustard. Cook on low heat until sirloin is tender, about 1 hour. Before serving add sour cream and mix well. May be served over rice or noodles.

When I can find my way, Emmanuel, I know it's because you've gone ahead of me. Amen.

In Your love You lead the people you have redeemed;
In Your strength You guide them to Your holy abode.
Exodus 15:13 JPS

Big Burger

Crust:
2 c. all-purpose flour
2 c. instant mashed-potato flakes
¾ c. butter or margarine, softened
¾ c. milk

Preheat oven to 425 degrees. Mix flour and potato flakes in large bowl. Cut in butter with fork. Stir in milk. Press half of dough into 10-inch circle on ungreased baking sheet.

Filling:
1 lb. ground beef
1 T. ketchup
1 T. mustard
1 can condensed cheddar cheese soup
¼ c. chopped onion
½ tsp. salt
½ tsp. pepper

In saucepan brown ground beef. Drain. Stir in remaining ingredients. Mix well. Spread to within ¼ inch of dough edge.

Topping:
2 T. milk
2 T. butter or margarine, melted
¼ c. mashed potato flakes

On waxed paper roll out remaining half of dough into 11-inch circle. Place over filling. Seal edge and brush with milk. In small bowl mix butter and potato flakes. Sprinkle mixture on dough. Bake 20 to 25 minutes until golden brown.

Covenant of the People, I trust you to put me where you want me. Amen.

In the evening quail appeared and covered the camp; in the morning there was a fall of dew about the camp.
                                              Exodus 16:13 JPS

Braised Steak
2 lbs. round steak
3 T. butter or oil
3 T. flour
3 T. chopped onion
1 tsp. lemon juice
2 cloves
1 tsp. salt
⅛ tsp. pepper

Cut meat into 4-inch squares. Melt butter in skillet. Add meat and brown well on both sides. Remove meat. Stir in flour, blending well. Add onion, lemon juice, cloves, salt and pepper. Mix well. Return meat to skillet. Cover with boiling water. Simmer 2½ hours. Remove cloves before serving.

Your provision is enough, Living Bread. Amen.

And all the congregation of the children of Israel journeyed from the wilderness of Sin . . . . Exodus 17:1a KJV

Cheesy Barbecued Meatballs
Meatballs:
2 c. corn flakes
2 eggs
⅓ c. milk
½ tsp. salt
⅛ tsp. pepper
½ lb. ground beef
1 c. shredded cheddar cheese, about 4 oz.

Preheat oven to 350 degrees. Coat 9 by 13-inch baking pan. In medium bowl lightly crush corn flakes. Add eggs, milk, salt and pepper. Mix well. Let stand 5 minutes or until cereal softens. Add ground beef and cheese. Mix well. Shape into 1-inch balls. Place in single layer in prepared pan. Bake 10 minutes or until brown. Remove from oven and immediately remove meatballs from pan before combining with sauce.

Sauce:
1 c. ketchup
¾ c. water
2 T. cider vinegar
3 T. brown sugar
1 T. minced onion
1 tsp. salt
1 tsp. celery seed

In large saucepan combine all ingredients. Mix well. Bring to boil over medium heat. Reduce heat to low. Add meatballs and cook, uncovered, 15 minutes. May be served over spaghetti, noodles or rice.

God the Purifier, my life is a journey toward you. Amen.

You shall have no other gods besides Me.

Exodus 20:3 JPS

Cola Pot Roast
4 lbs. beef roast
3 stalks celery, chopped
3 carrots, chopped
1 clove garlic, minced
1 pkg. dry brown gravy mix
2 T. water
1 pkg. dry onion soup mix, about 1 oz.
1 can condensed cream of mushroom soup
10 oz. cola

Preheat oven to 350 degrees. Place beef in roasting pan. Sprinkle carrots, celery and garlic around beef. In medium bowl make paste of gravy mix and water. Add soup mix, mushroom soup and cola. Mix well. Pour over beef. Cover pan and roast 1 hour. Reduce heat to 225 degrees and roast 2 hours. Remove from oven, turn meat over so top is covered with gravy. Cover and bake at least 2 more hours until meat is fork-tender. Remove from oven and let stand at least 10 minutes before slicing and serving.

Ruler over Kings of Earth, help the nations to hold you higher than all else. Amen.

Remember the Sabbath day and keep it holy.

Exodus 20:8 JPS

Enchiladas
1 lb. ground beef
1 onion, chopped
1 can enchilada sauce, about 10 oz.
1 can condensed cream of mushroom soup
1 can condensed tomato soup
1 pkg. soft tortillas
8 oz. shredded cheddar cheese
Sour cream (optional)

Preheat oven to 425 degrees. In skillet saute ground beef and onion. In bowl combine enchilada sauce, mushroom soup and tomato soup. Fill each tortilla with 1 tablespoon browned meat and 1 tablespoon sauce mixture. Wrap tortilla and secure with toothpick. Place tortillas in 9 by 13-inch baking pan. Spread remaining sauce over tortillas. Top with cheese. Cover pan. Bake 20 to 25 minutes. Serve warm with sour cream.

I rest in you, Shepherd of Souls. Amen.

~~~

Honor your father and your mother . . . .

Exodus 20:12a JPS

Gone All Day Stew
1 can condensed tomato soup
1 soup can water
¼ c. flour
2 lbs. stew beef
3 carrots, cut in small chunks
6 onions, quartered
4 potatoes, cubed
12 whole large fresh mushrooms
2 beef bouillon cubes
1 T. Italian seasoning
3 grinds fresh pepper

In Dutch oven or slow cooker combine soup, water and flour. Mix well. Add beef, carrots, onions, potatoes, mushrooms, bouillon cubes, Italian seasoning and pepper. Mix well. Cover. Bake 4 to 5 hours in oven at 275 degrees or 4 to 5 hours in slow cooker on low setting.

I want to bless my parents, God Who Knows. Show me how. Amen.

~~~

You shall not murder.   Exodus 20:13a JPS

Ham Barbecue
1 T. butter
1 onion, minced
1 tsp. dry mustard
1 tsp. celery salt
Brown sugar
1 tsp. paprika
1 c. ketchup
⅓ c. cider vinegar
½ c. water
6 whole cloves or 1 tsp. ground cloves
1 lb. chipped ham

In large skillet or saucepan heat butter and brown onion. Add remaining ingredients and stir well. Bring to boil. Reduce heat and simmer, uncovered, ½ hour.

Remove my wrong thoughts, Lord Our Righteousness. Amen.

You shall not commit adultery. Exodus 20:13b JPS

Ham Cassoulet
¼ c. butter or margarine
1 lb. ground pork sausage
1 c. chopped onion
¾ c. chopped carrot
½ c. chopped celery
1 large clove garlic, minced
2 c. cooked ham, cubed
2 cans navy beans, undrained, about 15 oz. each
¾ c. chicken broth or water
2 bay leaves
2 T. or more water

Preheat oven to 325 degrees. In large skillet heat butter and cook sausage, onion, carrot, celery and garlic over moderate heat, stirring occasionally, until sausage is brown and vegetables are tender. Stir in ham, beans, broth, bay leaves and water. Pour into large casserole dish. Adjust water if necessary to achieve stewlike consistency. Bake about 45 minutes or until heated through. Remove bay leaves before serving.

The spouse of my heart, God Who Joins, is a gift from you. Amen.

~~~

You shall not steal. Exodus 20:13c JPS

Ham Loaf
1 lb. ground ham
1½ lbs. ground pork
1 c. milk
1 c. bread crumbs
2 eggs
Salt (optional)
Pepper (optional)
1 c. firmly packed brown sugar
¼ c. cider vinegar

1 tsp. mustard
¼ c. water
Pineapple chunks (optional)

Preheat oven to 350 degrees. In large bowl mix ham, pork, milk, crumbs, eggs, salt and pepper. Shape into 1 large or 2 small loaves and place in loaf pans. In medium saucepan mix and heat brown sugar, vinegar, mustard and water. Pour mixture over loaves. Bake 1 hour or until done, basting loaves occasionally with sauce. Let stand at least 10 minutes before slicing to serve. Garnish with pineapple chunks.

I repent of my greed, Root of David. Amen.

~~~

You shall not bear false witness against your neighbor.
                                                Exodus 20:13d JPS

Hawaiian Kielbasa
4 lbs. smoked kielbasa or sausage
½ c. firmly packed brown sugar
1 can crushed pineapple, undrained, about 20 oz.
1 bottle chili sauce, about 12 oz.

Preheat oven to 350 degrees. Cut kielbasa in ¾-inch to 1-inch pieces and place in 9 by 13-inch baking pan. In medium bowl mix brown sugar, pineapple and chili sauce. Pour mixture evenly over kielbasa. Cover and bake 1 hour. Remove kielbasa from oven and uncover. Increase temperature to 400 degrees. Bake 15 to 20 minutes or until sauce is no longer runny, stirring occasionally.

Only Begotten Son, let my words honor you and my neighbors. Amen.

You shall not covet . . . . Exodus 10:14a JPS

Honey Glazed Baked Ham
1 T. flour
Whole or half ham, ready to eat
⅛ c. prepared yellow mustard
Whole cloves
¾ c. firmly packed brown sugar
3 T. honey

Preheat oven to 325 degrees. Place flour in extra-large oven bag for whole ham or large oven bag for half ham. Place bag in 9 by 13-inch baking pan. Insert ham in bag, fat side up. Close bag with twist tie. Pierce top of bag 6 to 8 times. Bake 12 minutes per pound. Remove from oven 30 minutes before baking time is complete and increase temperature to 375 degrees. Carefully slit bag down center and sides to expose ham. Remove any skin. Score fat in diamond shapes ¼ inch deep. Brush entire top of ham with mustard. Insert clove in each diamond. Sprinkle brown sugar on top. Drizzle with honey. Return to oven and bake 30 minutes.

I have enough for today, and I thank you for it, God Who Mediates. Amen.

~~~

Your people will be my people and your God my God.
Ruth 1:16c NIV

Hungarian Pork Chops
1 small onion, chopped
1 clove garlic
3 T. butter
6 pork chops
1 bay leaf
¾ c. chicken bouillon
1 c. sour cream
2 tsp. paprika

In large skillet saute onion and garlic in butter over moderate heat. Add pork chops and brown. Pour off fat. Add bay leaf and bouillon. Cover and simmer 1 hour. Remove meat from skillet. Add sour cream and paprika to pan juices. Blend and heat through. Pour over chops.

Your arms reach around the world, God of Grace. Amen.

~~~

So Naomi returned from Moab accompanied by Ruth the Moabitess, her daughter-in-law . . . .
<div style="text-align: right;">Ruth 1:22a NIV</div>

Mock Cabbage Rolls
4 c. shredded cabbage
1½ c. sausage, browned
½ c. uncooked rice
1 T. chopped onion
1½ tsp. salt
1¼ tsp. pepper
½ tsp. paprika
1 can sauerkraut, drained, about 15 oz.
1 can tomato paste, about 6 oz.
1½ c. water
1 c. sour cream
1 can refrigerated crescent rolls

Preheat oven to 300 degrees. Spread cabbage in 9 by 13-inch baking pan. Add sausage, rice, onion, salt, pepper and paprika. Spread sauerkraut evenly on top. In small bowl mix tomato paste and water. Pour evenly over cabbage mixture. Cover and bake 1½ hours. Remove from oven and increase temperature to 400 degrees. Spread sour cream evenly on top. Form crescent rolls from dough, pinching seams to hold in place. Place rolls on top. Bake 8 to 10 minutes or until rolls are golden brown.

Help me, Horn of Salvation, to see the path you pick for me. Amen.

The Lord has not stopped showing his kindness to the living and the dead. Ruth 3:20b NIV

Norwegian Meatballs
¼ c. milk
½ c. cornstarch, divided
1 lb. ground chuck
1 medium onion, chopped
¾ tsp. salt
¼ tsp. pepper
½ tsp. ground nutmeg
1 egg, lightly beaten
2 T. vegetable oil
2 cans beef broth, about 13 oz. each
Hot mashed potatoes

In large bowl mix milk and ¼ cup cornstarch until well blended. Add ground chuck, onion, salt, pepper, nutmeg and egg. Mix well. Chill 20 minutes. Shape into 1-inch balls. In large skillet heat oil. Saute meatballs until brown, 8 to 10 minutes. Remove from heat. Drain meatballs on paper towels. Remove all but ¼ cup drippings from skillet. In medium bowl mix broth and remaining ¼ cup cornstarch until well blended. Pour into skillet. Cook over medium heat, stirring constantly, until broth boils and thickens. Add meatballs. Reduce heat and simmer 15 minutes. Spoon potatoes onto middle of platter. Using slotted spoon, arrange meatballs around potatoes. Serve gravy on side.

King of Kings, your loving kindness is the glue of life. Amen.

~~~

Today you are witnesses. Ruth 4:10b NIV

Poor People's Steak
3 lbs. ground beef
1 c. soda cracker crumbs
1 c. cold water or milk
1 T. salt
¼ tsp. pepper

1 onion, finely chopped
Oregano and sage (optional)
Flour for dredging
2 T. oil
1 can condensed cream of mushroom soup

In large bowl mix beef, crumbs, water, salt, pepper, onion, oregano and sage. Press mixture about ½ inch thick onto baking sheet. Refrigerate several hours or overnight.

Preheat oven to 325 degrees. Cut meat mixture into 2-inch to 3-inch pieces. Dredge pieces in flour. In large skillet heat oil and saute pieces on both sides. Place in roasting pan. In small bowl combine soup with 1 soup can of water. Pour mixture over meat. Bake 1½ hours.

I want to do things your way, Jealous God. Amen.

~~~

So Boaz took Ruth and she became his wife.
<div style="text-align: right;">Ruth 4:13a NIV</div>

Roast Beef

Beef roast, 3½ lbs. or larger
1 pkg. dry onion soup mix, about 1 oz.
1 can condensed cream of mushroom soup
1 can brown gravy, about 10 oz.
1 can mushrooms, drained
1 medium onion, sliced

Preheat oven to 225 degrees or set slow cooker on low heat. Place roast in roasting pan or slow cooker. Pour soup mix over roast. Top, in order, with mushroom soup, gravy, mushrooms and onion slices. Cover roasting pan with foil or slow cooker with lid. Cook 5 hours or longer. May be served with mashed potatoes, cooked rice or noodles.

Thank you, Lily of the Valley, for the wonder of marriage. Amen.

And the Lord enabled her to conceive, and she gave birth to a son. Ruth 4:13b NIV

Shish Kebab Formula
1¾ lbs. meat or seafood, cut into 1½-inch pieces
    (suggestions below)
1¾ lbs. vegetables or fruits, cut into 1-inch cubes
    (suggestions below)
1¼ tsp. salt
½ tsp. pepper
Flavored paste (suggestions below)
Lemon or lime wedges for garnish
Minced parsley or cilantro for garnish

Meat and seafood suggestions: skinless boneless chicken thighs or breasts, pork tenderloin, beef tenderloin, rib-eye steak, strip steak, lamb, kielbasa, Italian sausage (steamed until done), swordfish, salmon, tuna, large shrimp (leave whole).

Vegetable and fruit suggestions: white mushrooms (leave whole), zucchini, yellow squash, eggplant, bell peppers, onions and fennel (cut in 1-inch chunks 2 layers thick), apples, pineapple, apricots, plums.

Preheat gas grill or prepare charcoal grill as usual. Prepare one of the following pastes and set aside. Sprinkle meat, vegetables and fruit with salt and pepper and toss with the paste. Thread items onto eight 12-inch or six 14-inch skewers, alternating between 1 meat and 2 vegetable/fruit pieces and making sure not to thread too tightly. If using bamboo skewers, leave as little exposed wood as possible at each end to prevent charring.

Before grilling kebabs, use wire brush to clean grill grate, then use tongs to wipe oil-soaked rag over grate to prevent kebabs from sticking. Place skewers on grill, close lid and grill on high until spotty brown, about 4 minutes. To turn skewers (particularly bamboo ones, on which ingredients tend to twirl), grab as much of the kebab as possible from the side with tongs and turn quickly. Grill until spotty brown on the other side and food is cooked through, about 2 minutes for shrimp, 3 minutes for chicken breasts and fish, and 4 minutes for chicken thighs, pork, beef and lamb.

Let rest a few minutes before serving. If desired, serve with lemon or lime wedges and minced parsley or cilantro.

Pineapple Cumin Flavoring Paste: 1 tablespoon vegetable oil; 4 teaspoons ground cumin; ½ cup frozen pineapple juice concentrate, thawed.

Curried Apple Flavoring Paste: 1 tablespoon vegetable oil; 2 tablespoons curry powder; ½ cup frozen apple juice concentrate, thawed.

Jamaican Jerk-Style Flavoring Paste: 1 tablespoon vegetable oil; 1 tablespoon dried thyme leaves; 1 tablespoon dried oregano; 1 teaspoon ground coriander; 1 teaspoon ground allspice; 2 tablespoons Dijon mustard; 2 teaspoons hot red pepper sauce; ½ cup frozen limeade concentrate, thawed.

Orange Rosemary Flavoring Paste: 1 tablespoon vegetable oil; 2 tablespoons minced fresh rosemary; 2 teaspoons brown sugar; ½ cup frozen orange juice concentrate, thawed.

Moroccan-Style Flavoring Paste: 2 tablespoons vegetable oil; 1½ teaspoons paprika; 1 teaspoon each garlic powder, ground ginger and cumin; ½ teaspoon each ground cinnamon and ground cloves; ½ cup frozen limeade concentrate, thawed.

Asian-Style Flavoring Paste: 2 tablespoons sesame oil; 2 teaspoons garlic powder; 2 teaspoons ground ginger; 1 teaspoon hot red pepper flakes; 6 tablespoons soy sauce; ½ cup frozen pineapple juice concentrate, thawed.

The miracle of birth humbles us before you, O Giver of Life. Amen.

And they named him Obed. He was the father of Jesse, the father of David.
Ruth 4:17b NIV

Smothered Pork Chops
2 lbs. pork chops, cut thick
2 unpeeled lemons, sliced
1 large sweet onion, cut in rings
1 green pepper, cut in rings
1 tsp. salt
2 c. tomato juice
1 T. butter

Place chops in large skillet and cover with lemons, onion and pepper. Sprinkle with salt. Pour tomato juice over all and dot with butter. Cover and cook on top of stove 1½ hours or until meat is tender. Transfer to hot platter.

Our Faithful Commander, your battle plan is magnificent, strong and awesome. Amen.

All the articles of gold and silver numbered 5,400; Shesbazzar brought them all up with the exiles who went up from Babylon to Jerusalem. Ezra 1:11 NAS

Sukiyaki

3 T. oil
1½ lb. sirloin or round steak, sliced thin
2 T. sugar
½ c. soy sauce
⅓ c. water
1 can Chinese vegetables, including liquid, about 8 oz.
1 c. thinly sliced onions
1 c. sliced celery
½ c. canned mushrooms, about 4 oz.
¾ c. green onion and tops, cut in 1-inch lengths
¾ c. watercress (optional)
Hot cooked rice

Heat oil in large pot. Add steak and brown lightly, stirring often, about 10 minutes. In small bowl combine sugar, soy sauce and water. Add to meat. Bring to boil, cover and reduce heat. Simmer about 40 minutes. Add Chinese vegetables, onions, celery and mushrooms. Increase heat. Bring to boil, cover and cook 5 to 10 minutes. Add green onions and watercress. Uncover and cook 1 minute. Stir well. Serve over rice.

You manage our salvation with exquisite balance, God of Serenity, and we kneel in gratitude. Amen.

And all the people shouted with a great shout when they praised the Lord because the foundation of the house of the Lord was laid. Ezra 3:11b NAS

Sweet and Sour Meatballs
5 beef bouillon cubes, divided
¼ c. hot water
1½ lbs. ground beef
1 c. soft bread crumbs
¾ c. finely chopped onion
1 egg
Oil for sauteing
18-20 oz. pineapple chunks, juice reserved and divided
⅓ c. bottled lemon juice
3 T. brown sugar
2 T. soy sauce
1 tsp. ground ginger
2 T. cornstarch
1 large green pepper, chopped
Hot cooked rice

Dissolve 2 bouillon cubes in ¼ cup hot water. In large bowl combine beef, crumbs, onion, egg and bouillon liquid. Mix well. Shape into 18 meatballs. In large skillet heat oil and brown meatballs. Drain oil. In medium bowl mix ¼ cup pineapple juice, lemon juice, brown sugar, soy sauce, ginger and 3 remaining bouillon cubes. Add mixture to meatballs in skillet. Cover and simmer 20 to 25 minutes. In small bowl combine remaining pineapple juice and cornstarch. Stir into meatball mixture. Cook and stir until thickened. Add pineapple chunks and green pepper. Heat through. Serve with rice.

Living God, I shout your praises! Amen.

For Ezra had set his heart to study the law of the Lord, and to practice it, and to teach His statutes and ordinances in Israel.

Ezra 7:10 NAS

Teriyaki Steak
2½ lb. chuck steak, sliced thin
1 tsp. ginger
1 T. sugar
½ c. soy sauce
1 clove garlic or 1 tsp. garlic powder

Place all ingredients in slow cooker and cook on low 6 to 8 hours. May be served over rice or noodles.

Holy Teacher, may all who love you stand tall and speak straight. Amen.

~~~

Behold, we are before thee in guilt, for no one can stand before Thee because of this.

Ezra 9:15b NAS

Unstuffed Peppers
1 lb. ground beef
1 jar pasta sauce, 26 to 28 oz.
2 large bell peppers, any color, coarsely chopped
1½ tsp. salt
1¾ c. water
1 c. instant rice

In large nonstick skillet brown ground beef. Drain fat. Stir in pasta sauce, peppers, salt, water and rice. Bring to boil over high heat. Reduce heat to medium-low, cover and cook 20 minutes or until liquid is absorbed and rice is tender.

When I think of my guilt, Rose of Sharon, I am convinced of your love. Amen.

BEVERAGES

And I told them how the hand of God had been favorable to me . . . . Nehemiah 2:18a NAS

Berry Banana Smoothie
1 small banana, cut up and frozen
¼ c. fresh or frozen strawberries
1 c. orange juice
3 T. low-fat vanilla yogurt
Fresh strawberries for garnish (optional)

Combine all ingredients except garnish in blender. Cover and blend until smooth. Pour into glasses and garnish each with a fresh strawberry.

I told a friend about you today, Merciful God, and our friendship grew. Amen.

> Remember me, O my God, for good, according to all that I have done for this people.
> Nehemiah 5:19 NAS

Berry Smoothie

1½ c. fresh or frozen berries
¾ c. sugar
2 c. crushed ice
½ c. water or juice, any kind

Combine all ingredients in blender. Cover and blend until smooth. Pour into glasses and serve immediately.

For a freezer treat, pour smoothie mixture into plastic cups with sticks in the middle and freeze overnight.

I will be all right, Adonai, as long as you remember me. Amen.

~~~

> But now, O God, strengthen my hands.
> Nehemiah 6:9b NAS

"Champagne" Punch

64 oz. grape juice (½ gal.)
1 liter ginger ale, about 34 oz.
16 oz. white grape juice (2 c.)
16 oz. apple juice (2 c.)
¼ c. cider vinegar

In large container combine ingredients and mix well. Serve chilled.

May be frozen into ice ring with mint leaves and served with maraschino cherries for garnish.

I hold out my hands in hope of your strength, God Who Reaches Out. Amen.

And it came about when all our enemies heard of it, and the nations surrounding us saw it, they lost their confidence, for they recognized that this work had been accomplished with the help of our God.
Nehemiah 6:16 NAS

Cocoa Mix
2 c. powdered milk
¼ c. cocoa powder
1 c. powdered sugar (substitute may be used)
Dash salt

Mix all ingredients well and store in airtight container. To make cup of cocoa, place about 4 tablespoons of mixture into large mug and fill with boiling water. May be enhanced by adding whipped cream, ice cream, marshmallows, ⅓ cup powdered nondairy creamer, or 1 or 2 tablespoons of malted-milk powder.

God of Mighty Angels, all nations tremble before you. Amen.

~~~

Then Ezra the priest brought the law before the assembly of men, women, and all who could listen with understanding, on the first day of the seventh month.
Nehemiah 2:2 NAS

Cranberry Punch
4 c. cranberry juice
¼ c. sugar
4 c. pineapple juice
1 T. almond extract
8 c. ginger ale

In large container combine cranberry juice, sugar, pineapple juice and almond extract. Chill. Add ginger ale just before serving.

May each of us lift your word in our own part of your world, Lord Our Righteousness. Amen.

O may thy glorious name be blessed
And be exalted above all blessing and praise!
Nehemiah 9:5b NAS

Double Lime Punch
½ pt. lime sherbet, softened
1 can limeade concentrate, thawed, about 6 oz.
1 large bottle ginger ale, chilled
2 c. cold water

In punch bowl combine all ingredients. Serve chilled.

Most High God, you deserve all glory. Amen.

~~~

But they, our fathers, acted arrogantly….
<div align="right">Nehemiah 9:16a NAS</div>

Egg Nog
6 eggs
¼ c. sugar
¼ tsp. salt (optional)
4 c. milk, divided
1 tsp. vanilla

In large saucepan beat eggs, sugar and salt. Stir in 2 cups of the milk. Cook over low heat, stirring constantly, until mixture is thick enough to coat a metal spoon with a thin film and reaches at least 160 degrees. Remove from heat. Stir in remaining 2 cups milk and vanilla. Cover and refrigerate until thoroughly chilled, several hours or overnight. Just before serving, pour into bowl or pitcher.

Keep me humble, Lord of the High Places. Amen.

But when they cried to Thee in the time of their distress, Thou didst hear from heaven, and according to Thy great compassion Thou didst give them deliverers who delivered them from the hand of their oppressors. Nehemiah 9:27b NAS

Flavored Coffees
Mocha Coffee:
½ c. instant coffee granules
½ c. sugar or substitute
1 c. powdered milk or powdered creamer (nonfat okay)
2 T. cocoa powder

Viennese Coffee:
½ c. instant coffee granules
⅔ c. sugar or substitute
⅔ c. powdered milk or powdered creamer (nonfat okay)
½ tsp. ground cinnamon

Combine ingredients and mix well. Store in labeled airtight container. To make cup of coffee, place 2 rounded teaspoons, more or less, of the flavored blend in a cup and add 8 ounces boiling water.

I cry out to you, Lord Who Hears All, for you know my suffering. Amen.

One day as the angels came to present themselves before the Lord, Satan, the Accuser, came with them.

Job 1:6 LB

Friendship Tea
2 c. orange drink powder from jar
1 envelope unsweetened lemonade mix
½ c. sugar
½ c. instant tea powder
1 tsp. ground cinnamon
½ tsp. ground cloves
½ tsp. ground nutmeg

Mix all ingredients and store in airtight container. To serve, dissolve 2 heaping teaspoons of mix in 1 cup boiling water. Makes nice Christmas gift, in pretty jar, given along with recipe.

Keep me on guard in darkness, God of Light and Truth. Amen.

~~~

The Lord gave me everything I had, and they were his to take away.

<div align="right">Job 1:20b LB</div>

Fruit Punch for 75 People
2½ lbs. sugar
5 c. water
3 pkg. cherry drink mix
½ can grapefruit juice, about 23 oz.
1 can pineapple juice, about 46 oz.
Juice of 6 lemons
Juice of 12 oranges
6 qts. water
2 qts. ginger ale

In large pan boil sugar and 5 cups water 5 minutes. Add drink mix and cool. Add fruit juices and 6 quarts water. Chill. Add ginger ale just before serving.

Father in Heaven, all of this is yours. Amen.

In all of this, Job did not sin or revile God.

Job 1:22 LB

Hymn Book Punch
1 pt. punch concentrate (16 oz.)
2 qts. club soda (64 oz.)
1 small can frozen lemonade concentrate, about 6 oz.
1 small can frozen orange juice concentrate, about 6 oz.
1 large can pineapple juice, about 46 oz.
1 qt. lemon-lime soda (32 oz.)
Strawberries or orange slices for garnish

Place block of ice in punch bowl. Add punch concentrate and enough club soda to dissolve concentrate. Stir well. Mix in lemonade and orange concentrates, pineapple juice, lemon-lime soda and remaining club soda. Garnish.

I remember you, Lord Who Triumphs, when enemies surround me. Amen.

A wicked man is always in trouble throughout his life.
Job 15:21 LB

Kool Fruit Punch
3 pkg. unsweetened drink mix (enough to make 6 qts.)
¾ c. sugar or to taste
1 gal. cold water (128 oz.)
1 can pineapple juice (46 oz.)
12 oz. lemonade concentrate, mixed according to directions
12 oz. orange juice concentrate, mixed according to directions
4 liters lemon-lime soda or ginger ale, chilled
Ice or ice ring (optional)

In large container blend drink mix, sugar and water. Add pineapple juice, lemonade and orange juice. Mix well. Store in airtight containers until ready to serve. When ready to serve, add lemon-lime soda and ice.

My desire is to be right with you, O Lover of My Soul. Amen.

~~~

Yet, finally, the innocent shall come out on top....
Job 17:8b LB

Mock Champagne
2 c. sugar
2 c. water
1 can frozen grapefruit juice concentrate, about 6 oz.
1 can frozen orange juice concentrate, about 6 oz.
1 can frozen grape juice concentrate, about 6 oz.
2 qts. Lemon-lime soda, chilled (64 oz.)

In medium saucepan boil sugar and water until sugar is dissolved. Chill. When ready to serve, place sugar water in large serving container and add juice concentrates and soda. Mix well. Serve immediately.

You, Jesus the Christ, are my now and my future. Amen.

The righteous shall move onward and forward . . . .
                                         Job 17:9a LB

Orange Crush Punch
5 pkg. orange gelatin
1 qt. boiling water
4½ qts. cold water
5 c. sugar
1 small can frozen lemonade concentrate, about 6 oz.
1 can pineapple juice, about 46 oz.
1 can crushed pineapple, about 16 oz.
8 liters lemon-lime soda

In large container dissolve gelatin in boiling water. Add cold water, sugar, lemonade concentrate, pineapple juice and pineapple. Mix well. Freeze in four ½-gallon containers. Be sure frozen punch can be removed from containers. Set out to thaw 3 hours before using. To serve, place 1 block of frozen mixture in punch bowl. Crush a bit of block with spoon. Pour 2 liters lemon-lime soda over each block of frozen punch. Serve immediately.

It's exciting to journey with you, Savior Mine. Amen.

~~~

Those with pure hearts shall become stronger and stronger.
                                         Job 17:9b LB

Orange Julie
1 can frozen orange juice concentrate, about 6 oz.
1 c. milk
1 c. water
½ c. sugar or to taste
1 tsp. vanilla
1 tray ice cubes

Blend ingredients in blender until smooth. Serve immediately.

When I feel weak, you are my strength, O Giver of Life. Amen.

But as for me, I know that my Redeemer lives . . . .
                                              Job 18:25a LB

Orange Julius
1 can frozen orange juice concentrate, about 6 oz.
½ c. water
½ c. milk
¼ c. or less sugar
1 tsp. vanilla
4 to 6 ice cubes

Place all ingredients except ice cubes in blender and blend well. Add ice cubes, 1 at a time, blending well after each addition, until mixture is frothy. Serve immediately.

How sweet, in the midst of turmoil, is the knowledge of you, Redeeming God. Amen.

~~~

Wisdom is far more valuable than gold and glass.
                                              Job 28:17a LB

Orange Smoothie
¼ c. sugar
1 can frozen orange juice concentrate, about 6 oz.
1 c. milk
1 c. water
1 tsp. vanilla
10 ice cubes

In blender combine all ingredients. Cover and blend 30 seconds or until ice cubes are crushed. Serve immediately.

Lord of Mercies, help me to listen, to learn and to grow wise. Amen.

He makes the winds blow and sets the boundaries of the oceans.
   Job 28:25 LB

Party Punch
4 pkg. unsweetened cherry drink mix
2 large cans pineapple juice, about 46 oz. each
1 can frozen lemonade concentrate, about 6 oz.
2 large cans punch, about 46 oz. each
2 qts. ginger ale
16 oz. frozen strawberries

In large container prepare drink mix as directed. Add pineapple juice, lemonade concentrate and punch. When ready to serve, add ginger ale and strawberries.

God of the Elements, this breeze is sweet and fragrant. Amen.

~~~

He makes the laws of the rain and a path for the lightning.
   Job 28:26 LB

Presbyterian Punch
2 c. sugar
3 c. water
3 ripe bananas, mashed
¼ c. lemon juice
1 can frozen orange juice concentrate, about 6 oz.
1 can pineapple juice, about 46 oz.
3 qts. ginger ale

In medium saucepan boil sugar and water until mixture forms syrup. Cool. In large container mix bananas, lemon juice, orange juice concentrate and pineapple juice. Add cooled syrup and mix well. Freeze. When ready to serve, thaw to a slush and add ginger ale. Serve immediately. Main mixture may be frozen in containers with ginger ale added just before serving.

God Over Me, it's so silly for me to think I have control. Amen.

He knows where wisdom is and declares it to all who will listen.
Job 28:27 LB

Punch from Flavored Gelatin
2 large pkg. gelatin, any flavor
3 c. sugar
2 c. boiling water
1 can pineapple juice, about 46 oz.
1½ c. bottled lemon juice
2 qts. cold water
1 qt. ginger ale
3 qts. lemon-lime soda

In large container dissolve gelatin and sugar in boiling water. Add pineapple juice, lemon juice and cold water. Mix well. Freeze until ready to serve. Allow time for thawing. Punch should be slushy when served. Add ginger ale and lemon-lime soda before serving.

If I hear only one word, Precious God, let it be yours. Amen.

~~~

And this is what he says to all mankind: "Look, to fear the Lord is true wisdom; to forsake evil is real understanding."
Job 28:28 LB

Russian Tea
¾ c. instant tea powder with lemon
2 c. orange drink powder from jar
1¼ c. sugar
½ tsp. ground cloves
1 tsp. ground cinnamon

Mix all ingredients well and store in airtight container. To use, place 2 teaspoons of mix in cup with 1 cup boiling water.

I know when I sin, Chosen of God; help me to stop. Amen.

God is almighty and yet does not despise anyone.

Job 36:5a LB

Slush
2 c. sugar
3 c. lukewarm water
1 can orange juice concentrate, about 6 oz.
1 can crushed pineapple, about 20 oz.
8 bananas, peeled and mashed

In large container stir sugar and lukewarm water until sugar melts. Add orange juice concentrate and 3 canfuls of water. Stir. Add pineapple and bananas. Mix well. Freeze. Remove from freezer a few minutes before serving.

Thank you for your patience with us, Angel of His Presence. Amen.

~~~

Listen, O Job, stop and consider the wonderful miracles of God.

Job 37:14 LB

Spiced Tea Mix
1 c. lemon-flavored iced tea mix, artificially sweetened
5 T. orange drink powder from jar
1 T. apple pie spice
1 pkg. lemonade drink mix, artificially sweetened

In jar or plastic container, mix all ingredients well. Cover tightly and store. To serve, place 1¼ to 1½ teaspoons mix into cup or glass. Add either 1 cup hot water or 1 cup cold water and ice. Stir.

While I wait and watch, you are working miracles, Awesome God. Amen.

So the Lord blessed Job at the end of his life more than at the beginning.
Job 42:12a LB

Wassail
1 T. whole cloves
1 T. whole allspice
1 tsp. ground nutmeg
1½ gal. apple cider
½ c. firmly packed brown sugar
1 large can lemonade concentrate, about 12 oz.
1 small can orange juice concentrate, about 6 oz.
1 cinnamon stick for garnish

Combine cloves, allspice and nutmeg in cheesecloth and tie securely with string. Place spice bag, cider, brown sugar and juice concentrates in large saucepan. Simmer 45 minutes over medium-low heat. Serve warm with cinnamon stick.

I want to be faithful all my days, True Vine. Amen.

~~~

But thou, O Lord, art a shield for me; my glory, and the lifter up of mine head.
Psalm 3:3 KJV

Wedding Punch
10 qts. lime sherbet, cut in chunks
24 qts. ginger ale

Place sherbet in punch bowl. Pour ginger ale over sherbet. Let stand briefly. Stir slowly. Makes 250 servings.

My God, you are above me, beside me, beneath me and around me. Amen.

BREAD, ROLLS AND BISCUITS

Hear me when I call, O God of My Righteousness.
                                    Psalm 4:1a KJV

Angel Biscuits
1 pkg. dry yeast
¼ c. warm water
2½ c. flour
½ tsp. baking soda
1 tsp. baking powder
1 tsp. salt
2 T. sugar
½ c. shortening
1 c. buttermilk

In small bowl dissolve yeast in water. Set aside. In large bowl mix dry ingredients in order: flour, baking soda, baking powder, salt and sugar. Cut in shortening with fork or pastry tool until pea-size particles form. Add yeast mixture. Stir in buttermilk and blend well. Dough may be refrigerated in a covered container up to 3 days.

To make biscuits, preheat oven to 400 degrees. Coat baking sheet. Turn dough out on floured surface and knead lightly. Roll out and cut with biscuit cutter. Place biscuits on prepared baking sheet. Let dough rise slightly. Bake 12 to 15 minutes or until golden brown.

Hear my cry, for I am weary and sad, O Bread of Life. Amen.

My voice shalt thou hear in the morning, O Lord; for unto thee
will I pray. Psalm 5:3 KJV

Baking Mix
8 c. flour
⅓ c. baking powder
2 tsp. salt
8 tsp. sugar (optional)
1 c. shortening
⅓ c. milk for biscuits

In large bowl combine flour, baking powder, salt and sugar. Mix well. Cut in shortening with fork or pastry tool until mixture resembles coarse meal. Refrigerate in airtight container.

To make biscuits, preheat oven to 450 degrees. Coat baking sheet. Combine 1 cup mix with ⅓ cup milk. Knead dough lightly and turn out on lightly floured surface. Roll dough about ½ inch thick and cut with biscuit cutter. Bake 12 to 15 minutes or until golden brown.

When I am not faithful to you, My Deliverer, why are you faithful to me? Amen.

~~~

Have mercy upon me, O Lord; for I am weak . . . .
 Psalm 6:2a KJV

Baking Powder Biscuits
2 c. flour
4 tsp. baking powder
½ tsp. salt
4 T. shortening
¾ c. milk

Preheat oven to 450 degrees. Coat baking sheet. Into large bowl sift flour, baking powder and salt. Rub in shortening with fingertips. Add milk slowly and mix to soft dough. Roll out about

½ inch think on lightly floured surface. Cut with biscuit cutter. Bake 10 to 15 minutes or until golden brown.

Variation: For sweet biscuits, roll Baking Powder Biscuits dough ¾ inch thick. Cut into circles with biscuit cutter. With thumb make indentation in center of each biscuit. Into each indentation place ½ teaspoon butter, 1 teaspoon sugar and three sprinkles of ground cinnamon. Sprinkle all over with granulated sugar. Bake as for Baking Powder Biscuits.

Sometimes I feel as if I can't go on, Man of Sorrows. Amen.

~~~

O Lord, heal me; for my bones are vexed.
<div style="text-align:right">Psalm 6:2b KJV</div>

Breakfast Sticky Buns
2 loaves frozen bread dough, thawed
1 small box cooked-style butterscotch pudding mix, uncooked
¼ c. melted margarine
1 c. firmly packed brown sugar
2 T. milk
½ c. pecans
1 tsp. ground cinnamon

Coat Bundt or tube pan. Divide each dough loaf into 16 pieces. Place 16 pieces in pan. In large bowl combine pudding mix, margarine, brown sugar, milk, pecans and cinnamon. Mix well. Spoon mixture over dough. Place remaining 16 pieces on top. Let rise 2 hours, or cover and refrigerate overnight and let rise before baking. Bake 30 minutes at 350 degrees.

My complaints are tiring to all but you, Jesus My Rock. Amen.

O Lord my God, in thee do I put my trust . . . .

Psalm 7:1a KJV

Bride's Bread or Rolls
2 c. boiling water
2 T. shortening
1½ tsp. salt
½ c. sugar
2 pkg. dry active yeast
2 eggs, well beaten
5½ c. flour

In large bowl combine water, shortening, salt and sugar. Mix well. Cool to lukewarm. Add yeast and eggs and mix well. Add flour 1 cup at a time, mixing well after each addition. Do not knead. Cover and refrigerate until ready to use. Can be kept up to 1 week.

To bake, preheat oven to 325 degrees for bread or 350 degrees for rolls. Coat 2 large loaf pans for bread or two 9-inch pans for rolls. Shape into loaves or rolls. Let rise to about double in bulk. Bake bread 30 to 35 minutes. Bake bread 15 minutes.

I'm a little tree leaning into a hard wind, Shepherd of Life, and yours are the arms that hold me tight. Amen.

O Lord our Lord, how excellent is thy name in all the earth!
Psalm 8:1a KJV

Buttermilk Cornbread
½ c. butter
⅔ c. sugar
2 eggs
1 c. buttermilk
½ tsp. baking soda
1 c. cornmeal
1 c. flour
½ tsp. salt

Preheat oven to 375 degrees. Coat 8-inch pan. Melt butter in large skillet. Remove from heat and stir in sugar. Quickly add eggs and beat until well blended. In small bowl combine buttermilk with baking soda. Stir into mixture in skillet. Stir in cornmeal, flour and salt until well blended and few lumps remain. Pour batter into prepared pan. Bake 30 to 40 minutes or until tester inserted in center comes out clean.

Would all the world speak your name in confidence, All-Knowing God. Amen.

I will praise thee, O Lord, with my whole heart . . . .
                                                    Psalm 9:1a KJV

Butterscotch Rolls

Rolls:
2 c. flour
5 tsp. baking powder
1 tsp. salt
2 T. sugar, divided
3 T. shortening
⅔ c. milk
1 tsp. melted butter
¼ c. raisins
¼ c. chopped nuts
½ tsp. ground cinnamon

Sauce:
1 c. firmly packed brown sugar
2 T. butter
1 T. cold water

Preheat oven to 375 degrees. Coat deep baking pan. To make rolls, in large bowl mix flour, baking powder, salt and 1 tablespoon of the sugar. Cut in shortening with knife or rub in with fingertips. Add milk gradually and mix to soft dough. Roll out on lightly floured surface. Brush with butter. Sprinkle with raisins, nuts, remaining tablespoon sugar and cinnamon. Roll like jelly roll, starting with long side, and cut into ¾-inch slices.

To make sauce, in medium bowl cream brown sugar with butter and water. Spread mixture into prepared pan. Lay dough slices on mixture. Bake 20 to 25 minutes. Transfer rolls to plate and serve hot.

How wonderful, gracious, awesome, inspiring and beautiful you are, O Prince of Peace. Amen.

How long wilt thou forget me, O Lord? Psalm 13:1a KJV

Cheese Boereg

Filling:
1½ lb. grated brick cheese
3 eggs, beaten
¼ c. chopped parsley
1 T. flour

Dough:
1½ c. melted butter
1 box filo dough

Preheat oven to 375 degrees. Coat baking sheet. In large bowl mix all filling ingredients well. Place dough on clean towel to prevent drying. Allow dough to thaw if frozen. With sharp knife cut dough into 3 by 12-inch strips. Using 2 layers of a strip at a time, place 1 heaping tablespoonful of filling at end of strip and fold in triangle shape. Place on prepared sheet and brush with melted butter. Repeat until dough and filling are used. Bake 20 to 25 minutes or until golden brown. Leftovers may be wrapped tightly and frozen.

Can you hear me, Word of Life? Amen.

Preserve me, O God . . . . Psalm 16:1a KJV

Cinnamon Raisin Biscuits
1⅔ c. all-purpose flour
1½ c. sifted cake flour
¼ c. sugar
1 T. baking powder
1 tsp. salt
1½ tsp. ground cinnamon
½ c. plus 1 T. margarine
1 c. raisins
1 c. plus 1 to 2 T. milk, divided
3 T. melted margarine
1 c. sifted powdered sugar

Preheat oven to 400 degrees. Grease baking sheets. In large bowl combine flours, sugar, baking powder, salt and cinnamon. Cut in margarine with pastry blender until mixture resembles coarse meal. Add raisins and 1 cup milk. Stir just until dry ingredients are moistened.

Turn dough out on lightly floured surface. Knead lightly 10 times. Roll dough ¾ inch thick. Cut with 2-inch biscuit cutter. Arrange biscuits on prepared sheets. Alternately, drop dough by spoonfuls onto baking sheets.

Brush biscuits lightly with margarine. Bake 15 minutes.

Combine powdered sugar and remaining 1 to 2 tablespoons milk, stirring until smooth. Drizzle over warm biscuits.

I'm in a fix, Precious Savior, that only you can mend. Amen.

The Lord is my rock, and my fortress, and my deliverer; my God, my strength, in whom I will trust; my buckler, and the horn of my salvation, and my high tower.
                                                Psalm 18:2 KJV

Cream of Tartar Biscuits
3 c. flour
1 tsp. salt
2 tsp. cream of tartar
1½ T. shortening
1 tsp. baking soda
1 c. milk

Preheat oven to 425 degrees. Coat baking pan. In large bowl mix flour, salt and cream of tartar. Work in shortening with fingertips. In small bowl mix baking soda and milk. Add to flour mixture and mix thoroughly. Form into ball and knead on lightly floured surface until satiny. Roll ¾ inch thick. Cut with biscuit cutter. Place on prepared pan. Bake 15 minutes or until golden brown.

Glorious Lord, you are my cathedral, my shield of steel, my beacon of peace, my cradle of love, my crucible of power and the wellspring of my strength. Amen.

The heavens declare the glory of God . . . .　　Psalm 19:1 KJV

English Muffins
¼ c. boiled diced potatoes, firmly packed
1 c. boiling water
1 tsp. salt
1 cake compressed yeast, crumbled
2 c. sifted flour

In large bowl mix potatoes and boiling water. Cool until lukewarm. Add salt, yeast and flour. Beat thoroughly, about 2 minutes. Cover and let rise in warm place until double in bulk. Turn dough out on floured surface and dust lightly with flour. Shape dough into mounds 3 inches across and ¼ inch thick. Place on lightly greased baking sheet and let rise until double in bulk. Carefully slip spatula under muffin and place on lightly greased hot griddle. Dough is very soft and falls easily. Bake 15 minutes at 350 degrees. Turn and bake other side 15 minutes.

In the sky I see your palette, God of the Cosmos. Amen.

~~~

The Lord is my shepherd; I shall not want.
　　　　　　　　　　　　　　　　　Psalm 23:1 KJV

Garlic Biscuits
2 c. baking mix
⅔ c. milk
½ c. shredded cheddar cheese
2 T. butter or margarine, melted
½ tsp. garlic powder

Preheat oven to 375 degrees. In large bowl combine baking mix, milk and cheese into soft dough. Drop by large spoonfuls onto ungreased baking sheet. Bake 8 to 10 minutes or until golden brown. In small bowl mix butter and garlic powder. Brush on warm biscuits.

We are lost, Jesus Our Guide, until we walk with you. Amen.

Who shall ascend the hill of the Lord?
  And who shall stand in his holy place?
Those who have clean hands and pure hearts,
  who do not lift up their souls to what is false,
  and do not swear deceitfully.

Psalm 24:3, 4 NRSV

Garlic Pizza Crust

2 T. dry yeast
2 c. warm water
2 T. sugar
½ c. olive oil
1 tsp. salt
3 T. minced garlic
6 c. flour

Coat large bowl with oil. Coat 2 large (10 by 13-inch or larger) baking sheets with olive oil. In small bowl dissolve yeast in warm water. Add sugar. Set aside a few minutes. Add oil, salt and garlic. Stir in flour, using hand if necessary to stir in last cup. Form dough ball and place on lightly floured surface. Knead until smooth. Place in greased bowl and turn to grease all sides of dough. Cover bowl with plastic wrap. Place bowl in warm spot and let rise to double in bulk. Punch down. Place half of dough on each baking sheet and spread to fit. Let dough rise 15 minutes. Adjust dough as needed to fit baking sheet. Bake crusts at 425 degrees 10 to 12 minutes or until light brown. Remove from oven. Cool slightly. Crust may be wrapped and frozen. If desired, add toppings immediately and bake at 425 degrees 10 to 12 minutes or until toppings are cooked.

Holy and High God, I want to be worthy to meet you face to face. Amen.

Make me to know your ways, O Lord;
  teach me your paths.   Psalm 25:4 NRSV

Garlic Toast
½ c. margarine
½ tsp. onion salt
½ tsp. Italian seasoning
½ tsp. garlic powder
8 to 12 slices bread

Preheat oven to 300 degrees. In small saucepan soften margarine. Stir in remaining ingredients. Spread on both sides of bread. Cut bread into strips. Place on ungreased baking sheet. Bake until bread is toasted. Turn over and toast other side.

  Your way, Lord Jesus Christ, is my way. Amen.

> The Lord is my light and my salvation;
>   whom shall I fear?
>
> Psalm 27:1a NRSV

Hoagie Buns

2 T. dry yeast
2 c. lukewarm water
½ c. sugar
2 tsp. salt
2 eggs, beaten
½ c. shortening, melted
7 to 7½ c. flour

Grease large bowl and set aside. In another large bowl dissolve yeast in water. Stir in sugar, salt, eggs and shortening. Gradually stir in flour until soft dough forms. Turn out onto floured surface and knead until elastic and smooth. Place in prepared bowl, turning to grease top of dough. Let dough rise until double in bulk. Punch down and shape into buns as desired. Place buns on coated baking sheet. Let rise until double in bulk. Bake 25 to 30 minutes at 350 degrees.

My fears are under your feet, God of the Mighty Waves. Amen.

In you, O Lord, I seek refuge	Psalm 31:1a NRSV

Honey Cornbread
1 c. sifted flour
¾ c. yellow cornmeal
1 T. baking powder
½ tsp. salt
1 egg, beaten
¼ c. honey
2 T. melted butter
1 c. milk

Preheat oven to 400 degrees. Coat 8-inch baking pan. In large bowl mix flour, cornmeal, baking powder and salt. In small bowl combine egg, honey, butter and milk. Add egg mixture to flour mixture. Stir to moisten. Pour into prepared pan. Bake 30 minutes.

Running to you is better than running away, God of Truth. Amen.

You are indeed my rock and my fortress . . . .
              Psalm 31:3 NRSV

Hush Puppies
2 c. yellow cornmeal
¾ c. flour
1 tsp. salt
1 medium onion, minced
1 T. baking powder
2 eggs, lightly beaten
1 c. milk or water (approximate)

In medium bowl mix cornmeal, flour, salt, onion and baking powder. Add eggs. Mix well. Stir in enough milk, beginning with ¾ cup, to make thick batter that holds shape on spoon. Drop by heaping tablespoonfuls into deep hot fat. Flip when puppies float. Fry until golden brown all over. Drain on paper towels.

I am shamed, Lord Who Sees, by the things I trust. Amen.

~~~

Happy are those whose transgression is forgiven, whose sin is covered.   Psalm 32:1 NRSV

Kentucky Spoon Bread
½ c. margarine, melted
1 can cream corn
1 can whole-kernel corn, drained
1 egg, beaten
1 c. sour cream
1 small box corn muffin mix, about 8.5 oz.

Preheat oven to 375 degrees. Butter 2-quart baking dish. In large bowl mix margarine, corn, egg and sour cream. Add muffin mix and mix well. Pour into prepared dish. Bake 35 to 40 minutes or until golden brown.

I rest without worry because of my God's salvation. Amen.

Do not forsake me, O Lord;
  O my God, do not be far from me;
make haste to help me,
  O Lord, my salvation.   Psalm 38:21-22 NRSV

Never Fail Bread

4 c. warm water
1 T. salt
½ c. sugar
1 c. vegetable oil
2 pkg. dry yeast (4 T.)
3 eggs, used separately
14 c. sifted flour, divided
1 teaspoon water
Sesame or poppy seeds (optional)

In large bowl mix warm water, salt, sugar, oil, yeast, 2 of the eggs and 6 cups of the flour. Mixer may be used. Add remaining 8 cups flour, 1 cup at a time, mixing after each addition. Knead until all flour is blended and dough is smooth. Place in large greased bowl and turn to grease all sides of dough. Let rise 2 hours or until double in bulk. Punch down gently. Shape into 6 loaves, 6 dozen rolls or a combination of loaves and rolls. Let rise 1 hour or until double in bulk. In small bowl beat remaining egg and 1 teaspoon water. Brush mixture on top of dough. Sprinkle with sesame seeds. Bake in middle of top rack of oven at 350 degrees 20 to 30 minutes or until bread makes hollow sound when tapped.

Your family has no orphans, God the Father, and I delight in being your child. Amen.

Why are you cast down, O my soul,
   and why are you disquieted within me?
Hope in God; for I shall again praise him,
   my help and my God.   Psalm 42:11 NRSV

Oatmeal Bread

1 c. quick-cooking rolled oats
½ c. whole wheat flour
½ c. firmly packed brown sugar
1 T. salt
2 T. butter
2 c. boiling water
1 pkg. dry yeast
½ c. warm water
About 5 c. all-purpose flour

In large bowl combine oats, whole wheat flour, brown sugar, salt and butter. Pour boiling water over all. Cool to lukewarm. In small bowl dissolve yeast in warm water. Add yeast mixture to flour mixture. Gradually add enough all-purpose flour to form smooth, elastic dough. Place in greased bowl, turning to coat top of dough. Let rise until double in bulk. Shape into 2 loaves and place in greased loaf pans. Let rise until double in bulk. Bake at 350 degrees about 30 minutes or until bread makes hollow sound when tapped. Remove loaves from pans. Butter tops for soft crust. Cover with cloth until cool.

Note: More whole wheat flour and less all-purpose flour may be used if desired.

Sometimes, Jesus Who Walks With Us, I feel so sad; but then I remember you and am glad. Amen.

God is king over the nations;
God sits on his holy throne.   Psalm 47:8 NRSV

Raisin Bread
3½ c. flour, divided
4½ tsp. baking powder
1 tsp. salt
½ c. sugar
1½ c. milk
1 egg, beaten
1 T. oil or melted shortening
1 c. chopped raisins, dates or figs

Into large bowl sift 3¼ cup of the flour, baking powder, salt and sugar. Add milk, egg and oil. Beat well. Into small bowl sift reserved ¼ cup flour over raisins and stir well. Stir raisins into dough. Place in greased bread pan and let stand 20 minutes. Bake at 350 degrees 45 to 60 minutes or until lightly browned and tester inserted in center comes out clean.

You, Holy Judge, are highest of all, and I adore you. Amen.

~~~

Have mercy on me, O God, according to your steadfast love.
                                           Psalm 51:1a NRSV

Sixty Minute Rolls
2 pkg. dry yeast (4 T.)
½ c. warm water
1 c. buttermilk
4 T. sugar
¾ tsp. salt
2 T. butter
4 to 4½ c. flour

Coat 1 large or 2 small baking pans. In small bowl dissolve yeast in warm water. In large saucepan combine buttermilk, sugar, salt and butter. Heat until warm. Add yeast mixture. Stir in flour. Cover. Set in warm spot and let rise 15 minutes. Pinch to form 20 to 24 small balls. Place in prepared pans. Let rise 15 minutes. Bake at 450 degrees 10 to 12 minutes or until golden brown.

I was wrong, Jesus Our Bridegroom, to do what I did. I repent and trust your forgiveness. Amen.

~~~

Lead me to the rock that is higher than I.
                                                Psalm 61:2a NRSV

Smoky Mountain Cornbread
2 c. buttermilk
2 c. yellow cornmeal
1 c. flour
2 T. melted shortening
1 tsp. salt
1 tsp. baking soda
1 tsp. baking powder
1 egg, beaten

Preheat oven to 450 degrees. Place greased cast-iron skillet in oven 10 minutes to preheat. In large bowl mix all ingredients until moistened. Do not beat. Pour into hot skillet. Bake 15 to 20 minutes until golden brown.

I rely on your strength today, Rock of Ages. Amen.

Wisdom is a tree of life . . . . Proverbs 3:18a LB

Sour Milk Biscuits
2 c. flour
1 T. baking powder
1 tsp. salt
2 T. shortening
½ tsp. baking soda
¼ c. sour milk

Preheat oven to 450 degrees. Coat baking pan. In large bowl sift and mix flour, baking powder and salt. Cut in shortening. In small bowl mix baking soda and sour milk. Add slowly to flour mixture. Mix to form soft dough. Roll out ½ inch thick on floured surface. Cut into circles. Bake 12 minutes or until golden brown.

Light of the World, let me learn one thing today from you. Amen.

~~~

Have two goals: wisdom . . . and common sense.
Proverbs 3:21 LB

Spoon Bread
1 c. cornmeal
¾ c. boiling water
1 tsp. salt
1 T. sugar
1 beaten egg
½ tsp. baking soda
1 c. buttermilk
1½ T. shortening, melted and slightly cooled

Preheat oven to 375 degrees. Coat deep baking dish. In bowl mix cornmeal and hot water. Cover and cool. Stir in salt, sugar and egg. In small bowl mix baking soda and buttermilk. Stir lightly into cornmeal mixture. Mix in shortening. Pour into prepared dish. Bake 30 to 35 minutes or until golden brown.

You are the center of my universe, Jesus the Door. Amen.

BROWNIES AND BARS

The rich man's wealth is his only strength. The poor man's poverty is his only curse.   Proverbs 10:13 LB

Blondies
⅔ c. melted butter
2 c. firmly packed brown sugar
2 eggs
2 c. flour
1 tsp. baking powder
¼ tsp. baking soda
2 tsp. salt

Preheat oven to 350 degrees. Coat 9 by 13-inch pan. In large bowl mix all ingredients with spoon. Pour batter into prepared pan. Bake 20 to 25 minutes or until lightly browned. Do not overbake. Let cool and cut into squares.

We are poor, Shepherd of Souls, until we know your care. Amen.

A wise man holds his tongue. Only a fool blurts out everything he knows; that only leads to sorrow.

>Proverbs 10:14 LB

Bunny Delights
½ c. margarine
½ c. firmly packed brown sugar
1⅓ c. flour
⅓ c. granulated sugar
⅔ c. light corn syrup
6 oz. chocolate chips (1 c.)
½ c. chunky peanut butter
2 c. corn flakes

Preheat oven to 350 degrees. In medium bowl cream margarine and brown sugar. Stir in flour until mixture is crumbly. Press into ungreased 9 by 13-inch baking pan. Bake 15 minutes. Cool. In medium saucepan mix granulated sugar and corn syrup. Bring to boil. Remove from heat and add chocolate chips and peanut butter. Stir until melted. Stir in corn flakes. Top baked mixture with chocolate mixture. Cool. Cut into squares.

What folly it is when my mouth is open and my mind is shut, God of Knowledge. Amen.

It is possible to give away and become richer!
Proverbs 11:24 LB

Caramel Chocolate Bars
14 oz. light caramels, about 50
⅓ c. evaporated milk
1 German chocolate cake mix
1 c. chopped nuts
1 T. water
½ c. margarine or butter, softened
1 c. semisweet chocolate chips

Preheat oven to 350 degrees. Grease and flour 9 by 13-inch baking pan. In heavy saucepan combine caramels and evaporated milk. Cook over low heat, stirring constantly, until caramels melt. Keep warm. In large bowl combine cake mix, nuts, water and margarine. Stir with fork until mixture crumbles. Press half of dough into prepared pan. Bake 6 minutes. Sprinkle chocolate pieces over baked crust. Spread caramel mixture on chocolate. Spread remaining half of dough over caramel mixture and bake 15 to 20 minutes. Cool completely before cutting into bars.

Word of Life, the more I share you, the richer I feel. Amen.

To learn, you must want to be taught.

> Proverbs 12:1a LB

Caramel Oatmeal Squares

½ c. butter, softened
1 c. sugar
1 egg
½ tsp. vanilla
1½ c. rolled oats
1¼ c. flour
½ tsp. baking powder
¼ tsp. baking soda
½ tsp. salt
1 tsp. ground cinnamon
½ c. semisweet chocolate chips
12 caramel candies
2 tsp. water

Preheat oven to 375 degrees. Lightly coat 8-inch square baking pan. In medium bowl beat butter and sugar until fluffy. Beat in egg and vanilla. In separate bowl mix oats, flour, baking powder, baking soda, salt and cinnamon. Add dry ingredients to butter mixture. Beat until well blended. Press half of dough into baking pan. Sprinkle with chocolate chips.

Combine caramels and water in microwave-safe bowl. Heat in microwave oven at 50 percent power until caramels are melted. Drizzle caramel over chocolate. Crumble remaining dough on top. Bake 18 to 22 minutes or until top is lightly browned. Cool completely before cutting into squares.

Okay, Ensign God, you opened my heart with your love, and now you're opening my mind with your truth. Joy is mine! Amen.

The backslider gets bored with himself; the godly man's life is exciting.   Proverbs 14:14 LB

Chocolate Revel Bars
Batter:
1 c. butter
2 c. firmly packed brown sugar
2 eggs
2 tsp. vanilla
2½ c. flour
1 tsp. baking soda
1 tsp. salt
3 c. rolled oats

Preheat oven to 350 degrees. Coat 10 by 15-inch baking pan. In large bowl cream butter and brown sugar. Add eggs and vanilla. Beat until fluffy. Stir in flour, baking soda, salt and oats. Set aside.

Chocolate filling:
12 oz. chocolate chips
1 can sweetened condensed milk
2 T. butter, softened
½ tsp. salt
1c. chopped nuts
2 tsp. vanilla

In double boiler or microwave oven melt chocolate chips. Stir in condensed milk, butter, salt, nuts and vanilla. Spread two-thirds of batter in prepared pan. Cover with chocolate mixture. Dot with remaining one-third of batter. Bake 30 minutes or until tester inserted in center comes out clean.

My Lord and my God, what a good time we have as we live in you. Amen.

A soft answer turns away wrath, but harsh words cause quarrels.
Proverbs 15:1 LB

Colonial Pumpkin Bars
¾ c. margarine
2 c. sugar
2 c. canned pumpkin
4 eggs
2 c. flour
2 tsp. baking powder
1 tsp. ground cinnamon
½ tsp. baking soda
½ tsp. salt
¼ tsp. ground nutmeg
1 c. chopped nuts
Vanilla Cream Cheese Frosting

Preheat oven to 350 degrees. Grease and flour 10 by 15-inch jellyroll pan. In large bowl cream margarine and sugar until light and fluffy. Blend in pumpkin and eggs. In another bowl combine dry ingredients. Add dry mixture to creamed mixture. Mix well. Stir in nuts. Spread batter into prepared pan. Bake 30 to 35 minutes or until tester inserted in center comes out clean. Frost with Vanilla Cream Cheese Frosting and cut into bars.

Vanilla Cream Cheese Frosting
3 oz. cream cheese, softened
⅓ c. margarine
1 tsp. vanilla
3 c. powdered sugar

In small bowl combine cream cheese, margarine and vanilla. Blend well. Gradually add sugar, mixing well after each addition.

The next time—the very next time—I want to say something mean, God Who Listens, I promise to remember instead that you want me to speak softly. Amen.

Only the good can give good advice. Rebels can't.
Proverbs 15:7 LB

Date Bars
1 c. nuts, chopped
1 c. stoned dates, chopped
1 c. plus about ½ c. powdered sugar .
2 eggs, beaten
1 T. lemon juice
¼ c. flour
1 T. melted shortening
½ tsp. salt

Coat large shallow baking pan. In large bowl combine nuts, dates, 1 cup of the powdered sugar and eggs. Mix well. Add lemon juice, flour, shortening and salt. Mix thoroughly. Spread about ¼ inch thick in prepared pan. Bake at 350 degrees 20 to 25 minutes. While hot, cut into strips or bars and roll in remaining ½ cup powdered sugar.

Jesus the Teacher, point out to me the ones whose wisdom I should trust. Amen.

A mocker stays away from wise men because he hates to be scolded.
                                                  Proverbs 15:12 LB

Date Chews
¾ c. butter or margarine, melted
¾ c. whole pitted dates
1 egg
1 tsp. vanilla
1¾ c. rolled oats
½ c. flour
½ c. granulated sugar or firmly packed brown sugar
1 tsp. ground cinnamon
½ tsp. baking soda
½ tsp. salt

Preheat oven to 350 degrees. Coat 9 by 13-inch baking pan. Place butter, dates, egg and vanilla in blender and blend 5 to 10 seconds or until dates are coarsely chopped. In large bowl mix oats, flour, sugar, cinnamon, baking soda and salt. Add date mixture to flour mixture and mix well. Spread evenly in prepared pan. Bake 18 to 20 minutes or until golden brown. Cool and cut into bars. Store in airtight container.

If I must be scolded, God Who Chastens, I pray to be humble enough to recognize truth and open enough to learn. Amen.

~~~

Dishonest money brings grief to all the family . . . .
                                                  Proverbs 15:27a LB

Dirt Bars
1 German chocolate cake mix
¾ c. margarine, melted
1 c. chopped nuts
50 caramel candies
1 small can evaporated milk, about 5 oz.
1 c. chocolate chips

Preheat oven to 350 degrees. Coat 9 by 13-inch baking pan. In large bowl blend cake mix, margarine and nuts. Press half of mixture into prepared pan. Bake 6 minutes. In small saucepan melt caramels with milk. Sprinkle chocolate chips over cake in pan. Cover with melted caramel mixture. Spread remaining cake mixture on top. Bake additional 15 to 20 minutes or until cake is firm to touch and pulls away from sides of pan.

Lord Who Sweeps Clean, the broom is in your hands. Amen.

~~~

We can make our plans, but the final outcome is in God's hands.   Proverbs 16:1 LB

English Toffee
2 c. sugar
6 T. water
1 tsp. vanilla
2 c. butter, softened
1 c. coarsely chopped pecans
12 oz. chocolate chips
½ c. finely chopped pecans

Butter 9 by 13-inch pan. In 4-quart saucepan combine sugar, water and vanilla. Cook over medium heat until sugar dissolves. Add butter gradually, stirring constantly, over medium heat. Cook to 260 degrees on candy thermometer. Add coarsely chopped pecans. Cook to 300 degrees. Spread in prepared pan. Sprinkle chocolate chips on top. Spread chocolate when melted. Sprinkle finely chopped pecans on top. With large sharp knife, score while hot into 1-inch squares. Cut when toffee is cooled and chocolate is set.

What do you have in store for us, O God of Tomorrow? We wait eagerly. Amen.

Better poor and humble than proud and rich.
>Proverbs 16:19 LB

Fig Newsomes
½ c. shortening
1½ c. sugar, divided
1 egg, well beaten
½ c. milk
1 tsp. vanilla
3 c. flour
½ tsp. salt
3 tsp. baking powder
1 c. figs, chopped
1 c. boiling water

Preheat oven to 400 degrees. In large bowl cream shortening and 1 cup of the sugar. Add egg and beat until light. In small bowl mix milk and vanilla. Into separate bowl sift flour, salt and baking powder. Add flour mixture and milk mixture alternately to creamed mixture, blending well after each addition. Shape into ball and place on lightly floured surface. Roll into rectangle ½ inch thick. Cut dough into 2 equal pieces. Place figs in saucepan with remaining ½ cup sugar and boiling water. Boil 5 minutes. Cool. Spread cooked mixture over half of dough. Cover with other half of dough. Cut into bars. Bake 12 to 15 minutes or until golden brown.

What a surprise it was to learn that the world does not revolve around me, Lord of All. Amen.

~~~

Kind words are like honey—enjoyable and healthful.
>Proverbs 16:24 LB

Fruit and Chocolate Dreams
Crust:
1¼ c. flour
½ c. sugar
½ c. butter, softened

Preheat oven to 350 degrees. Coat 9-inch square pan. In medium bowl combine flour, sugar and butter. Mix into fine crumbs. Press into prepared pan. Bake 20 to 25 minutes. Remove from oven.

Topping:
½ c. seedless raspberry jam
10 oz. milk chocolate chips
⅔ c. flour
6 T. butter, softened
6 T. sugar
½ c. chopped nuts
½ tsp. vanilla

Spread jam on baked crust. Sprinkle chocolate chips evenly on jam. In medium bowl mix flour, butter, sugar, nuts and vanilla. Spread on chocolate chips. Bake 15 to 20 minutes. Cool. Cut into squares.

Whether or not I hear kind words from others, Mighty One of Israel, let me utter them. Amen.

Only that shall happen
Which has happened,
Only that occur
Which has occurred,
There is nothing new
Beneath the sun!

Ecclesiastes 1:9 JPS

Fudge Nut Orange Bars

Crust:
1 butter-recipe yellow cake mix
1 c. rolled oats
⅓ c. margarine, softened
1 egg

Filling:
1 c. chocolate chips, about 6 oz.
½ c. sugar
½ c. margarine, softened
2 eggs
1 c. chopped pecans
2 tsp. grated orange peel
¼ c. orange juice

Glaze:
½ c. chocolate chips
2 T. margarine
1 tsp. orange juice

To make crust, preheat oven to 350 degrees. Coat 9 by 13-inch pan. In large bowl combine cake mix, oats and margarine at low speed until crumbs form. Reserve 1 cup crumbs for filling. To remaining crumbs add 1 egg and mix well. Press crumb-egg mixture into bottom of prepared pan.

To make filling, in medium saucepan heat chocolate chips, sugar and margarine over low heat, stirring constantly, until chips melt. Remove from heat. Add eggs and mix well. Stir in pecans, orange peel and orange juice. Pour evenly over prepared crumb crust. Sprinkle with reserved crumbs. Bake 30 to 40 minutes until center is set. Cool completely.

To make glaze, in small saucepan heat chocolate chips, margarine and orange juice, stirring until smooth. Immediately drizzle over filling in crisscross design. Cut into 36 bars.

You mean this isn't the first time a person has felt lost and lonely, God of Hiding Places? Amen.

~~~

Wisdom is superior to folly
As light is superior to darkness.
<div align="right">Ecclesiastes 12:13 JPS</div>

Happy Squares
1 c. butter, softened
1 c. firmly packed brown sugar
2 egg yolks
Pinch of salt
2 c. flour
6 to 8 regular chocolate bars
¼ c. ground nuts (optional)

Preheat oven to 350 degrees. Butter 10 by 15-inch rimmed baking sheet. In large bowl cream butter, brown sugar, yolks, salt and flour. Spread evenly on prepared baking sheet. Bake 20 to 25 minutes or until lightly browned. Remove from oven. Place chocolate bars on top. When melted, smooth with knife. Cool. Cut into squares. Sprinkle nuts on top. May be frozen.

If I can't be wise about all things, God Who Loves Me, then let me be wise about one thing. Amen.

A time for being born and a time for dying,
A time for planting and a time for uprooting the planted.
Proverbs 3:2 JPS

Kate's Brownies
1 c. unsalted butter or non-dairy margarine suitable for baking
2 c. sugar
1¼ c. cocoa
1 tsp. salt
1 tsp. baking powder
1 T. vanilla
4 large eggs, lightly beaten
1 c. unbleached all-purpose flour
½ c. whole wheat pastry flour
1 c. chocolate chips

Preheat oven to 350 degrees. Coat 9 by 13-inch baking pan. Melt butter in medium saucepan over low heat. Add sugar and stir about 30 seconds. Remove from heat briefly. Return mixture to heat and cook just until hot but not bubbling. (Mixture will look shiny.) Remove from heat and stir in cocoa, salt, baking powder and vanilla. Add eggs and stir until smooth. Add flour and stir until smooth. Spoon batter into prepared pan. Bake about 25 minutes or until cake tester inserted in center comes out clean. Remove from oven. Sprinkle chocolate chips on top. Cool on rack before cutting into bars or squares.

Wonderful Counselor, I'm still learning to hold each minute as a gift from you. Amen.

A time for slaying and a time for healing,
A time for tearing down and a time for building up.
Proverbs 3:3 JPS

Lemon Bars
2½ c. flour, divided
½ c. powdered sugar
1 c. soft butter
4 eggs, beaten
2 c. granulated sugar
½ tsp. salt
6 T. lemon juice
1½ c. shredded or flaked coconut (optional)
Powdered sugar for dusting

Preheat oven to 350 degrees. In large bowl mix 2 cups of the flour, powdered sugar and butter. Press into ungreased 9 by 13-inch pan. Bake 15 to 20 minutes. In medium bowl mix eggs, granulated sugar, remaining ½ cup flour, salt, lemon juice and coconut. Pour mixture over baked crust. Bake 25 to 30 minutes. Cool and cut into bars. Dust with powdered sugar. Best if made a day ahead.

We remember yesterday and sorrow, but you remember yesterday and call us to tomorrow, God of All Days. Amen.

A time for weeping and a time for laughing,
A time for wailing and a time for dancing.

> Proverbs 3:4 JPS

Lemon Chiffon Dessert

Crust:
1½ c. graham crackers, crushed (about 24 squares)
⅓ c. sugar
½ c. butter, melted

Coat 9 by 13-inch pan or dish. Combine ingredients and mix until crumbly. Set aside 3 tablespoons for topping. Press remainder into prepared pan.

Filling:
3 oz. package lemon gelatin
1 c. boiling water
8 oz. plus 3 oz. cream cheese
1 c. sugar
1 tsp. vanilla
8 oz. frozen whipped topping

In bowl combine gelatin and boiling water. Mix well. Set aside to cool. In small bowl beat cream cheese until soft. Add sugar and vanilla. Slowly add gelatin. Mix well. Slowly fold in frozen whipped topping. Spread evenly over crust. Sprinkle with reserved crumbs. Cut into squares. Cover. Refrigerate at least 3 hours before serving.

Note: Other gelatin flavors may be substituted as desired.

I know when to cry, God the Word; help me learn to laugh. Amen.

A time for throwing stones and a time for gathering stones,
A time for embracing and a time for shunning embraces.
Proverbs 3:5 JPS

Minty Refrigerator Brownies
1 c. chopped walnuts
2 c. miniature marshmallows
4 c. graham cracker crumbs (about 52 squares)
1 c. powdered sugar
12 oz. chocolate chips
1 c. evaporated milk
¾ tsp. peppermint extract

Coat 9 by 13-inch pan or dish. In large bowl mix walnuts, marshmallows, graham cracker crumbs and powdered sugar. Set aside. In double boiler heat chocolate chips with evaporated milk until chips melt. Remove from heat and stir in peppermint extract. Reserve ½ cup chocolate mixture. Stir remaining chocolate mixture into crumb mixture until well moistened. Press into prepared pan. Pour reserved ½ cup chocolate mixture on top. Cut into bars. Refrigerate at least 3 hours before serving.

You have time-stamped my life, God of Creation. Amen.

A time for seeking and a time for losing,
A time for keeping and a time for discarding.

> Proverbs 3:6 JPS

Oatmeal Toffee Bars
Crust:
8 c. oatmeal
1 c. granulated sugar
1⅓ c. butter, softened
2 c. firmly packed brown sugar
1 tsp. vanilla

Topping:
12 oz. chocolate chips
1 c. peanut butter

Preheat oven to 375 degrees. Coat two 10 by 15-inch baking pans. In large bowl combine oatmeal, granulated sugar, butter, brown sugar and vanilla. Mix well. Spread thinly into prepared pans. Bake 10 minutes. In small saucepan melt chocolate chips and peanut butter over low heat. Mix well. Spread on bars immediately after bars are removed from oven. Cut into bars while warm.

See all this junk around me, God of Order? I know you hate it, and now I do, too. Amen.

A time for ripping and a time for sewing,
A time for silence and a time for speaking.

> Proverbs 3:7 JPS

O-Henriettas

Crust:
⅔ c. margarine
1 c. firmly packed brown sugar
4 c. quick-cooking rolled oats
½ c. light corn syrup
1 tsp. vanilla
Dash salt

Topping:
6 oz. chocolate chips
⅔ c. crunchy peanut butter

Preheat oven to 350 degrees. Coat 9 by 13-inch baking pan. In large bowl cream margarine and brown sugar. Add oats, corn syrup, vanilla and salt. Blend well. Pat mixture into prepared pan. Bake 12 to 15 minutes or until lightly brown and firm to the touch. Cool.

For topping, melt chocolate chips with peanut butter in top of double boiler. Spread mixture evenly over crust. Cover and refrigerate until chocolate sets. Cut into bars. Store in refrigerator.

That's the hardest one, Jesus the Firstborn, the one about speaking sometimes and not other times. Amen.

A time for loving and a time for hating;
A time for war and a time for peace.

Proverbs 3:8 JPS

Peanut Butter Brownies
¼ c. shortening
½ c. peanut butter
1½ c. granulated sugar
¾ c. firmly packed brown sugar
3 eggs
1½ tsp. vanilla
2 c. flour
2¼ tsp. baking powder
¾ tsp. salt
¼ c. chopped peanuts (optional)

Preheat oven to 350 degrees. In large bowl cream shortening and peanut butter. Add granulated sugar and brown sugar and beat well. Add eggs and vanilla. Beat until creamy. Add flour, baking powder and salt. Mix well. Add peanuts and mix well. Spread evenly into prepared pan. Bake 30 to 35 minutes or until tester inserted in center comes out clean. Cool. Cut into bars.

What do you mean, God the Eternal One, that there is a time for war? I need to know. Amen.

~~~

Whatever God has brought to pass will recur evermore:
   Nothing can be added to it
   And nothing can be taken from it. Proverbs 3:14 JPS

Peanut Butter Fudgy Bars
1 yellow cake mix
1½ c. crunchy peanut butter, divided
⅓ c. water
1 egg
1 can prepared chocolate frosting
1 c. candy-coated chocolate pieces
½ c. chopped peanuts

Preheat oven to 350 degrees. Coat 9 by 13-inch baking pan. In large bowl combine cake mix, 1 cup of the peanut butter, water and egg. Mix 1 minute on low speed, then 2 minutes on medium speed. Spread into prepared pan. Bake 20 to 25 minutes or until puffed and light golden brown. Cool completely.

In small bowl blend frosting with remaining ½ cup peanut butter. Spread over cooled bars. Top with candy pieces and peanuts.

What a joy it is, Gracious God, to be part of your plan. Amen.

~~~

Keep your mouth from being rash.
<div align="right">Proverbs 5:1a JPS</div>

Pecan Turtle Bars
2 c. flour
1½ c. firmly packed brown sugar, divided
½ c. plus ⅔ c. margarine, softened
1 c. pecan halves
1 c. milk chocolate chips

Preheat oven to 350 degrees. In medium bowl mix flour, 1 cup of the brown sugar and ½ cup of the margarine. Pat firmly into ungreased 9 by 13-inch pan. Sprinkle with pecan halves. In small saucepan combine remaining ½ cup brown sugar and remaining ⅔ cup margarine. Cook over medium heat, stirring constantly, until bubbly, 30 to 60 seconds. Pour over pecans in crust. Bake 20 minutes or until top layer is bubbly and crust is golden brown. Remove from oven and sprinkle with milk chocolate chips. Allow chips to melt slightly, swirling as they melt. Cut into bars.

Loving God, help me to pray quickly, not to speak quickly. Amen.

A lover of money never has his fill of money . . . .
>
> Proverbs 5:9a JPS

Seven Layer Bars
¼ c. butter
1 c. graham cracker crumbs
1 c. flaked or shredded coconut
1 c. chocolate chips
1 c. white chocolate chips
1 c. chopped walnuts
1 can sweetened condensed milk

Preheat oven to 350 degrees. Melt butter in 9-inch square pan. Spread graham cracker crumbs in pan. Spread coconut, chocolate chips, white chocolate chips and walnuts in layers over crumbs. Pour condensed milk on top. Bake 30 minutes.

The love you spend on this world outshines all the money ever made or spent, God Who Is, Who Was and Who Is to Come. Amen.

A good name is better than fragrant oil, and the day of death than the day of birth.

Proverbs 7:1 JPS

Valentine Fudge Brownies
1 c. butter or margarine, melted
1 c. unsweetened cocoa powder
1¼ c. firmly packed dark brown sugar
1 c. granulated sugar
½ tsp. salt
4 eggs
1¼ c. flour
6 oz. semisweet chocolate chips
1 c. chopped nuts (optional)
Sweetened whipped cream or ice cream for topping (optional)

Preheat oven to 350 degrees. Coat 9 by 13-inch baking pan. In large bowl combine butter and cocoa and mix well. Add brown sugar, granulated sugar and salt. Mix well. Add eggs, one at a time, blending after each addition. Add flour and mix well. Stir in chocolate chips and nuts. Spread evenly in prepared pan. Bake 30 minutes or until edges pull away slightly from pan. Top with whipped cream or ice cream to serve.

My favorite name is Christian, and you're the reason, Jesus the Christ of Humanity. Amen.

CAKES AND FROSTINGS

It is better to listen to a wise man's reproof than to listen to the praise of fools. Proverbs 7:5 JPS

Apple Dapple Cake
Batter:
1½ c. vegetable oil
2 c. sugar
3 eggs
2 tsp. vanilla
3 c. flour
1 tsp. salt
1 tsp. baking soda
1⅓ c. chopped nuts
3 c. peeled apples, chopped
Whipped topping or ice cream for topping

Sauce:
1 c. firmly packed brown sugar
½ c. margarine
¼ c. milk or cream

Preheat oven to 350 degrees. Coat 9 by 13-inch baking pan. In large bowl cream oil, sugar, eggs and vanilla. In separate bowl stir flour, salt and baking soda. Add to creamed mixture. Blend well. Fold in nuts and apples. Pour into prepared pan. Bake 60 to 75 minutes or until tester inserted in center comes out clean.

For sauce, combine brown sugar, margarine and milk in small saucepan and cook 3 minutes. Pour hot sauce over hot cake. Cool in pan 2 hours. Serve warm with whipped topping or ice cream.

When I don't know which way to turn, let me turn to the wise, Guiding God. Amen.

The race is not won by the swift, nor the battle by the valiant;
Nor is bread won by the wise, nor wealth by the intelligent,
Nor favor by the learned, for the time of mischance comes to all.
                                        Proverbs 9:11 JPS

Banana Cake with Olive Oil
2 c. flour
1¼ c. sugar
1½ tsp. baking powder
¾ tsp. baking soda
½ tsp. salt
1 c. mashed ripe banana
½ c. buttermilk or sour milk
¼ c. plus 2 T. extra-light olive oil
2 eggs or equivalent egg substitute
1 tsp. vanilla

Preheat oven to 350 degrees. Coat two round 8-inch cake pans. In large bowl sift flour, sugar, baking powder, baking soda and salt. Add banana, buttermilk, oil, eggs and vanilla. Beat on low speed 3 to 4 minutes or until well blended. Divide batter between prepared pans. Bake 30 minutes or until tester inserted in center comes out clean. Cool cakes in pans for a few minutes. Turn cakes out onto racks. Cool completely. Frost as desired. May be filled with Banana Butter.

Banana Butter
4 ripe bananas
1 c. sugar
2 eggs, well beaten
2 T. butter
Grated rind and juice of 1 lemon

In bowl mash bananas well. Add sugar, eggs, butter, lemon rind and lemon juice. Place mixture in saucepan and cook until thick, stirring constantly. Cool and spread between cake layers.

You are the author of completion, God Our Crown. Amen.

Send your bread forth upon the waters; for after many days you will find it.   Proverbs 11:1 JPS

Blackberry Jam Cake
1 c. butter
2 c. sugar
1 tsp. baking soda
1 c. buttermilk
4 eggs, separated
3 c. flour
2 tsp. ground cinnamon
1 tsp. ground nutmeg
1 tsp. ground cloves
1 tsp. ground allspice
1 c. blackberry jam
1 tsp. vanilla

Preheat oven to 300 degrees. Butter and flour large tube pan or Bundt pan. In large mixer bowl cream butter and sugar. In small bowl dissolve baking soda in buttermilk. Add 4 egg yolks and mix well. Into separate bowl sift flour, cinnamon, nutmeg, cloves and allspice. Add buttermilk mixture and flour mixture alternately to butter mixture, mixing well after each addition. Add jam and vanilla and mix well. In separate bowl beat the 4 egg whites until stiff but not dry. Fold gently into batter. Bake at 300 degrees for 15 minutes, at 350 degrees for 15 minutes, and finally at 360 degrees for 30 to 40 minutes or until tester inserted in center comes out clean. Remove from oven and cool 20 minutes before removing from pan.

Note: For a tasty icing, heat ½ cup blackberry jam with ½ cup powdered sugar until melted. Pour over cooled cake.

I stand casting crusts at the shore of faith, and I trust in you, Morning Star. Amen.

As an apple tree among the trees of the wood,
so is my love among young men.
In his delightful shade I sit,
and his fruit is sweet to my taste.

The Song of Songs 1:2 NJB

Brownie Cheesecake
1 pkg. (9 by 13-inch pan size) brownie mix
32 oz. cream cheese, softened
1 c. sugar
1 tsp. vanilla
½ c. sour cream
3 eggs
2 squares semisweet baking chocolate, melted, cooled slightly

Preheat oven to 350 degrees. Line 9 by 13-inch baking pan with foil, with ends of foil extending over sides of pan. Coat with cooking spray. Prepare brownie batter as directed on package. Pour into prepared pan. Bake 15 minutes or until top of batter is shiny and center is almost set.

Meanwhile, in large bowl beat cream cheese, sugar and vanilla on medium speed until well blended. Add sour cream and mix well. Add eggs, one at a time, mixing after each addition just until blended. Pour over partially baked brownie batter in pan. Filling will come almost to top of pan. Bake 40 minutes or until center is almost set.

Let stand at room temperature 30 minutes before serving. Lift cheesecake from pan using foil "handles." Drizzle with chocolate. Let stand until chocolate is firm. Cut into 16 squares. Refrigerate leftover cheesecake.

God Our Rainbow, you think of everything. Amen.

A capable wife, her husband's crown,
a shameless wife, a cancer in his bones.

> Proverbs 12:4 NJB

Caramel Pecan Coffee Cake

Batter:
1¾ c. flour
2 pkg. fast-rise yeast
2 T. sugar
½ tsp. salt
¾ c. very warm water (120 to 130 degrees)

Sugar Topping:
¼ c. sugar
1 tsp. ground cinnamon

Caramel Pecan Topping:
⅓ c. light or dark corn syrup
⅓ c. firmly packed brown sugar
2 T. butter, melted
½ c. chopped pecans

Coat 9-inch deep-dish pie plate. For batter, combine flour, yeast, sugar, salt and water in prepared plate.

Combine Sugar Topping ingredients in small bowl and stir well. Sprinkle mixture evenly over batter.

Combine Caramel Pecan Topping ingredients in small bowl and mix well. Pour over batter. Place cake in cold oven. Set oven to 350 degrees. Bake 25 minutes or until lightly browned and firm in center. Cool slightly before serving

O God, Our Dove, grant the unwed wisdom in choosing mates. Amen.

The fool shows anger straightaway . . . .
Proverbs 12:16a NJB

Caramel White Chocolate Cheesecake

1¼ c. graham cracker crumbs
¼ c. sugar
½ tsp. ground cinnamon
¼ c. butter, melted
12 oz. white chocolate, divided
½ c. whipping cream
16 oz. cream cheese, softened
4 eggs
1 T. vanilla
1½ c. caramel apple dip, divided

Preheat oven to 300 degrees. Coat springform pan. In medium bowl combine graham cracker crumbs, sugar, cinnamon and butter. Press onto bottom of prepared pan to form crust. In microwave or on stovetop, melt 10 ounces of the white chocolate with the whipping cream. Cool. In large mixer bowl beat cream cheese until fluffy. Beat in eggs one at a time until well blended. Stir in white chocolate mixture and vanilla. Remove one cup of batter and mix with one cup of the caramel dip. Spoon cream-cheese batter and cream-cheese/caramel batter alternately over crust. Cut through batter with table knife to marble. Bake 55 minutes or until set. Center will be slightly soft. Turn off oven and leave cheesecake in oven one hour. Cool completely. Chill.

To make sauce, in microwavable bowl combine remaining 2 ounces white chocolate and remaining ½ cup caramel dip. Cook on high power 40 seconds. Serve over chilled cheesecake.

Thank you, Christ the Forerunner, for the gift of emotions and the power of patience. Amen.

For the diligent hand, authority;
   for the slack hand, forced labour.   Proverbs 12:24 NJB

Carrot Cake
2 c. sugar
4 eggs
1½ c. vegetable oil
3 c. flour
2 tsp. baking soda
2 tsp. ground cinnamon
1 tsp. salt
1 c. crushed pineapple with juice
3 c. raw grated carrots
1 c. chopped nuts
2 tsp. vanilla
½ c. flaked or shredded coconut

Preheat oven to 350 degrees. Coat two small pans or one 9 by 13-inch pan. In large bowl beat sugar, eggs and oil. Into medium bowl sift flour, baking soda, cinnamon and salt. Blend into creamed mixture. Mix in pineapple and carrots. Stir in nuts, vanilla and coconut. Pour into pans. Bake 1 hour or until tester comes out clean. Cool. Good with Waldorf White Cake Icing.

Waldorf White Cake Icing
¼ c. flour
½ tsp. salt
1 c. milk
1 c. granulated sugar
1 c. shortening
1 tsp. vanilla

Mix flour and salt in medium saucepan. Slowly stir in milk until smooth. Cook over medium heat until very thick. Cool. In mixer bowl cream sugar and shortening. Gradually add cooled flour mixture to creamed mixture, beating until satiny. Stir in vanilla.

My heart, my voice, my feet, my hands—all are yours, Prince of Peace. Amen.

The light of the upright is joyful,
 the lamp of the wicked goes out.   Proverbs 13:9 NJB

Chocolate Skinny Cake
¾ c. unsweetened cocoa powder
¼ c. sugar
½ c. boiling water
1 angel food cake mix
1¼ c. water
1 T. instant coffee granules
1½ c. skim milk
1 pkg. whipped topping mix, about 1⅓ oz.
1 small pkg. sugar-free instant chocolate pudding mix

Preheat oven to 350 degrees. Line 10 x 15-inch jelly roll pan with waxed paper. In medium bowl whisk cocoa, sugar and boiling water. Cool to lukewarm. In large bowl prepare cake mix as directed on package, using 1¼ cup water. Add cocoa mixture and mix well. Spread batter evenly in prepared pan. Bake 20 minutes or until top looks slightly dry. Invert onto large wire rack. Remove pan and waxed paper. Cool.

In medium mixer bowl dissolve coffee in skim milk. Add topping and pudding mixes. Beat on low speed until moistened. Beat at high speed until soft peaks form. Chill 5 minutes. Cut cake crosswise into thirds. Cover each layer with topping. Stack. Chill 2 hours.

You put me in this place to shine for you. I'm sure of it, God Our Promised Land. Amen.

Contempt for the word is self-destructive,
   respect for the commandment wins salvation.
Proverbs 13:13 NJB

Cinnamon Crunch Coffeecake

Batter:
2 c. whole wheat flour
2½ tsp. baking powder
1 tsp. ground cinnamon
½ tsp. salt
¼ tsp. ground nutmeg
¾ c. honey
⅓ c. butter, softened
1 c. milk
2 eggs

Topping:
⅔ c. firmly packed brown sugar
2 T. all-purpose flour
2 T. butter
1 c. chopped pecans

Preheat oven to 350 degrees. Grease and flour 9 by 13-inch pan. In large bowl mix whole wheat flour, baking powder, cinnamon, salt and nutmeg. Blend in honey, ⅓ cup butter and milk. Beat 90 seconds. Add eggs and beat 1 minute. Spread one-third of batter in pan.

In small bowl combine brown sugar and all-purpose flour. Cut in 2 tablespoons butter until mixture is crumbly. Stir in pecans. Sprinkle half of topping on batter in pan. Carefully spread remaining batter over topping. Sprinkle with remaining topping. Bake 30 to 35 minutes or until tester inserted in center comes out clean. Serve warm.

Your word first, Heavenly Parent. Amen.

Whoever walks with the wise becomes wise,
whoever mixes with fools will be ruined.
Proverbs 13:20 NJB

Coconut Cake
1¾ c. sifted cake flour
2¼ tsp. baking powder
¾ tsp. salt
½ c. butter
1 c. plus 2 T. sugar
2 eggs
⅔ c. milk
1 tsp. vanilla
⅔ c. coconut

Preheat oven to 350 degrees. Coat two 8-inch cake pans. Into large bowl sift cake flour, baking powder and salt. In another large bowl cream butter and sugar. Add eggs one at a time, beating well after each. Alternately add flour mixture and milk to creamed mixture, beating well after each addition. Stir in vanilla and coconut. Spread in pans. Bake 30 to 35 minutes or until tester comes out clean. Good with Caramel Coconut Frosting.

Caramel Coconut Frosting
1½ c. firmly packed brown sugar
¾ c. cream or milk
2 T. butter
½ tsp. vanilla
1 c. moist shredded or flaked coconut

In heavy 2-quart saucepan combine brown sugar and cream. Cook over medium-low heat, stirring constantly, until a drop of mixture forms soft, pliable ball when dropped in cold water. Remove from heat. Stir in butter and vanilla. Cool to lukewarm. Beat to spreading consistency. Frost cake. Sprinkle with coconut and place under broiler until coconut is delicately browned.

Sometimes, Sovereign God, I worry about all the decisions you have left up to me. Amen.

Evil will pursue the sinner,
   but good will reward the upright.

> Proverbs 13:21 NJB

Cola Cake

Batter:
¾ c. margarine, melted
3 oz. unsweetened chocolate, melted
2¼ c. sugar
3 eggs
2¼ c. flour
1½ tsp. baking soda
2¼ c. cola beverage
1½ c. chopped pecans

Frosting:
⅓ c. margarine
1½ oz. unsweetened chocolate
1½ c. sugar
¾ tsp. salt
¾ c. evaporated milk
1½ tsp. vanilla

Preheat oven to 350 degrees. Grease and flour 9 by 13-inch pan. To make batter, in large bowl cream margarine, chocolate, sugar and eggs. In another bowl stir flour and baking soda. Add to margarine mixture. Stir in cola and pecans. Batter will be thin. Pour batter into prepared pan and bake 30 to 40 minutes or until tester inserted in center comes out clean.

To make frosting, melt margarine and chocolate in large saucepan over low heat. Blend in sugar and salt. Slowly add milk, stirring to keep mixture smooth. Bring to boil. Cook 2 minutes, stirring frequently. Remove from heat. Stir in vanilla.

Remove cake from oven. Poke all over with fork. Pour frosting on top. Cool.

I am run ragged but cannot stop, God My Altar. Amen.

Mastery of temper is proof of intelligence . . . .
Proverbs 14:29a NJB

Dark Applesauce Cake
¾ c. shortening
1½ c. sugar
2 eggs
2 c. applesauce
2¼ c. flour
1½ c. baking soda
½ tsp. salt
1½ tsp. ground cinnamon
¾ tsp. ground cloves
1½ c. raisins
1½ c. chopped nuts

Preheat oven to 350 degrees. Coat angel food cake pan. In large bowl cream shortening. Gradually beat in sugar and eggs. Add applesauce and beat 2 minutes. In separate bowl mix flour, baking soda, salt, cinnamon and cloves. Add dry ingredients slowly to creamed mixture and blend well. Stir in raisins and nuts. Pour batter into prepared pan. Bake 70 to 75 minutes or until tester inserted in center comes out clean. Turn cake out onto rack to cool completely. Top with Butterscotch Sauce or Caramel Frosting.

Butterscotch Sauce
1 c. firmly packed light brown sugar
¼ c. half-and-half
2 T. butter
2 T. light corn syrup

Combine all ingredients in heavy saucepan. Bring to boil over medium heat, stirring occasionally. Do not overcook. Serve over Dark Applesauce Cake or other desserts.

Caramel Frosting

½ c. butter (not margarine)
1 c. firmly packed brown sugar
¼ tsp. salt
¼ c. milk
2½ c. powdered sugar, sifted
1 tsp. vanilla

Melt butter in large saucepan. Blend in brown sugar and salt. Cook over low heat, stirring constantly, 2 minutes, until sugar dissolves. Add milk. Continue to stir until mixture boils. Remove from heat. Gradually blend in powdered sugar. Add vanilla and mix well. Thin with more milk or thicken with more powdered sugar to reach spreading consistency.

I'm sorry for losing my temper today, Jesus My Redeemer. Amen.

Wash yourselves; make yourselves clean;
  remove the evil of your doings
  from before my eyes;
cease to do evil,
  learn to do good;
seek justice,
  rescue the oppressed,
defend the orphan,
  plead for the widow.   Isaiah 1:16, 17 NRSV

Maude's Fudge Batter Pudding Cake

2 T. melted butter
1 c. sugar, divided
1 tsp. vanilla
1 c. sifted flour
8 T. cocoa, divided
1 tsp. baking powder
¾ tsp. salt, divided
½ c. milk
½ c. chopped nuts (optional)
1⅔ c. boiling water

Note: When baked, this pudding has a chocolate sauce on the bottom and a cake on top.

Preheat oven to 350 degrees. Coat 9-inch baking pan. In large bowl mix butter, ½ cup of the sugar and vanilla. Into separate bowl sift flour, 3 tablespoons cocoa, baking powder and ½ teaspoon of the salt. Add alternately with milk to butter mixture. Blend well and stir in nuts.

In another bowl blend remaining ½ cup sugar, remaining 5 tablespoons cocoa, remaining ¼ teaspoon salt and boiling water. Turn mixture into prepared pan. Drop first mixture by tablespoonfuls into chocolate liquid. Bake 40 to 45 minutes. Serve while warm, spooning out a portion of cake and covering it with sauce. If served cold, serve with whipped cream, pour-cream or top-milk because the sauce becomes quite thick.

Sometimes I forget what's important to you, Yahweh. Amen.

In days to come
   the mountain of the Lord's house
shall be established as the highest of the mountains,
   and shall be raised above the hills;
all the nations shall stream to it.   Isaiah 2:2 NRSV

Overnight Coffeecake
¾ c. butter or margarine, softened
1 c. sugar
2 eggs
2 c. flour
1 tsp. baking soda
1 tsp. ground nutmeg
½ tsp. salt
1 c. sour cream
¾ c. firmly packed brown sugar
½ c. chopped pecans or walnuts
1 tsp. ground cinnamon
1½ c. powdered sugar
3 T. milk

Coat 9 by 13-inch baking pan. In large bowl cream butter and sugar. Add eggs one at a time, beating well after each addition. In another bowl combine flour, baking soda, nutmeg and salt. Add to creamed mixture alternately with sour cream. Pour batter into prepared pan. In small bowl combine brown sugar, pecans and cinnamon. Sprinkle over cake batter. Cover and refrigerate overnight. Remove from refrigerator 30 minutes before baking. Preheat oven to 350 degrees. Bake 35 to 40 minutes or until tester inserted in center comes out clean. Cool on wire rack 10 minutes. In small bowl combine powdered sugar and milk. Drizzle over warm cake.

Note: May be baked immediately; does not have to be refrigerated.

You, God of the Cosmos, are the reason we hope. Amen.

For out of Zion shall go forth instruction,
and the word of the Lord from Jerusalem.

Isaiah 3:3c NRSV

Pineapple Orange Sunshine Cake

Batter:
1 yellow cake mix
¼ c. applesauce
4 eggs
1 c. mandarin oranges in light syrup

Frosting:
1 tub light whipped topping, thawed, about 8 oz.
1 small pkg. vanilla pudding mix
1 can crushed pineapple in juice, about 16 oz.

Preheat oven to 350 degrees. Coat 9 by 13-inch baking pan. In large bowl combine all batter ingredients. Beat by hand 2 minutes. Pour batter into prepared pan. Bake 30 to 40 minutes or until tester inserted in center comes out clean. Cool. For frosting, blend all frosting ingredients in large bowl. Spread on cooled cake.

We know not what to think, to do, to plan unless you instruct us, God Our Dove. Amen.

He shall judge between the nations,
   and shall arbitrate for many peoples;
they shall beat their swords into plowshares,
   and their spears into pruning hooks;
nation shall not lift up sword against nation,
   neither shall they learn war any more.
Isaiah 2:4 NRSV

Pumpkin Pie Cake

1 large can pumpkin, about 29 oz.
1 can evaporated milk, about 13 oz.
2 tsp. ground cinnamon
¾ c. firmly packed brown sugar
¾ c. granulated sugar
4 eggs
Dash salt
1 yellow cake mix
½ c. margarine

Preheat oven to 350 degrees. Coat 9 by 13-inch baking pan. In large bowl combine pumpkin, milk, cinnamon, brown sugar, granulated sugar, eggs and salt. Pour into prepared pan. In separate bowl crumble margarine into cake mix and cut into fine particles. Sprinkle evenly over pumpkin mixture. Bake 1 hour.

Optional: Add ½ cup chopped pecans and 1 teaspoon cinnamon to cake topping before sprinkling over pumpkin mixture.

Help us, Lord Over Life and Death, to neither teach nor learn war. Amen.

Then I heard the voice of the Lord saying, "Whom shall I send, and who will go for us?"
And I said, "Here am I; send me!" Isaiah 6:8 NRSV

Quick Pineapple Coffee Cake
1 can crushed pineapple, about 16 oz.
2 c. baking mix
¼ c. sugar
1 egg
¼ c. firmly packed brown sugar
Ground cinnamon or ground nutmeg

Preheat oven to 400 degrees. Coat 8-inch or 9-inch baking pan. Drain crushed pineapple, reserving juice. In medium bowl mix ⅔ cup of the juice with baking mix, sugar and egg. Pour into prepared pan. Top with pineapple. Sprinkle with brown sugar and cinnamon. Bake 25 to 30 minutes or until tester inserted in center comes out clean. Serve warm.

I'm here, too, Lord Who Seeks the Lost. Amen.

~~~

Therefore, the Lord himself will give you a sign: Look, the young woman is with child and shall bear a son, and shall name him Immanuel. Isaiah 7:14 NRSV

Ring of Coconut Fudge Cake
2 c. sugar
1 c. cooking oil
2 eggs
¾ c. unsweetened cocoa powder
1 c. hot coffee or water
1 c. buttermilk or sour milk
1 tsp. vanilla
3 c. flour
2 tsp. baking soda
1½ tsp. salt
½ c. chopped nuts

Preheat oven to 350 degrees. Generously grease and lightly flour 10-inch tube or Bundt pan. In large mixer bowl combine sugar, oil and eggs. Beat 1 minute at high speed. Add cocoa, coffee, buttermilk, vanilla, flour, baking soda and salt. Beat 3 minutes at medium speed, scraping bowl occasionally. Stir in nuts by hand.

Filling:
8 oz. cream cheese, softened
¾ c. sugar
1 tsp. vanilla
1 egg
½ c. flaked coconut
6 oz. chocolate chips

Prepare filling by beating cream cheese, sugar, vanilla and egg until smooth. Stir in coconut and chocolate chips. Set aside.

Pour half of batter into prepared pan. Add filling and top with remaining batter. Bake 70 to 75 minutes or until top springs back when touched lightly. Cool upright in pan 15 minutes. Remove from pan and cool completely.

If desired, drizzle with glaze made by combining 1 cup powdered sugar, 3 tablespoons softened butter, 2 teaspoons vanilla and 1 to 3 tablespoons hot water.

Thank you, Creator God, for your mercy to us. Amen.

The people who walked in darkness
   have seen a great light;
those who lived in a land of deep darkness—
   on them light has shined.   Isaiah 9:2 NRSV

Spanish Bar Cake
1 c. raisins
1¼ c. sifted flour
1 tsp. baking soda
1 tsp. ground cinnamon
½ tsp. ground nutmeg
½ tsp. ground cloves
½ tsp. salt
½ c. shortening
½ c. firmly packed dark brown sugar
1 egg
1 c. unsweetened applesauce
½ c. chopped walnuts

Preheat oven to 350 degrees. Coat 8-inch cake pan or loaf pan. In small bowl cover raisins with hot water and soak until plump. Drain and set aside. Into large bowl sift flour, baking soda, cinnamon, nutmeg, cloves and salt three times. Set aside. In large mixer bowl cream shortening and brown sugar. Add egg and beat well. Fold in applesauce. Add flour mixture one-third at a time, stirring after each addition. Fold in walnuts and raisins. Pour batter into prepared pan. Bake 45 minutes or until tester inserted in center comes out clean. Cool 10 minutes before serving. Frost with Vanilla Glaze or Caramel Frosting if desired.

Vanilla Glaze
1 c. powdered sugar
1 tsp. vanilla
1 T. mayonnaise
1 T. water

In small bowl combine all ingredients and mix until smooth. Spread over cooled cake.

Caramel Frosting
1 c. butter
2 c. light brown sugar
½ c. evaporated milk
½ tsp. vanilla
4 c. powdered sugar

In 2-quart saucepan melt butter over low heat. Add brown sugar and evaporated milk. Cook 2 minutes over medium heat, stirring constantly. Remove from heat. Stir in vanilla and pour over powdered sugar. Beat until smooth. Cool slightly before frosting cake. Refrigerate unused portion.

We thank you, God, for turning on The Light. Amen.

For the yoke of their burden,
> and the bars across their shoulders,
> the rod of their oppressors,
> you have broken as on the day of Midian.

Joel 9:4 NRSV

Texas Sheetcake
1 c. butter
1 c. water
¼ c. cocoa
2 c. flour
2 c. sugar
2 eggs
1 tsp. vanilla
1 tsp. baking soda
¾ tsp. salt
½ c. sour cream

Preheat oven to 350 degrees. Coat 10 by 15-inch rimmed cookie sheet. In large saucepan boil butter, water and cocoa. Mix in remaining ingredients. Pour into prepared pan. Bake 20 minutes. Cool. Frost with Chocolate Sour Cream Frosting or Minute Fudge Frosting if desired.

Chocolate Sour Cream Frosting
1¼ lb. milk chocolate, finely chopped
10 oz. semisweet chocolate, finely chopped
3 c. sour cream
2 tsp. vanilla

Melt milk chocolate and semisweet chocolate in double boiler or large metal bowl set over saucepan of simmering water, stirring occasionally. Remove bowl from heat. Whisk in sour cream and vanilla. Cool to room temperature, stirring occasionally. When frosting becomes thick enough to spread, work quickly to frost cake before frosting becomes too thick. If icing becomes too thick, reheat over simmering water, cool and try again.

Minute Fudge Frosting
3 T. cocoa
⅓ c. milk
¼ c. butter
1 c. sugar
¼ c. shortening
¼ tsp. salt
1 tsp. vanilla

Place cocoa, milk, butter, sugar, shortening and salt in medium saucepan. Bring to boil, stirring constantly. Boil 1 minute. Remove from heat and beat until lukewarm. Stir in vanilla. Spread evenly over cooled cake.

All that we carried has been lifted by you, Lion of Judah. Amen.

For a child has been born for us,
   a son given to us;
authority rests upon his shoulders;
   and he is named
Wonderful Counselor, Mighty God,
   Everlasting Father, Prince of Peace.

Isaiah 9:6 NRSV

Turtle Cake

1 German chocolate cake mix
14 oz. caramels
½ c. butter or margarine
½ c. evaporated milk
1 c. chocolate chips
1 c. chopped pecans

Preheat oven to 350 degrees. Coat 9 by 13-inch baking pan. In large bowl prepare cake mix according to package directions. Pour half of batter into prepared pan. Bake 15 minutes. Melt caramels and butter in double boiler or microwavable bowl. Stir in evaporated milk. Pour over baked portion of cake. Sprinkle chocolate chips and pecans on top. Pour remaining batter on top and bake 15 minutes or until tester inserted in center comes out clean. Frost if desired.

Advisor, Coach, Awesome Re-creator, Gracious Governor, Thoughtful Provider. Amen.

> A shoot shall come out from the stump of Jesse,
> and a branch shall grow out of his roots.
>
> Isaiah 11:1 NRSV

Twinkles

Cake:
1 yellow cake mix
½ c. shortening
4 eggs
1 small pkg. vanilla instant pudding mix
1 c. water

Filling:
3 T. flour
1 c. milk
½ c. margarine or butter
½ c. shortening
1 c. sugar
1 tsp. vanilla

Preheat oven to 350 degrees. Line two rimmed cookie sheets with wax paper. Grease and flour the wax paper. In large bowl combine cake ingredients and mix well. Pour into prepared cookie sheets. Bake 15 to 20 minutes. Cool.

For filling, in medium saucepan cook flour and milk until thick. Cool. Add margarine, shortening, sugar and vanilla. Beat until thick. Spread on one cake. Place second cake on top. Cut into bars.

When I think of your brilliance, Shining Star, I feel faint with wonder. Amen.

The spirit of the Lord shall rest on him,
   the spirit of wisdom and understanding,
   the spirit of counsel and might,
   the spirit of knowledge and the fear of the Lord.

Isaiah 11:2 NRSV

Unfrosted Oatmeal Cake

1 c. oatmeal
1½ c. boiling water
1 c. granulated sugar
1 c. firmly packed brown sugar
½ c. butter
2 eggs
1 tsp. baking soda
½ tsp. salt
1 T. cocoa
1½ c. flour
1 c. chocolate chips, divided
1 c. chopped nuts, divided

Preheat oven to 350 degrees. Coat 9 by 13-inch baking pan. Place oatmeal in large bowl and cover with boiling water. Let stand 10 minutes. Add granulated sugar, brown sugar and butter. Beat well. Add eggs and beat well. Add baking soda, salt, cocoa, flour, ½ cup of the chocolate chips and ½ cup of the nuts. Mix well. Pour into prepared pan. Top with remaining ½ cup chocolate chips and remaining ½ cup nuts. Bake 30 to 35 minutes or until tester inserted in center comes out clean.

Your Spirit rests upon our Savior, and we see light beyond the tunnel. Amen.

The wolf shall live with the lamb,
  the leopard shall lie down with the kid,
the calf and the lion and the fatling together,
  and a little child shall lead them. — Isaiah 11:6 NRSV

Upside Down German Chocolate Cake

Topping:
½ c. firmly packed brown sugar
¼ c. butter or margarine
⅔ c. pecan halves
⅔ c. flaked coconut
¼ c. evaporated milk

Cake:
⅓ c. butter or margarine, softened
1 c. sugar
4 oz. German sweet chocolate, melted
2 eggs
1 tsp. vanilla
1½ c. flour
½ tsp. baking soda
½ tsp. baking powder
½ tsp. salt
¾ c. buttermilk
Whipped topping (optional)

Preheat oven to 350 degrees. Coat 9-inch baking pan. For topping, in saucepan over low heat, stir brown sugar and butter until sugar dissolves and butter melts. Spread into prepared pan. Top with pecans and coconut. Drizzle on evaporated milk. Set aside. For cake, in mixer bowl cream butter and sugar. Beat in chocolate, eggs and vanilla. In separate bowl mix flour, baking soda, baking powder and salt. Add to creamed mixture alternately with buttermilk. Pour over topping in pan. Bake 40 to 45 minutes or until cake is firm and shrinks from edges of pan. Cool 5 minutes. Invert onto serving plate. Serve with whipped topping.

Wondrous are your promises, God of All That Is. Amen.

I will exalt you, I will praise your name;
for you have done wonderful things,
    plans formed of old, faithful and sure.   Isaiah 25:1 NRSV

Vanilla Texas Sheetcake

2⅔ c. flour
2 c. sugar
½ c. margarine
½ c. oil
1 c. water
2 eggs
1½ tsp. baking soda
⅔ c. buttermilk
2 tsp. vanilla
2 tsp. ground cinnamon

Preheat oven to 350 degrees. Coat 10 by 15-inch rimmed cookie sheet. In large bowl combine flour and sugar. In saucepan bring margarine, oil and water to boil. Pour over flour mixture. Beat thoroughly. Beat in eggs, baking soda, buttermilk, vanilla and cinnamon. Pour into prepared pan and bake 20 to 25 minutes or until cake is firm to the touch. Cool slightly. Frost with Vanilla Cream Cheese Frosting.

Vanilla Cream Cheese Frosting

½ c. margarine
1 tsp. vanilla
8 oz. cream cheese
1 lb. powdered sugar
Chopped nuts (optional)

In large mixer bowl cream margarine, vanilla and cream cheese. Blend in powdered sugar, beating until light and fluffy. Spread over warm cake. Mix nuts into frosting or sprinkle on top of frosting.

Nothing on Earth is better—or older—than you, God of Truth. Amen.

CANDY

Temperature Testing of Cooked Candy

Soft Ball Stage
- 235 degrees to 240 degrees Fahrenheit
- Bead of hot sugar syrup dropped into cold water forms soft, flexible ball. Removed from water, ball flattens after a few moments in the hand.

Firm Ball Stage
- 245 degrees to 250 degrees Fahrenheit
- Bead of hot sugar syrup dropped into cold water forms firm ball that will not flatten when taken out of water but remains malleable and will flatten when squeezed.

Hard Ball Stage
- 250 degrees to 265 degrees Fahrenheit
- Bead of hot sugar syrup forms thick, ropy threads as it drips from spoon and forms hard ball when dropped into cold water. Removed from water, ball will not flatten but will change shape when squeezed.

Soft Crack Stage
- 270 degrees to 290 degrees Fahrenheit
- Bead of hot sugar syrup forms threads when dropped into cold water. Removed from water, threads are flexible and will bend before breaking.

Hard Crack Stage
- 300 degrees to 310 degrees
- Bead of hot sugar syrup, when dropped into cold water, forms hard, brittle threads that break when bent.

See, a king will reign in righteousness . . . .
Isaiah 32:1a NRSV

Butterscotch Fudge

1 c. granulated sugar
1 c. firmly packed brown sugar
¾ c. sour cream
½ c. butter
1 tsp. vanilla
1 c. chopped pecans or walnuts, toasted

Butter 8-inch square pan. Combine granulated sugar, brown sugar, sour cream and butter in large heavy saucepan. Cook over medium heat, stirring constantly, until sugar dissolves and mixture comes to boil. Cover and cook 2 to 3 minutes to wash down sugar crystals from sides of pan. Uncover and cook, stirring occasionally, until mixture reaches soft-ball stage, 235 to 240 degrees Fahrenheit. Remove from heat and cool 30 minutes. Add vanilla. Beat with wooden spoon until mixture thickens and begins to lose gloss. Stir in nuts. Pour into prepared pan. Cool completely. Cut into squares.

The world needs leaders who reflect your righteousness, Holy Governor. Amen.

Then the eyes of those who have sight will not be closed,
  and the ears of those who have hearing will listen.
                              Isaiah 32:3 NRSV

Caramels
1 c. butter
2¼ c. firmly packed light brown sugar
2 c. light corn syrup
1 can sweetened condensed milk, about 14 oz.

Butter 9 by 13-inch pan. Mix ingredients in big heavy saucepan. Boil 16 minutes, stirring constantly, until mixture reaches firm-ball stage, 245 to 250 degrees Fahrenheit. Pour into prepared pan. Cool. Cut and wrap each piece in waxed paper.

You, O God, are my Physician. Amen.

~~~

The minds of the rash will have good judgment . . . .
                              Isaiah 32:4a NRSV

Caramel Fudge
3 c. firmly packed brown sugar
3 T. corn syrup
⅔ c. milk or cream
3½ T. butter
1 tsp. vanilla
½ c. chopped nuts (optional)
¼ c. cocoa (optional)

Butter 8-inch pan or dish. In large heavy saucepan combine brown sugar, corn syrup, milk, butter and vanilla. Stir to blend. Cook over medium-low heat, stirring constantly, until mixture reaches soft-ball stage, 235 to 240 degrees Fahrenheit. Remove from heat. Add nuts and cocoa. Beat until creamy. Pour into prepared pan. Cool. Cut into squares.

O Morning Star, make even me new. Amen.

My people will abide in a peaceful habitation,
> in secure dwellings, and in quiet resting places.
>
> Isaiah 32:18 NRSV

Caramel Turtles
60 pecan halves
12 soft caramel candies
1 bar (15 oz.) milk chocolate, broken into 12 squares

Preheat oven to 350 degrees. Spread pecans on baking sheet. Toast nuts until fragrant, 5 to 7 minutes. Cool. Maintain oven temperature. Line baking sheet with parchment paper. Arrange pecans in clusters of five (1 for head, 2 for arms, 2 for legs). Unwrap caramels and flatten each with hands to 1¼-inch square. Lightly press caramel on top of each nut cluster. Bake until caramel is soft and shiny but not runny, 3 to 4 minutes. Remove baking sheet from oven. Place one piece of chocolate on top of each caramel. Return to oven until chocolate melts, about 30 minutes. Remove from oven. Smooth chocolate over caramel with small spoon. Cool completely. Refrigerate until chocolate hardens, about 15 minutes. Store in airtight container at room temperature up to 3 days.

We work so hard and have so little, Hand of Mercy, because we forget that only you will prosper us. Amen.

~~~

> A highway shall be there,
> and it shall be called the Holy Way.
>
> Isaiah 35:8 NRSV

Chocolate Big Batch Fudge
5 c. sugar
1 can evaporated milk, 12 to 13 oz.
½ c. butter or margarine
12 oz. miniature marshmallows or marshmallow creme
1 tsp. salt
1 tsp. vanilla
1 c. broken walnuts
24 oz. semisweet chocolate chips

Butter two 9-inch square pans or one 9 by 13-inch pan. In large heavy saucepan combine sugar, evaporated milk, butter, marshmallows and salt. Stir over low heat until blended. Bring to boil over moderate heat. Boil slowly, stirring constantly, 5 minutes. Remove from heat. Stir in vanilla, walnuts and chocolate chips. Stir until chips melt. Pour into prepared pans. Chill until firm. Cut into squares. Makes 5 pounds.

We long to tread the path to you, Word of Life. Amen.

~~~

The Lord will save me . . . .   Isaiah 38:20a NRSV

Chocolate Covered Cherries
8 T. oil or melted butter
6 T. corn syrup
1 can sweetened condensed milk, about 14 oz.
1 tsp. vanilla
3 lbs. powdered sugar
Maraschino cherries
12 oz. chocolate chips
1 square paraffin wax

Cover baking sheet with waxed paper. In medium bowl combine oil, corn syrup, sweetened condensed milk, vanilla and powdered sugar. Mix well. Form into small balls with cherry in center of each. Place candy on prepared sheet. Freeze 1 hour. In small saucepan melt chocolate chips and paraffin wax. Dip frozen candy into chocolate mixture and place on waxed paper.

You did save me, you have saved me, you will save me, Maker of Salvation. Amen.

Comfort, O comfort my people,
   says your God.   Isaiah 40:1 NRSV

Chocolate Fantasy Fudge
3 c. sugar
¾ c. butter or margarine
⅔ c. evaporated milk
12 oz. semisweet chocolate chunks or chips
7 oz. marshmallow crème
1 c. chopped walnuts
1 tsp. vanilla

Line 9-inch square pan with foil. Place sugar, butter and evaporated milk in heavy 3-quart saucepan. Bring to rolling boil over medium heat, stirring constantly. Boil and stir constantly about 4 minutes or until mixture reaches soft-ball stage, 235 to 240 degrees Fahrenheit. Remove from heat. Add chocolate chunks and marshmallow crème. Stir until melted. Add walnuts and vanilla. Mix well. Pour immediately into prepared pan. Spread evenly. Cool at room temperature at least 2 hours. Cut into squares. Store at room temperature in airtight container.

Peanut Butter Fudge—Substitute peanut butter chips for chocolate chips. Omit nuts.

Cookies and Cream Fudge—Substitute white chocolate chips for chocolate chips. Substitute 1 cup crushed Oreos for nuts.

Creamy Orange Fudge—Substitute white chocolate chips for chocolate chips. Substitute 2 teaspoons orange extract for vanilla. Omit nuts. Pour half of prepared fudge into pan. Stir 4 drops yellow and 3 drops red food coloring into remaining fudge. Pour orange fudge over plain fudge. Use knife to marble fudge.

Mocha Fudge—Stir ¼ cup prepared instant coffee into pan with chocolate chips. Omit nuts.

Chocolate Mint Fudge—Substitute 2 teaspoons peppermint extract for vanilla. Substitute ¼ cup crushed candy canes for nuts.
Almond Fudge—Substitute 2 teaspoons almond extract for vanilla. Substitute ½ cup chopped almonds for walnuts.

Maple Fudge—Substitute white chocolate chips for chocolate chips. Substitute 1 teaspoon maple flavoring for vanilla.

Sometimes, Great Shepherd, I am stubborn and won't let you comfort me. I am sorry. Amen.

~~~

"In the wilderness prepare the way of the Lord,
    make straight in the desert a highway for our God."

Isaiah 40:3 NRSV

Chocolate Yummies
1 c. semisweet chocolate chips
⅓ c. butter or margarine
16 large marshmallows
2 c. quick-cooking rolled oats
1 c. flaked coconut
½ tsp. vanilla

Line baking sheets with waxed paper or parchment paper. In medium saucepan over low heat melt chocolate chips, butter and marshmallows. Stir until smooth. Stir in oats, coconut and vanilla. Mix well. Drop by rounded spoonfuls onto prepared sheets. Chill 30 minutes or until set. Makes about 4 dozen.

We are hacking through a jungle, O Righteousness, and yearn to rest. Amen.

All people are grass,
   their constancy is like the flower of the field.

Isaiah 40:6b NRSV

Clark Larks
1 c. margarine
1 lb. crunchy peanut butter
2½ c. powdered sugar
3 tsp. vanilla
1 lb. graham crackers, crushed
Melted chocolate for dipping

In large bowl combine margarine, peanut butter, powdered sugar, vanilla and graham crackers. Mix well. Shape into small balls and dip in melted chocolate. Cool on waxed paper until coating is firm.

I am only what I am in you, Son of the Blessed One. Amen.

~~~

Yet I planted you a choice vine,
A completely faithful seed.

<div align="right">Jeremiah 2:21a NAS</div>

Coconut Cremes
3 T. butter, softened
3 T. corn syrup
1 tsp. vanilla
¼ tsp. salt
2½ c. powdered sugar
1¼ c. flaked coconut, minced
12 oz. milk chocolate bits
1 T. vegetable oil

Line baking sheets with waxed paper. In large bowl combine butter, corn syrup, vanilla and salt. Mix well. Gradually add powdered sugar while mixing well. Mixture will be crumbly. Add coconut and mix well. Shape into ball. Turn out onto smooth surface and knead until smooth and pliable. Roll into about thirty 1-inch balls and freeze 10 minutes. In small saucepan melt chocolate bits and oil together and mix until smooth. Dip frozen balls in chocolate. Shake off excess chocolate and place balls on prepared sheets. Chill 20 to 30 minutes.

I only planted the seed that you made, Righteous Branch. Amen.

~~~

"Let us lie down in our shame, and let our humiliation cover us; for we have sinned against the Lord our God, we and our fathers, since our youth even to this day. And we have not obeyed the voice of the Lord our God."

<p align="right">Jeremiah 3:25 NAS</p>

Fanny Farmer Fudge

4½ c. sugar
1 c. butter
1 can evaporated milk, about 13 oz.
18 oz. chocolate chips
3 tsp. vanilla
2 c. chopped nuts

Butter square or rectangular pan. In large heavy saucepan boil sugar, butter and evaporated milk 10 minutes, stirring constantly. Remove from heat. Add chocolate chips and vanilla. Stir until smooth. Add nuts. Pour into prepared pan. Cool at room temperature. Cut into squares.

None of us has listened to you in all things, Savior of Creation. Amen.

How long will your wicked thoughts
Lodge within you?   Jeremiah 4:14b NAS

Honey Nut White Fudge
2 T. butter or margarine
⅔ c. evaporated milk
1½ c. sugar
2 c. miniature marshmallows
1 pkg. white chocolate chips, 11 or 12 oz.
1½ c. honey-roasted peanuts, divided
2 tsp. vanilla

Line 9-inch square pan with foil. Combine butter, evaporated milk and sugar in heavy 3-quart saucepan. Bring to boil over medium heat, stirring constantly. Boil, stirring constantly, 4½ to 5 minutes. Remove from heat. Stir in marshmallows, white chocolate chips, 1 cup of the peanuts and vanilla. Stir vigorously 1 minute or until marshmallows melt. Pour into prepared pan. Coarsely chop remaining nuts. Sprinkle over fudge, pressing to adhere. Chill until firm. Remove from pan. Remove foil. Cut into squares.

Variations: Chocolate chips or butterscotch chips with pecans or walnuts; peanut butter chips with peanuts.

I am confused about my wicked thoughts because I do not want to have them, True Vine. Amen.

My soul, my soul! I am in anguish! Oh my heart!
My heart is pounding in me;
I cannot be silent . . . . Jeremiah 4:19a NAS

Martha's Fudge
1 lb. butter
1 lb. boxed processed cheese
1 tsp. vanilla
1 c. unsweetened cocoa powder
4 lbs. powdered sugar, sifted
1 c. chopped nuts (optional)

Butter 12 by 17-inch jelly roll pan. Cut butter and cheese into cubes. Place in large heavy saucepan over low heat. Stir until melted and smooth. Stir in vanilla and cocoa powder. Stir in powdered sugar. Mixture will be very thick. Add nuts and stir well. Pour into prepared pan. Refrigerate. Cut into squares. Makes about 6½ pounds.

Root of David, I am in pain all day and all night. Amen.

O Lord, do not Thine eyes look for truth?
Jeremiah 5:3a NAS

Microwave Caramels
1 c. butter
2¼ c. firmly packed brown sugar
1 c. light corn syrup
1 can sweetened condensed milk, about 14 oz.
Pinch salt
1 tsp. vanilla

Line 8 by 12-inch baking pan with lightly buttered aluminum foil. Place butter in large glass bowl. Microwave on high 1 to 2 minutes or until melted. Blend in brown sugar, corn syrup, sweetened condensed milk and salt. Cover with plastic wrap. Microwave on high 10 to 12 minutes or until bubbly and thick. Uncover. Stir well. Microwave on medium-high 16 to 20 minutes or until drop of candy forms soft ball when dropped into cold water and flattens when removed. Mix in vanilla. Pour into prepared pan. Cool at room temperature. Invert pan, peel off foil and cut candy into 1-inch squares. Wrap each in waxed paper or plastic wrap. Store covered at room temperature.

O Son of Man, the wicked prosper at my expense. Amen.

~~~

Thus says the Lord,
"Stand by the ways and see and ask for the ancient paths,
Where the good way is, and walk in it;
And you shall find rest for your souls."
Jeremiah 6:16 NAS

Molasses Fudge
1 c. granulated sugar
1 c. firmly packed brown sugar
½ c. cream
¼ c. molasses
¼ c. melted butter
2 oz. unsweetened chocolate, grated
1½ tsp. vanilla

Butter 9-inch pan or dish. In heavy saucepan combine granulated sugar, brown sugar, cream, molasses and butter. Bring to boil and cook 2 minutes. Add chocolate. Boil 5 minutes, stirring until well blended and then only enough to prevent burning. Remove from heat. Add vanilla. Stir until creamy. Turn into prepared pan. Chill and cut into squares.

Others hide the truth, Lord the Lawgiver, but you do not. Amen.

~~~

O that my head were waters,
   And my eyes a fountain of tears,
   That I might weep day and night
   For the slain of the daughter of my people.
                                                    Jeremiah 9:1 NAS

Never Fail Chocolate Fudge
18 oz. semisweet chocolate chips
1 can sweetened condensed milk, about 14 oz.
⅛ tsp. salt
¾ c. chopped nuts
1½ tsp. vanilla or 1 tsp. vanilla and ½ tsp. almond extract

Line 8-inch or 9-inch square pan with waxed paper. Melt chocolate chips with sweetened condensed milk in large heavy saucepan over low heat. Remove from heat. Stir in salt, nuts and vanilla. Spread evenly in prepared pan. Chill until firm. Turn out fudge on hard surface. Peel off paper. Cut into 1-inch squares. Refrigerate in airtight container. Makes about 2 pounds.

Chocolate Mint Fudge: Substitute ½ teaspoon mint extract for ½ teaspoon vanilla.

You bear the weight of my sins past and present, and I am grateful, my Jesus. Amen.

Thus says the Lord, "Do not learn the way of the nations, and do not be terrified by the signs of the heavens, although the nations are terrified by them." Jeremiah 10:2 NAS

Old Time Peanut Butter Fudge
2 c. sugar
⅔ c. milk
2 T. light corn syrup
2 T. butter
4 T. peanut butter
1 tsp. vanilla

Butter small pan or dish. In medium saucepan combine sugar, milk and corn syrup. Bring to boil over medium heat, stirring constantly. Cook to soft-ball stage, 235 degrees to 240 degrees Fahrenheit. Remove from heat. Add butter, peanut butter and vanilla. Stir until fudge loses sheen. Spread into prepared pan. Cool and cut into squares.

The ways of the nations are wicked, O Nazarene, and I reject them. Amen.

~~~

Correct me, O Lord, with your words of justice.
Jeremiah 10:24a NAS

Pastel Butter Mints
2 lbs. powdered sugar
½ c. butter, melted
5 to 6 T. cold water
Red and green food coloring
3 tsp. peppermint extract, divided

Line two baking sheets with waxed paper. In large bowl combine powdered sugar, butter and water. Mix well. Turn out onto smooth surface and knead until smooth. Divide in half. Add several drops red food coloring and 1½ teaspoons of the peppermint extract to half of the mixture and mix well. To the other half of the mixture, add several drops green food coloring and remaining 1½ teaspoons peppermint extract and mix well. Shape candy into thin round patties and place on prepared sheets. Press flat with fork tines. Refrigerate in airtight container.

Were my words wrong today, Master? Amen.

~~~

"Behold, like the clay in the potter's hand, so are you in My hand . . . ."   Jeremiah 18:6b NAS

Pecan Logs

7 oz. marshmallow crème
3½ c. powdered sugar
1 tsp. vanilla
¼ tsp. almond extract
1 lb. caramels
2½ c. chopped pecans

In large bowl combine marshmallow crème, powdered sugar, vanilla and almond extract. Knead until mixture is smooth. Shape into logs 8 inches long and 1 inch across. Wrap in plastic and freeze until very hard. Spread pecans in large shallow pan or flat dish. In saucepan at least 9 inches wide, melt caramels over low heat. Using spatulas, dip frozen logs in caramel. Roll logs in nuts. Wearing disposable gloves to avoid burns, carefully press nuts in with hands.

Shape me according to your will, Lord of Glory. Amen.

"Thus says the Lord who made the earth, the Lord who formed it to establish it—the Lord is His name,
'Call to Me, and I will answer you, and I will tell you great and mighty things, which you do not know.'"
Jeremiah 33:2, 3 NAS

Penuche
½ c. evaporated milk
2 c. firmly packed brown sugar
2 T. butter
1 tsp. vanilla
⅛ tsp. salt
1 c. broken nuts

Butter 9-inch pan or dish. Stir evaporated milk and brown sugar in medium saucepan. Cook slowly, stirring only until sugar is dissolved, until mixture reaches soft-ball stage, 235 to 240 degrees Fahrenheit. Add butter. Cool slightly. Add vanilla, salt and nuts. Beat until creamy. Pour into prepared pan. Cut and chill.

If I don't know, Captain of the Lord's Host, it's only because I didn't ask you. Amen.

~~~

Bitterly she weeps at night,
tears are upon her cheeks.
<p align="right">Lamentations 1:2a NIV</p>

Seafoam Fudge
3 c. light brown sugar
1 c. cold water
1 T. cider vinegar
2 egg whites
1 tsp. vanilla
1 c. chopped nuts (optional)

Line 2 baking sheets with waxed paper. In large heavy saucepan combine brown sugar, water and vinegar. Bring to boil. Do not stir once mixture boils. Boil steadily over moderate heat to soft-ball stage, 235 to 240 degrees Fahrenheit. Remove from heat. In large bowl beat egg whites until stiff. When cooked mixture has stopped bubbling, pour onto beaten egg whites. Beat well. When mixture begins to stiffen, stir in vanilla and nuts. Drop by teaspoonfuls onto prepared sheets. Cool.

I lost everything in that season of my life, Bread of the World. Amen.

~~~

Is any suffering like my suffering
that was inflicted on me,
that the Lord brought on me
in the day of his fierce anger?

Lamentations 1:12b NIV

Soda Cracker Candy
35 to 40 soda crackers
1 c. butter
1 c. firmly packed brown sugar
1½ c. semisweet chocolate chips
1½ c. chopped nuts

Preheat oven to 350 degrees. Line rimmed 10 by 15-inch baking pan with foil and coat with nonstick spray. Place crackers in row on foil. In saucepan melt butter with brown sugar. Boil 3 minutes. Pour over crackers. Bake 5 minutes. Remove from oven. Turn oven off. Sprinkle chocolate chips on baked crackers. Return to oven 3 minutes to melt chocolate. Remove from oven. Spread chocolate. Sprinkle with nuts. Cut while warm.

God of the Whole Earth, I was so stubborn that I had to learn from you the hard way. Amen.

"My sins have been bound into a yoke . . . ."
Lamentations 1:14a NIV

Sweetened Condensed Milk
1 c. powdered milk
⅓ c. boiling water
⅓ c. sugar
3 T. butter

Mix ingredients in blender until sugar dissolves. If necessary, add a few drops of water to achieve desired consistency. Refrigerate in covered container.

Those sins, Lord, the ones you hate—you've covered them with the blood of your Son, Jesus the Christ, and they no longer oppress me. Hallelujah! Amen.

~~~

The Lord has done what he planned;
he has fulfilled his word,
which he decreed long ago.
<div align="right">Lamentations 2:17a NIV</div>

Vanilla Caramels
2 c. granulated sugar
1 c. firmly packed brown sugar
1 c. light corn syrup
1 c. sweetened condensed milk
1½ c. milk
⅓ c. butter
¼ tsp. salt
1½ tsp. vanilla

Butter 9-inch square pan. In large heavy saucepan combine granulated sugar, brown sugar, corn syrup, sweetened condensed milk and milk. Cook, stirring constantly, until sugar is dissolved. Continue cooking, stirring only enough to prevent burning, to firm-ball stage, 245 to 250 degrees Fahrenheit.

Remove from heat and add butter, salt and vanilla. Mix well. Pour into prepared pan. Chill. Remove from pan, cut into cubes and wrap each piece in waxed paper.

You've never let your people down, Faithful Witness. Amen.

~~~

The hearts of the people
cry out to the Lord.   Lamentations 2:18a NIV

Vanilla Fudge
2 c. sugar
⅔ c. milk
2 T. corn syrup
2 T. butter
1½ tsp. vanilla

Butter 9-inch pan. In heavy saucepan combine sugar, milk and corn syrup. Stir until sugar dissolves. Cook slowly to soft-ball stage, 235 to 240 degrees Fahrenheit. Remove from heat. Add butter and stir. Cool to lukewarm. Add vanilla and beat until thick. Pour into prepared pan. Chill. Cut into squares when firm.

Sometimes I think you aren't listening, Lord Our Righteousness, but then you show me that I was wrong. Amen.

Arise, cry out in the night,
as the watches of the night begin;
pour out your heart like water
in the presence of the Lord.

Lamentations 2:19a NIV

White Candy Fantasy Clusters

4 c. rice square cereal
2 c. pretzel sticks, coarsely broken
1 c. cashews, coarsely chopped
8 oz. vanilla-flavored candy coating
½ c. semisweet chocolate chips, melted

Coat 9 by 13-inch pan. In large bowl mix cereal, pretzels and cashews. Set aside. Melt candy coating in 2-quart saucepan over low heat, stirring constantly. Pour over cereal mixture, stirring until evenly coated. Press into prepared pan. Drizzle with melted chocolate chips. Let stand until chocolate is firm. Break into about 24 clusters. Store in airtight container.

Finally I realize, Redeemer, that I have to tell you when things are wrong. Amen.

CASSEROLES

He has walled me in so I cannot escape;
he has weighed me down with chains.

Lamentations 3:7 NIV

Armenian Pizza
1 lb. ground lamb or beef
1 c. parsley, chopped fine
2 c. onions, chopped fine
1 c. green peppers, chopped fine
4 cloves garlic, chopped fine
3 oz. tomato paste
3 oz. tomato sauce
Salt and pepper
1 pkg. small (6-inch) flour tortillas

Preheat oven to 350 degrees. In large bowl combine all ingredients except tortillas. Set aside. Place tortillas on greased cookie sheets. Spread meat filling to edge of each tortilla. Bake 15 minutes. Serve warm. May be frozen in separate sandwich bags and reheated as needed.

Running away from you isn't an option, is it, Son of God? Amen.

He has barred my way with blocks of stone;
he has made my paths crooked.

Lamentations 3:9 NIV

Baked Potato Skin Casserole
10 to 12 medium potatoes, unpeeled
1 lb. bacon
½ c. margarine
1 lb. boxed processed cheese, sliced

Scrub potatoes. Boil with skins on and cool. Cut into small chunks. Cook bacon until crisp. Drain grease and mince bacon. Melt margarine. Preheat oven to 350 degrees. Grease large casserole dish. Layer in dish, in order: half of potatoes, half of bacon, half of cheese and half of margarine. Repeat layers. Bake 15 to 20 minutes.

Things feel wrong when they aren't of you, Wisdom of God. Amen.

~~~

Because of the Lord's great love
   we are not consumed,
for his compassions never fail.

<div align="right">Lamentations 3:22 NIV</div>

Big Deal Mexican Dish
2 c. baking mix
1 c. water
2 cans refried beans, about 15 oz. each
2 lbs. ground beef, seasoned, cooked and drained
1 jar salsa, about 16 oz.
3 c. shredded cheddar cheese
16 oz. sour cream
3 c. shredded lettuce
2 c. diced tomatoes

Preheat oven to 350 degrees. Coat 9 by 13-inch baking pan with nonstick spray. In large bowl combine baking mix, water and beans. Mix well. Spread in prepared pan. Sprinkle cooked ground beef on top. Spread salsa and shredded cheese on top. Bake 30 minutes. Top with sour cream, lettuce and tomatoes just before serving.

Thank you, Bright and Morning Star, for outlasting sin. Amen.

~~~

The Lord is good to those whose
   hope is in him,
to the one who seeks him....

<div align="right">Lamentations 3:25 NIV</div>

Block Party Beans
2 lbs. ground beef
2 c. chopped onion
1 c. chopped celery
1 can condensed tomato soup, about 10 oz.
1 can tomato paste, about 6 oz.
½ c. ketchup
1 can green beans, drained, about 16 oz.
1 can lima beans, drained, about 16 oz.
1 can wax beans, drained, about 16 oz.
1 can chili beans, undrained, about 16 oz.
1 can pork and beans, undrained, about 16 oz.
½ c. firmly packed brown sugar
2 T. mustard

Preheat oven to 350 degrees. In medium saucepan simmer ground beef, onion, celery, tomato soup, tomato paste and ketchup 15 minutes. In large casserole dish blend beans, brown sugar and mustard. Pour meat mixture over beans and mix well. Bake 1 hour.

I repent of relying on my bank account, Alpha and Omega. Amen.

Though he brings grief, he will
   show compassion,
so great is his unfailing love.

Lamentations 3:32 NIV

Cabbage Casserole
1 large head cabbage, shredded
1 onion, chopped
6 T. butter, divided
1 can condensed cream of mushroom soup, undiluted
8 oz. American cheese, cubed
Salt and pepper
¼ c. bread crumbs

Cook cabbage in salted water until tender. Drain. In skillet saute onion in 5 tablespoons of the butter until tender. Add soup and mix well. Add cheese. Heat until melted. Remove onion mixture from heat. Stir in cabbage, salt and pepper. Place in ungreased 2-quart baking dish. Preheat oven to 350 degrees. In small skillet melt remaining 1 tablespoon butter. Add bread crumbs and brown lightly. Sprinkle bread crumbs over casserole. Bake uncovered 20 to 30 minutes.

Nothing is ever so wrong that you cannot overcome it, Chosen of God. Amen.

<div align="center">~~~</div>

Who can speak and have it happen
if the Lord has not decreed it?

Lamentations 3:37 NIV

Cavatini
1 lb. sausage
1 small onion, chopped
8 oz. spiral macaroni
1 jar spaghetti sauce, about 28 oz.
8 oz. mushrooms
1 pkg. sliced pepperoni, about 4 oz.
2 c. mozzarella cheese, shredded

Brown sausage and onion in skillet. Drain off fat. Cook macaroni according to package directions and drain. Place macaroni in 9 by 13-inch baking dish. In large bowl mix browned sausage and onion with spaghetti sauce and mushrooms. Pour over macaroni. Spread pepperoni slices on top. Sprinkle cheese on pepperoni. Cover with foil and bake at 350 degrees 30 minutes. Uncover and let stand 10 minutes before serving.

You want what is good, and you are reliable, Living Stone. Amen.

~~~

I called on your name, O Lord,
from the depths of the pit.

> Lamentations 3:55 NIV

Cheeseburger Casserole
1 lb. ground beef
1 medium onion, chopped
Salt and pepper
½ c. ketchup
1 can condensed tomato soup
8 cheese slices
1 can refrigerated biscuit dough

Preheat oven to 375 degrees. Grease 2-quart casserole dish. In large skillet saute ground beef and onion. Drain fat. Add salt, pepper, ketchup and soup. Stir well and heat thoroughly. Pour into prepared dish. Top with cheese slices. Separate biscuits and place evenly on cheese. Bake 25 minutes.

King of Glory, I don't know how I got into this mess. Save me. Amen.

Woe to us, for we have sinned!

Lamentations 5:16b NIV

Cheese Potato Casserole

6 medium potatoes, washed, unpeeled
¼ tsp. salt
⅛ tsp. pepper
1 c. grated cheese
1 can condensed cream of mushroom soup
3 T. margarine or butter
¾ c. milk

Preheat oven to 350 degrees. Grease 2-quart casserole. Slice potatoes thinly. Layer in dish, in order: half each of potato slices, salt, pepper, cheese and soup. Dot with half the margarine. Repeat layers of potatoes, salt, pepper and soup, but not cheese. Dot with remaining 1½ tablespoons margarine. Pour milk into soup can and stir well. Pour over casserole and cover. Bake 1 hour or until potatoes are tender. Remove from oven. Top with remaining ½ cup cheese. Heat until cheese melts.

We dared to ignore you, Jehovah, and your anger is overwhelming. Amen.

~~~

In the thirtieth year, in the fourth month on the fifth day, while I was among the exiles by the Kebar River, the heavens were opened and I saw visions of God.

<p align="right">Ezekiel 1:1 NIV</p>

Cheesy Chicken and Rice

1 can condensed cream of chicken soup
1⅓ c. water
¾ c. uncooked long-grain white rice
2 c. chopped vegetables, fresh or frozen
½ tsp. onion powder
4 skinless boneless chicken breast halves
Salt and pepper
½ c. reduced-fat shredded cheddar cheese

Preheat oven to 375 degrees. Stir soup, water, rice, vegetables and onion powder in 9 by 13-inch baking pan. Top with chicken. Add salt and pepper to taste. Cover. Bake 45 minutes or until chicken is done. Top with cheese.

Your timing is perfect, King of Saints. Amen.

~~~

As I looked at the living creatures, I saw a wheel on the ground beside each creature with its four faces.

Ezekiel 1:15 NIV

Chicken Casserole
3 large chicken breasts
3 c. shredded cheese, divided
8 oz. sour cream
1 can condensed cream of chicken soup
Chicken broth as needed
1 stack round buttery crackers, crushed
Grated Parmesan cheese

Preheat oven to 350 degrees. Butter large baking dish. Boil and bone chicken. Place 2 cups of the shredded cheese in prepared dish. Cut chicken into serving pieces and place on cheese. In small bowl mix sour cream and soup. Add chicken broth if necessary to make mixture pourable. Pour over chicken. Top with crushed crackers. Sprinkle with remaining 1 cup shredded cheese and grated Parmesan cheese. Bake 30 to 40 minutes. Serve over rice or noodles.

You have showed humans your plan, and we stand in awe, God Our Savior. Amen.

Then he said to me, "Son of man, eat this scroll I am giving you and fill your stomach with it." So I ate it, and it tasted as sweet as honey in my mouth.
Ezekiel 3:3 NIV

Chicken Noodle Casserole
2 lbs. chicken
8 oz. noodles
1 small onion, minced
¼ tsp. garlic powder
8 oz. cream cheese
¼ tsp. salt
1 c. sour cream
2 cans condensed cream of mushroom soup
1 c. buttered bread crumbs

Boil chicken in large pot. Butter large casserole dish. Reserving broth in pot, bone chicken and cut into chunks. In chicken pot cook noodles in reserved chicken broth until slightly tender. Replace chicken in pot. Leave only enough broth in pot to cover chicken. Add onion, garlic powder and cream cheese. Stir until smooth. Add sour cream and soup. Mix well. Pour into prepared dish. Cover with buttered crumbs. Bake 1 hour at 325 degrees.

Yes, Messiah, your words are sweet and pleasant to me. Amen.

~~~

Then the Spirit lifted me up and brought me to the gate of the house of the Lord that faces east.
<div align="right">Ezekiel 11:1a NIV</div>

Creamy Mushroom Chicken
4 skinless boneless chicken breasts
2 tsp. vegetable oil, divided
10 oz. fresh mushrooms, sliced
1 medium onion, thinly sliced
¾ tsp. salt
½ c. sour cream
¼ c. water

In large pan saute chicken breasts in 1 teaspoon of the oil 8 to 10 minutes until golden brown. Remove chicken and keep warm. Increase heat to medium-high and add remaining 1 teaspoon oil to pan. Cook mushrooms with onion and salt until golden and tender. Reduce heat to low and stir in sour cream and water. Heat through. Pour over chicken and serve.

Holy Spirit, where would you take me today? Amen.

~~~

Therefore this is what the Sovereign Lord says: In my wrath I will unleash a violent wind, and in my anger hailstones and torrents of rain will fall with destructive fury.
<div align="right">Ezekiel 13:13 NIV</div>

Easy Potato Casserole

8 oz. cottage cheese
8 oz. sour cream
8 oz. sharp cheddar cheese, grated
32 oz. frozen hash brown potatoes
2 cans condensed cream of potato soup, undiluted
2 T. dried chives
1 green pepper, diced

Preheat oven to 350 degrees. Grease 9 by 13-inch baking dish. Mix all ingredients together and place in dish. Bake 1 hour.

I quake at the fullness of your power, Horn of Salvation. Amen.

This is what the Sovereign Lord says: Repent!
>
> Ezekiel 14:6b NIV

Houseboat Chicken
1½ lb. cooked chicken, cubed
1 can condensed cream of mushroom soup
1 c. sour cream
1 box chicken-flavored dressing mix
1⅔ c. chicken broth

Preheat oven to 350 degrees. In large bowl combine chicken, soup and sour cream and stir well. Pour into 3-quart baking dish. In large bowl combine dressing and broth. Spread over chicken mixture. Bake 30 to 40 minutes.

Have I waited too long to turn back, Holy One of God? Amen.

~~~

Now this was the sin of your sister Sodom: She and her daughters were arrogant, overfed and unconcerned; they did not help the poor and needy.
>
> Ezekiel 16:49 NIV

Hungarian Goulash
¼ c. shortening
2 lbs. stew beef
1 medium onion, sliced
1 green pepper, sliced
1½ c. water
1¼ c. ketchup
1 T. firmly packed brown sugar
2 T. Worcestershire sauce
2 tsp. salt
2 tsp. paprika
½ tsp. dry mustard
1 to 2 tsp. chili powder (optional)
Hot cooked noodles

Heat shortening in large saucepan or Dutch oven. Add beef, onion and green pepper and cook, stirring constantly, until beef is brown. Drain fat. Stir in water, ketchup, brown sugar, Worcestershire sauce, salt, paprika, dry mustard and chili powder. Heat to boiling. Reduce heat. Cover and simmer until beef is tender, 2 to 2½ hours, adding water as needed. Serve over noodles.

My selfishness weighs on me, Light of the World. Amen.

~~~

I will surely strike my hands together at the unjust gain you have made and at the blood you have shed in your midst.
Ezekiel 22:13 NIV

Meatloaf Casserole

Casserole:
1 lb. ground beef
1 onion, minced
½ c. cooked rice
1 egg, beaten
1 tsp. pepper
1 c. fresh bread crumbs
1 c. hot milk

Sauce:
1 c. condensed cream of mushroom soup
1 c. water
½ tsp. Worcestershire sauce

Preheat oven to 350 degrees. Butter large casserole dish. In large bowl lightly mix all casserole ingredients. Spread into prepared dish. In small saucepan combine all sauce ingredients. Heat over low heat and stir until smooth. Pour over meat mixture. Bake 1½ to 2 hours.

My Hope, our prizes have no real importance; liberate us from them, we pray. Amen.

I looked for a man among them who would build up the wall and stand before me in the gap on behalf of the land so I would not have to destroy it, but I found none.

Ezekiel 22:30 NIV

One Dish Casserole

2 or 3 sliced carrots
2 or 3 sliced potatoes
¼ c. uncooked long-grain rice
1 lb. ground beef, browned, drained, crumbled
1 onion, sliced thin
1 c. sliced celery
1 green pepper, sliced thick
1 to 3 c. tomatoes

Preheat oven to 350 degrees. Grease 2-quart casserole dish. Place all ingredients except tomatoes in dish in order given. Pour tomatoes on top. Bake 1½ hours.

Our knees are water and our feet are clay, Mighty God. Amen.

"Son of man, I have made you a watchman for the house of Israel; so hear the word I speak and give them warning from me."
　　　　　　　　　　　　　　　　　　　　　Ezekiel 33:7 NIV

Oven Baked Beef Stew

1 lb. beef stew meat, cut in ½-inch cubes
1 medium onion, chopped
30 baby carrots
1 can diced tomatoes with juice, about 14 oz.
1 can condensed beef broth, about 10 oz.
1 tsp. dried marjoram or 1 bay leaf
1 tsp. sugar
8 oz. tomato sauce
⅓ c. flour
1 T. Worcestershire sauce
1 tsp. salt
¼ tsp. pepper
12 red potatoes
1½ c. sliced mushrooms (optional)
½ c. frozen peas
1 tsp. hot sauce (optional)

Preheat oven to 325 degrees. Grease 4-quart baking dish. In large bowl combine all ingredients except potatoes, mushrooms, peas and hot sauce. Pour into prepared dish. Cover and bake 2 hours, stirring once. Stir in potatoes and mushrooms. Cover and bake 1 to 1½ hours or until beef and vegetables are tender. Stir in peas and hot sauce. Remove bay leaf if used. Cover and let stand 5 minutes.

How you must love us to warn us, Christ of the World. Amen.

Woe to the shepherds of Israel who only take care of themselves!

Ezekiel 34:1b NIV

Pizza Casserole

1 lb. ground chuck beef
1 lb. mild Italian sausage
1 large onion, diced
1 T. oregano
1 T. basil
1 tsp. salt
½ tsp. pepper
4 oz. sliced pepperoni
2 c. or more cooked spaghetti
4 oz. canned mushrooms
8 oz. sliced Swiss cheese
8 oz. grated mozzarella cheese
1 large jar spaghetti sauce, about 40 oz.
Parmesan cheese

Preheat oven to 350 degrees. Butter 9 by 14-inch casserole dish. In skillet brown ground beef, sausage and onion. Sprinkle with oregano, basil, salt and pepper. In small saucepan boil pepperoni 5 minutes. Drain fat. In prepared casserole dish place half each of the meat mixture, cooked spaghetti, mushrooms, pepperoni, Swiss cheese and mozzarella cheese. Sprinkle with half of the Parmesan cheese. Pour half of spaghetti sauce on top. Repeat layers. Bake 30 to 40 minutes or until heated through.

Strong and Mighty Lord, cure our generation of shepherds who hurt others. Amen.

I will judge between one sheep and another, and between rams and goats.
Ezekiel 34:17b NIV

Pork Chop Supper
5 pork loin chops
½ c. flour
2 T. olive oil or vegetable oil
2 tsp. dried thyme
2 tsp. salt
¼ tsp. pepper
4 large potatoes, peeled and cut into ¾-inch cubes
5 medium carrots, sliced in pieces ¼ inch thick
1 medium onion, cut into wedges
3 c. beef broth or bouillon

Dredge chops in flour. Heat oil in large skillet. Brown chops on both sides. Sprinkle with thyme, salt and pepper. Add potatoes, carrots and onion. Pour broth over all. Bring to boil. Reduce heat. Cover and simmer 40 to 50 minutes until all is tender.

We foolishly attempted to sidestep your judgment, Precious Cornerstone. Amen.

"And the name of the city from that time on will be: THE LORD IS THERE." Ezekiel 48:35b NIV

Spinach Meat Roll

10 oz. frozen chopped spinach
2 lbs. ground beef
2 eggs
¼ c. ketchup
¼ c. milk
¾ c. soft bread crumbs
1½ tsp. salt, divided
¼ tsp. pepper
¼ tsp. oregano
3 oz. smoked sliced ham
3 slices mozzarella cheese, cut in half diagonally

Preheat oven to 350 degrees. Grease 10 by 12-inch piece of aluminum foil. Quickly rinse spinach in hot water. In large bowl combine ground beef, eggs, ketchup, milk, bread crumbs, ½ teaspoon of the salt, pepper and oregano. Mix well. Flatten meat mixture on greased foil. Arrange spinach evenly on meat mixture, leaving ½-inch margin on edges. Sprinkle with remaining 1 teaspoon salt. Place ham slices on top. Carefully roll up, beginning at narrow end and using foil to lift meat. Remove foil. Press edges of meat roll to seal. Place on ungreased 9 by 13-inch pan. Bake 75 minutes. Overlap cheese slices on baked roll. Bake 5 minutes or until cheese melts.

Your presence is the holiest of imprints, Our Sanctuary. Amen.

Tell your children about it
and let your children tell their children,
and their children the next generation!   Joel 1:3 NJB

Stuffed Spaghetti Squash

1 medium spaghetti squash, halved lengthwise and seeded
4 oz. Italian sausage or 2 Italian sausage links, sliced
4 oz. sliced mushrooms
¼ c. diced onion
½ c. marinara sauce
2 oz. shredded mozzarella or provolone cheese
Grated Parmesan cheese

Preheat oven to 350 degrees. Place squash cut side down in baking pan with 1 inch water. Bake 35 to 45 minutes until tender. In skillet saute sausage, mushrooms and onion until sausage cooks through and mixture browns lightly. Remove from heat. Remove squash from pan and drain on paper towels. Preheat broiler. Place sausage mixture on squash. Top with sauce and mozzarella cheese. Sprinkle with Parmesan cheese. Broil until mozzarella bubbles and Parmesan starts to brown.

Let my mouth sow the seed of your Gospel, Shepherd and Overseer of Souls. Amen.

What the nibbler has left, the grown locust has eaten. . . .
>> Joel 1:4a NJB

Various Veggie Lasagna
4 c. cooked vegetables (choose 2 options below)
2 T. olive oil, divided
Salt and pepper
1 tsp. minced garlic, divided
4½ T. butter, divided
1 medium large onion, chopped
1½ T. salt
15 oven-ready lasagna noodles
2½ c. milk
1 c. canned chicken broth
6 cloves garlic, smashed
5 T. flour
1¼ c. grated Parmesan cheese, divided
¼ tsp. salt
Pepper
½ lb. fontina or provolone cheese, grated, about 2½ c.

Veggie Options (Choose 2)
1 lb. steam-sauteed asparagus, cut into 1-inch pieces
1 lb. steam-sauteed cauliflower, cut into medium florets
1 lb. steam-sauteed broccoli, cut into florets,
    stalks peeled and sliced into ¼-inch rounds
1 lb. steam-sauteed carrots, sliced into ¼-inch rounds
1 lb. steam-sauteed spinach, rinsed and tough stems removed
1 lb. sauteed white or cremini mushrooms, rinsed and sliced
1 lb. sauteed yellow or red bell peppers,
    seeded and cut into ¼-inch strips
1 lb. broiled eggplant, trimmed and sliced into ⅓-inch rounds
1 lb. broiled zucchini, trimmed and sliced into ⅓-inch rounds
1 lb. yellow squash, trimmed and sliced into ⅓-inch rounds

Toss each selected vegetable in separate bowl with 1 tablespoon of the olive oil, salt, pepper and scant ½ teaspoon of the minced garlic.

The Preacher Lady's Cookbook for the Hungry Heart

Heat 2 tablespoons of the butter over medium-high heat in large skillet. Add onion and cook 5 minutes or until soft and golden brown. Set aside. Mix 1½ tablespoons salt and 2 quarts very hot tap water in 9 by 13-inch baking pan. Add noodles and soak about 10 minutes or until soft and pliable. Drain and stack loosely. (Noodles tend to stick together as they dry but will pull apart easily.)

Begin making creamy Parmesan sauce by microwaving milk, broth and smashed garlic cloves in 1-quart microwavable bowl on high power about 8 minutes or until steaming hot. (Or slowly heat in medium saucepan over medium-low heat.) Remove garlic and discard.

In large saucepan melt remaining 2½ tablespoons butter over medium heat. When foaming subsides, whisk in flour and continue to cook, whisking constantly, until well blended. Pour in milk mixture all at once and whisk vigorously until sauce is smooth and starts to bubble and thicken. Stir in ½ cup of the Parmesan cheese, ¼ tsp. salt and pepper to taste. Remove from heat. Place plastic wrap directly on surface of sauce.

Adjust oven rack to upper middle position and preheat to 425 degrees. Smear ¼ cup of the sauce on bottom of pan. Assemble four sets of layers in order: 3 noodles, ⅔ cup Parmesan sauce, one-quarter of the onion slices, one-half of one of the cooked vegetables (alternating each layer), ½ cup fontina or provolone cheese, and 2 tablespoons Parmesan cheese. Assemble fifth layer with remaining noodles, sauce and cheeses. Seal with foil and bake about 35 minutes or until bubbly. Remove foil. Broil 5 to 7 minutes or until cheese is spotty brown. Let stand 10 to 15 minutes before serving.

Oh, Holy One, the yield of the land is diminished by our sins. Amen.

Wake up, you drunkards, and weep!   Joel 1:5a NJB

Veggie Casserole
1 can white corn, drained, about 11 oz.
1 can French-cut green beans, drained, about 14 oz.
½ c. chopped celery
2 T. chopped onion
½ c. sharp cheese, grated
½ c. sour cream
1 can condensed cream of celery soup
½ regular box round buttery crackers, crumbled
¼ c. butter, melted
½ c. almonds, slivered

Preheat oven to 325 degrees. Coat baking dish. Mix vegetables, cheese, sour cream and soup. Put in prepared dish. In bowl mix crackers, butter and almonds. Sprinkle on top. Bake 45 minutes.

When we slumber, wake us, Sun of Righteousness. Amen.

~~~

Even the wild animals pant loudly for you . . . .   Joel 1:20 NJB

Yum-A-Setta
2 lbs. ground beef
1 onion, chopped
Salt and pepper
1 tsp. brown sugar
1 can condensed tomato soup, undiluted
1 can condensed cream of chicken soup, undiluted
16 oz. egg noodles, cooked according to package directions
8 oz. shredded cheese

Preheat oven to 350 degrees. Saute beef and onion. Drain fat. Add salt, pepper, brown sugar and tomato soup. In bowl mix chicken soup and noodles. Layer in pan one-third each of beef mixture, cheese and noodles. Repeat twice. Bake 30 minutes.

Your hand, God of the Universe, holds our world's water. Amen.

CHICKEN AND TURKEY

Blow the ram's-horn in Zion,
sound the alarm on my holy mountain! Joel 2:1a NJB

Baked Chicken
3 lb. chicken, cut up
Salt
Pepper
Flour
Butter

Preheat oven to 450 degrees. Wash and dry chicken pieces. Sprinkle with salt, pepper and flour. Place in baking pan skin side up. Dot with butter. Add 2 cups hot water. Bake 15 minutes, turn once and sprinkle again with salt, pepper and flour. Baste. Reduce heat to 350 degrees and bake until tender, 1½ to 2 hours, basting every 15 minutes and turning when bottom side is well browned.

Make them listen as we shout your name, True God. Amen.

Let everybody in the country tremble,
for the Day of Yahweh is coming,
yes it is near.   Joel 2:1 NJB

Barbecued Turkey Meatballs

Meatballs:
3 lbs. ground turkey
1 can evaporated milk, about 12 oz.
1 c. rolled oats
1 c. cracker crumbs
2 eggs
½ c. chopped onion
½ tsp. garlic powder
2 tsp. salt
½ tsp. pepper
2 tsp. chili powder

Sauce:
2 c. ketchup
1 c. firmly packed brown sugar
½ tsp. liquid smoke (or adjust to taste)
½ tsp. garlic powder
¼ c. chopped onion

Line baking sheet with waxed paper. In large bowl combine all meatball ingredients. Mixture will be soft. Shape into walnut-size balls. Place meatballs in single layer on prepared baking sheet. Freeze until solid. Store frozen meatballs in freezer bags until ready to cook.

Preheat oven to 350 degrees. Combine all sauce ingredients in medium saucepan and stir until sugar dissolves. Place frozen meatballs in 9 by 13-inch baking dish. Cover with sauce. Bake 1 hour.

How foolishly we danced, Wonderful God, while you called us to service. Amen.

Yahweh's voice rings out
at the head of his troops!
For mighty indeed is his army,
strong, the enforcer of his orders,
for great is the Day of Yahweh,
and very terrible—who can face it?

Joel 2:11 NJB

Basic Stuffing for Birds

1 c. butter
2 c. chopped onion
1 c. chopped celery
16 to 20 slices white bread, cubed
3 T. sage
1 T. thyme
1 tsp. salt
½ tsp. pepper
1 can chicken broth, about 14 oz.

Pan method: Preheat oven to 325 degrees. Butter large pan or casserole dish. Melt butter in skillet. Saute onions and celery until onions are clear. In large bowl toss together cubed bread, sage, thyme, salt and pepper. Add onion-celery mixture to bread mixture. Place in prepared dish and pour chicken broth over stuffing until moist. Cover with foil and bake 30 minutes. Remove foil and bake 15 minutes or until brown.

Bird method: Combine all ingredients, including broth, and use to stuff 16- to 20-pound turkey before baking.

There is no escape from your justice, Most Holy. Amen.

> But now—declares Yahweh—
> come back to me with all your heart,
> fasting, weeping, mourning.
>
> Joel 2:12 NJB

Brined Turkey

Brine solution:
1 small onion, diced
1 stalk celery, diced
1 medium carrot, diced
3 cloves garlic, sliced
3 bay leaves
1 T. black peppercorns
3 sprigs each of sage, rosemary and thyme
6 sprigs Italian parsley
½ c. iodized salt
3 gallons cold water

Bird:
16 lb. turkey (neck and giblets removed and discarded)
Salt and pepper

In the bird:
2 carrots, coarsely chopped
2 celery stalks, coarsely chopped
1 apple, sliced into wedges
1 orange, peeled and sliced into wedges
4 cloves garlic, whole

Under the bird:
1 medium onion, diced
1 medium carrot, diced
1 stalk celery, diced
3 cloves garlic, whole
3 sprigs each of sage, rosemary and thyme
6 sprigs Italian parsley
3 bay leaves

On the bird:
¼ butter, unsalted, sliced into pats
5 c. chicken stock, divided

One day before baking turkey, prepare brine. Combine all brine ingredients. Place turkey in bucket or very large pot and cover with brine. Refrigerate 12 to 24 hours. Remove turkey from brine. Dry with paper towels. Discard brine.

On roasting day, preheat oven to 300 degrees. Salt and pepper brined turkey and cavity. In large bowl mix carrots, celery, apple, orange and garlic. Fill bird cavity with mixture. Bind legs with kitchen twine. On bottom of large roasting pan or disposable aluminum pan spread onion, carrot, celery, garlic, sage, rosemary, thyme, parsley and bay leaves. Place turkey atop bed of vegetables and herbs. Place butter pats on turkey or between skin and breast.

Roast 45 minutes. Pour half the chicken stock over turkey. Roast 45 minutes. Pour remaining stock over turkey and roast 45 minutes. Turkey will start turning golden brown. Baste with pan juices, cover loosely with foil and roast 45 minutes. When turkey reaches internal temperature of 165 to 175 degrees, remove from oven, keep covered and let rest at least 10 minutes before carving.

To make gravy, discard herbs and measure out 1 cup of vegetables and 3 cups of pan juices. Puree in blender. To thicken, add more vegetables. To thin, add more pan juice. Pour through mesh strainer to make gravy smooth. Makes about 4 cups.

Open all our eyes to the opportunities of your invitation, Lord Jesus Christ. Amen.

Land, do not be afraid;
be glad, rejoice,
for Yahweh has done great things.   Joel 2:21 NJB

Chicken and Chestnuts
2 c. cooked chicken, diced
1 medium onion, diced
2 or 3 celery stalks, diced
1 small pimiento
1 pkg. prepared chicken-flavored rice
1 can sliced water chestnuts
2 cans condensed cream of chicken soup
1 c. mayonnaise
1 T. lemon juice
2 c. croutons

Preheat oven to 375 degrees. Place all ingredients except croutons in 9 by 13-inch pan. Stir well. Top with croutons. Bake 30 to 40 minutes or until heated through.

Lord Over All, your wondrous results exceed my imagination. Amen.

The threshing-floors will be full of grain,
the vats overflow with wine and oil.

Joel 2:24 NJB

Chicken and Rice

1 can condensed cream of mushroom
 or low-fat cream of mushroom soup
1 c. water
¾ c. uncooked long-grain white rice
¼ tsp. paprika
¼ tsp. pepper
4 skinless boneless chicken breast halves

Preheat oven to 375 degrees. In shallow 2-quart baking dish mix soup, water, rice, paprika and pepper. Top with chicken. Season with additional paprika and pepper. Cover. Bake 45 minutes or until tender and cooked through.

Note: For creamier rice, increase water to 1⅓ cups.

You conquer even the fields and farms, Strong and Supreme Lord. Amen.

~~~

After this I shall pour out my spirit on all humanity.

Joel 3:1a NJB

Chicken Bake

4 skinless boneless chicken breast halves
1 can condensed cream of mushroom
 or reduced-fat cream of mushroom soup

Preheat oven to 400 degrees. Place chicken in shallow 2-quart baking dish. Spread soup evenly over chicken. Cover. Bake 25 minutes or until chicken is tender and cooked through.

Your spirit moves the world, Lord of Hosts. Amen.

Your sons and daughters shall prophesy,
your old people shall dream dreams,
and your young people see visions. Joel 3:1b NJB

Chicken Mozzarella
1 T. vegetable oil
⅔ c. baking mix
2 T. grated Parmesan cheese
2 tsp. Italian seasoning
1 tsp. paprika
¼ tsp. pepper
6 large chicken breast halves
6 T. chili sauce
6 slices mozzarella cheese

Preheat oven to 425 degrees. Place oil in 9 by 13-inch baking pan. In medium bowl combine baking mix, Parmesan cheese, Italian seasoning, paprika and pepper. Coat chicken with mixture. Place chicken in pan skin side down. Bake, uncovered, 45 minutes. Turn chicken over. Spoon 1 tablespoon chili sauce onto each piece of chicken. Top each piece with cheese slice. Continue baking until cheese melts.

Your day, O Power of God, beckons me to do what you made me to do. Amen.

~~~

I shall show portents in the sky
  and on earth,
blood and fire and columns of smoke. Joel 3:3 NJB

Chicken Noodles in the Slow Cooker
2 cans condensed cream of chicken soup, regular or low-fat
½ c. water
¼ c. lemon juice
1 T. Dijon mustard
1½ tsp. garlic powder
8 large carrots, thickly sliced
8 boneless chicken breast halves

8 c. hot cooked egg noodles
Chopped fresh parsley

In slow cooker mix soup, water, lemon juice, mustard, garlic powder and carrots. Add chicken and turn to coat. Cover and cook on low 7 to 8 hours or until tender and cooked through. May be served over noodles. Sprinkle with parsley.

Your salvation is a colossal upheaval, Mighty to Save. Amen.

~~~

The sun will be turned into darkness,
and the moon into blood,
before the Day comes,
that great and terrible Day.   Joel 3:4 NJB

Chicken Parmesan
1 egg, beaten
¾ c. Italian-style bread crumbs
4 skinless boneless chicken breast halves
1 jar pasta sauce, about 26 oz.
1 c. shredded mozzarella cheese, about 4 oz.

Preheat oven to 400 degrees. Place egg and bread crumbs in separate bowls. Dip chicken in egg, then in crumbs. Arrange chicken in 9 by 13-inch baking pan. Bake 20 minutes. Pour pasta sauce over chicken. Top with cheese. Bake 10 minutes or until chicken is cooked through. May be served over hot pasta.

The cosmos is at your fingertips, Liberator of the World. Amen.

Tear your hearts and not your clothes,
and come back to Yahweh your God,
for he is gracious and compassionate,
slow to anger, rich in faithful love,
and he relents about inflicting disaster. Joel 2:13 NJB

Chicken Pilau
3 lbs. chicken, cut up, washed and dried
2 c. rice
2 tsp. salt
½ tsp. pepper
2 T. butter
1 onion, chopped
½ c. celery, chopped
3 tomatoes, sliced
3 T. butter

Boil 2 quarts water in large saucepan. Add rice and chicken. Cover and simmer until chicken is nearly tender, about 1½ hours, adding salt and pepper in last 30 minutes of cooking. Melt butter in skillet and brown onion, celery and tomatoes. Add to chicken mixture. Cover and simmer 30 minutes.

When will we turn to you in disaster, Rose of Sharon? Amen.

~~~

All who call on the name of Yahweh
 will be saved . . . . Joel 3:5a NJB

Chicken Quicken
1 T. vegetable oil
4 skinless boneless chicken breast halves
1 can condensed cream of chicken
    or low-fat cream of chicken soup
1½ c. water
¼ tsp. paprika
¼ tsp. pepper
2 c. quick rice, uncooked
3 c. fresh or frozen broccoli flowerets (optional)

Heat oil in skillet. Brown chicken and remove from skillet. Add soup, water, paprika and pepper. Stir and heat to boil. Add rice and broccoli. Top with chicken. Add more paprika and pepper. Cover and cook on low 5 minutes or until cooked through.

Jesus, Redeemer, Friend, Anchor, My Sure Foundation. Amen.

~~~

Listen, all you peoples,
Give heed, O earth, and all it holds . . . .   Micah 1:2a JPS

Chicken Rollups
1 pkg. wild rice-mushroom stuffing mix, about 6 oz.
6 skinless boneless chicken breast halves
Pepper
2 T. butter or margarine, melted
2 T. Dijon mustard
1¼ c. ground pecans
3 T. vegetable oil
¾ c. chicken broth
¾ c. sour cream

Prepare stuffing mix according to package directions. Place chicken breasts between sheets of waxed paper. Use a meat mallet or rolling pin to pound ¼ inch thick. Divide stuffing evenly and place on top of each chicken piece. Fold sides of chicken over stuffing, roll up and secure with toothpicks. Sprinkle with pepper. In small bowl combine butter and mustard. Stir well. Brush over all sides of chicken. Roll chicken in pecans. Heat oil in skillet over medium-high heat. Add chicken. Brown well on all sides and transfer to paper towels to drain. Pour drippings from skillet. Return chicken to skillet. Add broth. Reduce heat and simmer 20 minutes or until chicken is cooked through. Transfer chicken to serving dish. Tent with foil to keep warm. Stir sour cream into broth in skillet. Cook on low heat, stirring constantly, until heated through. Spoon over chicken.

We hear but must also listen, Christ the Way. Amen.

The mountains shall melt under Him
And the valleys burst open—
Like wax before fire,
Like water cascading down a slope. Micah 1:4 JPS

Chicken Spaghetti
4 skinless boneless chicken breasts
7 oz. spaghetti
1 T. butter
1 onion, chopped
1 green pepper, chopped
1 lb. boxed processed cheese
10 oz. canned tomatoes or tomatoes with chilies
6 oz. canned mushrooms
1 can small peas
2 T. Worcestershire sauce
½ c. butter, melted

Grease large baking pan or casserole dish. Boil chicken in large saucepan until well done. Remove chicken from saucepan and save water. Cook spaghetti in chicken water. Melt 1 tablespoon butter in skillet. Lightly saute onion and green pepper. Melt cheese in large bowl and combine with onion mixture, tomatoes, mushrooms, peas, Worcestershire sauce and ½ cup melted butter. Cut cooled chicken into cubes and stir into cheese mixture. Spread evenly in prepared pan and bake 30 minutes at 250 degrees.

There is no hope for any who oppose you, Yahweh. Amen.

They covet fields, and seize them;
Houses, and take them away.
They defraud men of their homes,
And people of their land.   Micah 2:2 JPS

Chicken and Cashews
5 T. vegetable oil
2 to 2½ lbs. skinless boneless chicken breasts, cut in slivers
2 T. soy sauce
2 tsp. salt
1½ tsp. sugar
Pinch of pepper
¼ c. cornstarch
⅓ c. water
1 can chicken broth, about 14 oz.
1 can water chestnuts, drained, chopped, about 5 oz.
½ c. frozen peas, thawed, drained
1 c. thinly sliced celery
1 can whole mushrooms, drained, about 4 oz.
¾ c. toasted unsalted whole cashews, or more if desired
Hot cooked rice

Heat oil in large skillet. Add chicken, soy sauce, salt, sugar and pepper. Cook and stir a few minutes or until chicken is no longer pink. In small bowl make smooth paste of cornstarch and water. Stir into chicken mixture with broth, water chestnuts, peas, celery and mushrooms. Cook and stir until mixture is slightly thickened and translucent. Stir in cashews. Serve over rice.

I hate the thieves, too, God of the Beginning. Amen.

I will bring together the remnant of Israel . . . .
                                                  Micah 2:12b JPS

Church Supper Chicken Sandwiches
Large roasting or frying chicken
3 eggs, beaten
1 c. fine bread crumbs
Chicken broth
Salt and pepper

Boil chicken until tender. Remove meat from bones. Grind or chop meat into about 5 cups of meat. Mix in beaten eggs and bread crumbs. Slowly add broth to reach thick spreading consistency. Season with salt and pepper. Serve on buns.

You finish what you begin, God of Eternity. Amen.

~~~

But you hate good and love evil.   Micah 3:2a JPS

Company Chicken
1 pkg. chipped beef, about 4 oz.
4 strips bacon
8 chicken breast halves, boned and skinned
1 can condensed cream of mushroom soup
1 can condensed cream of chicken soup
1 c. sour cream

Preheat oven to 300 degrees. Cut beef in small places and place in bottom of 9 by 13-inch baking pan. Cut bacon strips in half and place half a strip around each chicken breast. Place chicken on beef. In large bowl mix mushroom soup, chicken soup and sour cream. Pour over chicken. Bake uncovered 3 hours. Chicken will be crisp. Dish may be prepared ahead and baked when needed. May be served over hot cooked rice.

Because of you, Emmanuel, I need not worry about who will win. Amen.

I am filled with strength by the spirit of the Lord . . . .
> Micah 3:8a JPS

Country Style Chicken

3 lbs. chicken pieces
2 tsp. salt, divided
½ c. flour
6 T. butter
6 medium potatoes, peeled and quartered
6 small onions, quartered
6 large carrots, quartered lengthwise
2 large green peppers, cut in ½-inch strips
1 T. sugar
¼ tsp. pepper
2½ c. canned or stewed tomatoes

Wash and dry chicken pieces. Mix ½ teaspoon of the salt with flour and roll chicken in mixture. Melt butter in frying pan and cook chicken on all sides, about 10 minutes, until browned. Place two-thirds of potatoes, onions, carrots and green peppers in bottom of large saucepan. Place chicken on top and add remaining one-third of vegetables. In small bowl mix remaining 1½ teaspoons salt, sugar and pepper with tomatoes. Pour tomato mixture and 3 cups boiling water over all. Cover tightly and bring to boil. Reduce heat and simmer until tender, about 1½ hours.

I was empty before you, God of Heaven and Earth. Amen.

In the days to come, the Mount of the Lord's House shall stand firm above the mountains . . . . Micah 4:1a JPS

Feta Chicken Bake
6 skinless boneless chicken breast halves
2 T. lemon juice, divided
¼ tsp. salt
¼ tsp. pepper
4 oz. crumbled feta cheese
¼ c. diced red bell pepper
¼ c. diced fresh parsley

Preheat oven to 350 degrees. Arrange chicken in 9 by 13-inch baking pan. Drizzle with 1 tablespoon of the lemon juice. Add salt and pepper. Top with feta cheese. Drizzle with remaining 1 tablespoon lemon juice. Bake 35 to 40 minutes or until chicken is cooked through. Sprinkle with red peppers and parsley.

When I look up, there you are, God of Knowledge. Amen.

~~~

Nation shall not take up
Sword against nation . . . . Micah 4:3c JPS

Meatloaf Sensation
2½ lbs. ground turkey
4 oz. salsa
1 envelope dry taco seasoning
1 egg, lightly beaten
1 c. bread crumbs
12 oz. shredded Mexican-blend cheese
2 tsp. salt
½ tsp. pepper

Combine all ingredients, using half of taco seasoning. Mix well. Shape into loaf. Place in slow cooker. Sprinkle with remaining taco seasoning. Cover. Cook on low 8 to 10 hours.

We love war, God of Our Salvation, but you do not. Amen.

We will walk
In the name of the Lord our God
Forever and ever.   Micah 4:5b JPS

Shredded Chicken Sandwiches
1 large can boneless chicken
1 can condensed cream of chicken, celery or mushroom soup
1 stack round buttery crackers, crushed
Pepper

Mix all ingredients together and heat in slow cooker.

My future is with you, God Who Is Near. Amen.

~~~

And you, O Bethlehem of Ephrath,
Least among the clans of Judah,
From you one shall come forth
To rule Israel for Me—
One whose origin is from of old,
From ancient times.   Micah 5:1 JPS

So Speedy Chicken
3 lbs. chicken pieces
1 small bottle Catalina salad dressing
1 can crushed pineapple
½ c. apricot jam

Preheat oven to 350 degrees. Place chicken in large shallow baking dish. In small bowl mix dressing, pineapple and jam. Spread mixture on chicken. Cover and bake 1 hour or until chicken is well cooked.

I weep with gratitude to know that you work with the least, Faithful God. Amen.

For lo, he shall wax great
To the ends of the earth . . . .   Micah 5:3b JPS

Sour Cream Chicken
12 pieces fryer chicken
2 T. butter
½ c. chopped celery
½ c. chopped onion
½ c. chopped green pepper
1 can condensed cream of mushroom soup
1 small can mushrooms
16 oz. sour cream

Preheat oven to 350 degrees. In 9 by 13-inch pan bake chicken in single layer about 45 minutes or until tender. Melt butter in medium saucepan. Saute celery, onion and green pepper until tender. In large bowl mix soup, mushrooms and sour cream. Add vegetable mixture. Stir well and spoon over baked chicken. Bake 30 minutes at 350 degrees. May be served with steamed rice, mashed potatoes or hot noodles.

Over all, under all, through all, with all—you, God of Fidelity. Amen.

"He has told you, O man, what is good
And what the Lord requires of you:
Only to do justice
And to love goodness,
And to walk modestly with your God;
Then will your name achieve wisdom."

Micah 6:8 JPS

Sweet and Sour Chicken

¼ c. butter
½ c. chopped onion
½ c. chopped green pepper (optional)
1 can pineapple chunks, juice reserved, about 15 oz.
¾ c. to 1 c. pineapple juice, reserved from pineapple chunks
¾ c. ketchup
¼ c. firmly packed brown sugar
2 T. cider vinegar
2 tsp. soy sauce
½ tsp. garlic salt
½ tsp. salt
¼ tsp. pepper
3 lbs. chicken, cut up

Preheat oven to 400 degrees. Melt butter in large skillet. Add onion and green pepper and cook 5 minutes, stirring occasionally. In small bowl combine pineapple juice, ketchup, brown sugar, vinegar, soy sauce, garlic salt, salt and pepper. Mix well. Add to onion mixture in skillet. Cook, stirring constantly, until mixture boils. Add pineapple chunks and mix well. Arrange chicken pieces skin side up in 9 by 13-inch baking pan. Pour sauce over chicken. Cover pan with aluminum foil. Bake 45 minutes. Remove foil and bake 35 minutes more, basting occasionally.

Note: To make in slow cooker, place chicken and onions in bottom, pour sauce over them, and top with pineapples and green peppers. Cook on low 8 to 10 hours.

I missed the marks of justice, goodness and humility today, Great God, and I ask forgiveness. Amen.

Hark! The Lord
Summons the city.... Micah 6:9b JPS

Turkey Meatloaf

1 envelope brown gravy mix
½ c. canned evaporated milk
1 tsp. minced onion
2 large eggs, lightly beaten
1 T. chopped parsley
2 T. soy sauce
1 tsp. garlic powder
½ tsp. salt
Pinch pepper
1 c. soft bread crumbs
2 lbs. ground turkey
½ c. bottled sweet and sour sauce

Preheat oven to 350 degrees. In large bowl blend gravy mix and milk. Add onion. Let stand several minutes. Add eggs, parsley, soy sauce, garlic powder, salt and pepper. Mix well. Stir in bread crumbs. Add ground turkey. Mix well. Shape into loaf. Place in shallow baking pan. Spread sauce on top. Bake 1 hour.

What would happen, God of Heights, if even one city gave itself to you? Amen.

COOKIES

They are eager to do evil:
The magistrate makes demands,
And the judge [judges] for a fee;
The rich man makes his crooked plea,
And they grant it. Micah 7:3 JPS

Applesauce Raisin Cookies
1 c. sifted flour
1½ tsp. baking powder
½ tsp. baking soda
¾ tsp. ground cinnamon
¼ tsp. ground nutmeg
⅛ tsp. ground cloves
⅛ tsp. cream of tartar
½ c. margarine, softened
⅓ c. brown sugar substitute
1 egg
1⅓ c. unsweetened applesauce
1½ tsp. vanilla
1¾ c. quick-cooking rolled oats
1 c. seedless raisins

Preheat oven to 375 degrees. Coat cookie sheets with nonstick spray. Into small bowl sift flour, baking powder, baking soda, cinnamon, nutmeg, cloves and cream of tartar. In large bowl cream margarine until fluffy. Blend in brown sugar substitute and egg. Alternately add dry ingredients and applesauce, blending well after each addition. Stir in vanilla, oats and raisins. Drop by tablespoonfuls onto prepared cookie sheets. Flatten each cookie with bottom of glass dipped in flour. Bake 12 to 15 minutes or until firm.

The highest are low when they do not honor you, God of the Universe. Amen.

The best of them is like a prickly shrub;
The [most] upright, worse than a barrier of thorns.
Micah 7:4a JPS

Best Oatmeal Cookies
3 eggs, well beaten
1 c. raisins
1 tsp. vanilla
1 c. butter
1 c. firmly packed brown sugar
1 c. granulated sugar
2½ c. flour
1 tsp. salt
1 tsp. ground cinnamon
2 tsp. baking soda
2 c. rolled oats
¾ c. chopped pecans or walnuts

Preheat oven to 350 degrees. In small bowl blend eggs, raisins and vanilla. Cover and refrigerate 1 hour. In large mixer bowl cream butter, brown sugar and granulated sugar. Add flour, salt, cinnamon and baking soda. Mix well. Blend in egg-raisin mixture, oats and nuts. Dough will be stiff. Drop by teaspoonfuls onto ungreased cookie sheets. Bake 10 to 12 minutes or until lightly browned.

I don't want to be a stumbling block, Lord of the Sabbath. Amen.

~~~

Yet I will look to the Lord,
I will wait for the God who saves me,
My God will hear me.
<div align="right">Micah 7:7 JPS</div>

Butterscotch Refrigerator Cookies
2 c. firmly packed brown sugar
1 c. butter
2 eggs, well beaten
1 tsp. baking soda
1 tsp. cream of tartar

3 c. flour, divided
1 c. chopped nuts (black walnuts best)
1 tsp. vanilla

In large mixer bowl cream brown sugar and butter. Add eggs and mix well. Into medium bowl sift baking soda, cream of tartar and 1 cup of the flour. Add to creamed mixture and mix well. Add remaining 2 cups flour, nuts and vanilla and mix well. Shape into long roll about 2 inches in diameter. Refrigerate overnight. Preheat oven to 350 degrees. Lightly coat cookie sheets. Slice dough about ⅜ inch thick with thin, sharp knife. Bake about 10 minutes or until golden brown.

Minute by minute—and year by year—I wait for you, Chief of Compassion. Amen.

~~~

Do not rejoice over me,
O my enemy!
Though I have fallen, I rise again....   Micah 7:8a JPS

Cake Mix Cookies
1 pkg. cake mix
2 eggs
½ c. vegetable oil
Chocolate chips, nuts, raisins (optional)

Preheat oven to 350 degrees. Coat cookie sheets. Mix ingredients well and drop by teaspoonfuls 2 inches apart on prepared sheets. Bake 8 to 10 minutes or until lightly browned.

Yes, All-Seeing God, I have fallen many times, but you always picked me up. Amen.

Though I sit in darkness, the Lord is my light.

Micah 7:8b JPS

Cranberry Sugar Cookies
1 pkg. cranberry quick bread or muffin mix
¾ c. butter, softened
3 T. sugar

Preheat oven to 350 degrees. In large bowl combine bread mix and butter. Mix well. Shape dough into 2-inch balls. Place 2 inches apart on ungreased cookie sheets. Flatten balls to ¼-inch thickness with bottom of glass dipped in sugar. Bake 9 to 11 minutes or until edges are light golden brown. Cool 2 minutes. Remove from cookie sheets.

Day Star, you light my way, my work and my wonder. Amen.

~~~

I will enjoy vindication by Him.

<p align="right">Micah 7:9c JPS</p>

Crunch Drop Cookies
2 c. flour
2 tsp. baking soda
½ tsp. salt
1 tsp. ground cinnamon
1 c. margarine
1 c. firmly packed brown sugar
1 c. granulated sugar
2 eggs
1 tsp. vanilla
1½ c. quick-cooking rolled oats
1½ c. puffed rice cereal
1 c. shredded coconut

Preheat oven to 350 degrees. Lightly coat cookie sheets. Into medium bowl sift flour, baking soda, salt and cinnamon. In large mixer bowl cream margarine, brown sugar and granulated sugar until fluffy. Add eggs to creamed mixture. Beat well. Stir in vanilla. Add flour mixture and mix well. Mix in oats, rice cereal and coconut. Drop by teaspoonfuls onto prepared sheets. Bake 12 to 15 minutes or until golden brown.

Only you know all my truth, God Blessed Forever. Amen.

~~~

When my enemy sees it,
She shall be covered with shame.   Micah 7:10a JPS

Date Pinwheels
1 c. shortening
¾ c. granulated sugar
¾ c. firmly packed brown sugar
2 eggs
2 tsp. vanilla
3 c. flour
2 tsp. baking powder
½ tsp. salt

Filling:
1 c. finely chopped dates
½ c. sugar
1 T. grated orange rind
½ c. water
½ c. chopped nuts

In medium bowl cream shortening, granulated sugar and brown sugar. Add eggs and vanilla. Mix well. In small bowl combine flour, baking powder and salt. Add to creamed mixture and mix well. Chill. In small saucepan blend filling ingredients. Cook, stirring constantly, until thick. Chill. On floured surface, roll out dough in rectangle about ¼ inch thick. Spread date mixture on top. Roll up, jellyroll style, starting with shorter end. Chill. Slice about ¼ inch thick with thin, sharp knife dipped in flour. Bake at 325 degrees 10 to 12 minutes or until light golden brown.

I laugh at the devil because of you, Chosen of God. Amen.

She who taunts me with "Where is He,
The Lord your God?"
My eyes shall behold her [downfall]....   Micah 7:10b JPS

Date Surprises

Filling:
2 c. chopped dates
⅓ c. sugar
⅔ c. boiling water
1 T. lemon juice
1 T. butter

Dough:
3½ c. sifted cake flour
1 T. baking powder
½ tsp. salt
½ c. shortening
½ c. firmly packed brown sugar
1 egg, well beaten
1 tsp. vanilla
⅓ c. milk

To make filling, combine dates, sugar and boiling water in medium saucepan. Cook 6 to 8 minutes or until thick. Remove from heat. Stir in lemon juice and butter. Cool.

To make dough, into large bowl sift cake flour, baking powder and salt. In large mixer bowl cream shortening and brown sugar until light and fluffy. Blend in egg and vanilla. Add dry ingredients alternately with milk, mixing well after each addition. Chill until firm.

Preheat oven to 425 degrees. Lightly coat cookie sheets. Roll out dough ⅛ inch thick. Cut with 2½- inch round cookie cutter or glass. Place 1 teaspoon filling in center of one dough circle. Top with another dough circle. Press edges together with fork. Repeat with remaining dough and filling. Arrange on prepared sheets. Bake 6 to 8 minutes or until light brown.

Infinite One, you will take care of the bullies. Amen.

Oh, shepherd Your people with Your staff,
Your very own flock.

Micah 7:14a JPS

Everyday Cookies

1 c. butter or margarine
1 c. granulated sugar
1 c. light brown sugar
1 c. vegetable oil
2 eggs
1 tsp. vanilla
3½ c. all-purpose flour
1 tsp. cream of tartar
1 tsp. baking soda
1 tsp. salt
1 c. crispy rice cereal
1 c. quick-cooking rolled oats
1 c. shredded coconut
½ c. chopped pecans

Preheat oven to 350 degrees. In large bowl cream butter, granulated sugar, brown sugar and oil. Add eggs and vanilla. Mix well, completely blending in oil. In medium bowl combine flour, cream of tartar, baking soda and salt. Mix well. Add flour mixture to creamed mixture. Mix well. Stir in rice cereal, oats, coconut and pecans. Drop by teaspoonfuls onto ungreased cookie sheets. Flatten slightly. Bake 9 to 10 minutes, watching carefully to prevent overbrowning. Remove cookies from oven and immediately remove cookies from baking sheets.

I appreciate the way you look after me, Author of All Things. Amen.

Who is a God like You,
Forgiving iniquity
And remitting transgression;
Who has not maintained His wrath forever . . . .
                                   Micah 7:18a JPS

Favorite Oatmeal Cookies
1 c. margarine
1 c. firmly packed brown sugar
½ c. granulated sugar
2 eggs
1 tsp. vanilla
1½ c. flour
1 tsp. baking soda
1 tsp. ground cinnamon
½ tsp. salt (optional)
2 c. rolled oats
1 c. shredded or flaked coconut
1 c. raisins

Preheat oven to 350 degrees. Coat cookie sheets. In large mixer bowl beat margarine, brown sugar, granulated sugar, eggs and vanilla until well blended. In separate large bowl combine flour, baking soda, cinnamon and salt. Add flour mixture to margarine mixture. Mix well. Stir in oats, coconut and raisins. Drop by tablespoonfuls 2 inches apart on prepared cookie sheets. Bake 10 to 12 minutes or until lightly browned. Cool 2 minutes on cookie sheets. Transfer to wire racks and cool completely.

I shake, Deliverer, when I think what my life would be without your forgiveness. Amen.

I will sweep the earth clean of all that is on it,
   says the Lord.

                                 Zephaniah 1:2a NEB

Forgotten Cookies
3 egg whites, beaten stiff
1 c. sugar
1 tsp. vanilla
1 c. chocolate chips
1 c. nuts

Preheat oven to 350 degrees. Line cookie sheet with foil. In large bowl fold together beaten egg whites, sugar and vanilla. Lightly stir in chocolate chips and nuts. Place by teaspoonfuls on prepared cookie sheet. Place in oven and turn off heat. Leave overnight. Remove from oven in morning.

The broom is in your hand, Consuming Fire. Amen.

The great day of the Lord is near,
  it comes with speed;
no runner so fast as that day,
  no raiding band so swift.   Zephaniah 1:14 NEB

Gingerbread Cookies
½ c. butter or shortening
½ c. sugar
½ c. molasses
1 egg
2 c. flour
1 tsp. baking soda
¼ tsp. salt
1 tsp. ginger
1 tsp. ground cinnamon
⅛ tsp. ground cloves

In large bowl beat butter with sugar and molasses. Mix in egg. Into separate bowl sift flour, baking soda, salt, ginger, cinnamon and cloves. Add to butter mixture and mix well. Chill 1 hour in freezer or 2 hours in refrigerator. Preheat oven to 350 degrees. Coat baking sheets. Remove portion of dough and return remainder to refrigerator. Roll out portion ¼ inch thick on lightly floured surface. Cut with cookie cutter. Place on prepared baking sheets. Decorate if desired. Bake 8 to 10 minutes or until lightly browned. Cool.

What will happen, Desired of All Nations, on your great day? Amen.

On the day of the Lord's wrath,
In the fire of His passion,
The whole land shall be consumed;
For He will make a terrible end
Of all who dwell in the land.

                                        Zephaniah 1:18b JPS

Grandma's Soft Sugar Cookies
1½ tsp. baking soda
1 c. sour cream
1½ c. sugar
1 c. shortening (not butter or margarine)
1 egg
1½ tsp. vanilla
1½ tsp. baking powder
1 pinch salt
About 3¼ c. flour, divided

Preheat oven to 375 degrees. Lightly coat cookie sheets. Do not use mixer. In small bowl combine baking soda and sour cream. Set aside. In large bowl cream sugar and shortening by hand. Add egg and vanilla. Mix well. In medium bowl combine baking powder, salt and 2 cups of the flour. Alternately add sour cream mixture and flour mixture to creamed mixture, stirring well after each addition. Add additional flour as needed to make soft dough suitable for dropping. Drop by teaspoonfuls onto prepared sheets. Bake 10 to 15 minutes or until light brown.

Hint: To keep cookies soft and moist, store in sealed container with piece of fresh white bread.

You made us, placed us, called us and completed us, High Priest Forever. Amen.

Seek the Lord,
all in the land who live humbly by his laws,
seek righteousness, seek a humble heart;
> it may be that you will find shelter
> in the day of the Lord's anger.

Zephaniah 2:3 NEB

Lemon Whippersnaps
1 lemon cake mix
1 egg
2 c. whipped topping, thawed
½ c. powdered sugar

Preheat oven to 350 degrees. Coat cookie sheets with nonstick spray. In large bowl combine cake mix, egg and whipped topping. Stir until well blended. Drop by teaspoonfuls into powdered sugar and roll to coat. Place balls on prepared cookie sheets. Bake 10 to 15 minutes until light brown.

Remembering you foils attacks of the enemy, Messenger of the Covenant. Amen.

~~~

Shame on the tyrant city, filthy and foul!

<div align="right">Zephaniah 3:1 NEB</div>

Neverland Cookies
2¼ c. flour
1 tsp. baking powder
1 tsp. baking soda
1 tsp. salt
1½ c. creamy peanut butter
1 c. margarine, softened
1 c. granulated sugar
1 c. firmly packed brown sugar
1 tsp. vanilla
2 large eggs, lightly beaten
1 pkg. white baking morsels, about 12 oz.
1⅓ c. macadamia nuts, coarsely chopped

Preheat oven to 350 degrees. In small bowl blend flour, baking powder, baking soda and salt. In large mixer bowl beat peanut butter, margarine, granulated sugar, brown sugar and vanilla until creamy. Add eggs and blend well. Gradually add flour mixture and beat well. Stir in morsels and nuts. Drop by rounded tablespoonfuls onto ungreased cookie sheets 1½ inches apart. Bake 15 to 16 minutes or until lightly browned. Cool 5 minutes on cookie sheets. Transfer to wire rack and cool completely.

Without you, shame; with you, glory, Power of God. Amen.

~~~

But the Lord in her midst is just;
   he does no wrong;
morning by morning he gives judgment,
   without fail at daybreak.   Zephaniah 3:5 NEB

Outrageous Chocolate Chip Cookies

½ c. granulated sugar
⅓ c. firmly packed brown sugar
½ c. margarine or butter, softened
½ c. peanut butter
½ tsp. vanilla
1 egg
1 c. flour
½ c. rolled oats
1 tsp. baking soda
¼ tsp. salt
6 oz. chocolate chips

Preheat oven to 350 degrees. In medium bowl, using wooden spoon, beat granulated sugar, brown sugar, margarine, peanut butter, vanilla and egg until creamy and well blended. Mix in flour, oats, baking soda and salt. Stir in chocolate chips. Drop by rounded tablespoonfuls 2 inches apart on ungreased cookie sheets. Bake 10 to 12 minutes or until lightly browned.

Spirit of God, you are as faithful as the sunrise. Amen.

I will give all peoples once again pure lips,
   that they may invoke the Lord by name
   and serve him with one consent.

Zephaniah 3:9 NEB

Peanut Butter Cutouts

½ c. creamy peanut butter
½ c. butterlike spread
½ c. firmly packed brown sugar
½ c. granulated sugar
1 egg
½ tsp. vanilla
1½ c. flour
¾ tsp. baking soda
½ tsp. baking powder
¼ tsp. salt

In large mixer bowl beat peanut butter, spread, brown sugar, granulated sugar, egg and vanilla at medium speed until smooth. Beat in flour, baking soda, baking powder and salt at low speed just until blended. Divide dough in half. Chill 1 hour. On well-floured surface with well-floured rolling pin, roll each dough portion about ⅛ inch thick. Preheat oven to 375 degrees. Cut dough into shapes with cookie cutters or knife. Arrange on ungreased cookie sheets. Bake 8 to 10 minutes or until lightly golden. Let stand on cookie sheets 2 minutes. Transfer to wire racks and cool completely. Reroll dough trimmings to make additional cookies. Decorate with sprinkles and candies if desired.

Oh, Carpenter's Son, to speak of you with one voice, what joy! Amen.

The Lord your God is in your midst,
   like a warrior, to keep you safe . . . .

Zephaniah 3:17a NEB

Shortbread Cookies

1⅓ c. cornstarch
2 c. flour
⅔ c. powdered sugar, sifted
2 c. butter
1½ tsp. grated lemon peel
½ tsp. vanilla

Preheat oven to 350 degrees. In medium bowl combine cornstarch, flour and powdered sugar. In large mixer bowl beat butter at medium speed until softened and smooth. Add cornstarch mixture, lemon peel and vanilla. Beat until well blended. If necessary, refrigerate dough 1 hour or until easy to handle. Shape dough into 1-inch balls. Place 1½ inches apart on ungreased cookie sheets. Bake 10 to 12 minutes or until edges are lightly browned. Cool completely on wire racks. Decorate with icing. Store in airtight container.

Icing:
⅓ c. butter
1 tsp. grated lemon peel
4 c. powdered sugar, sifted
⅓ c. lemon juice

In medium bowl beat butter and lemon peel until butter is softened. Add powdered sugar and beat well. Add lemon juice and beat well. Decorate cookies with icing.

We are secure because you are fighting for us, Holy Advocate. Amen.

I will rescue the lost and gather the dispersed;
I will win my people praise and renown
in all the world where once they were despised.
Zephaniah 3:19 NEB

Slice and Bake Lemon Crisps
¾ c. unsalted butter, softened
1 c. sugar
1 egg
1 T. grated lemon peel
1½ c. flour
Sugar, granulated or powdered

In large mixer bowl beat butter and sugar at medium speed until creamy, scraping bowl often. Add egg and lemon peel. Beat well. Reduce speed to low. Add flour and beat until soft dough forms. Divide dough in half. On lightly floured surface, shape each half into 8-inch log about 1½ inches in diameter. Wrap tightly in plastic wrap. Refrigerate until firm, 2 hours or overnight.

Preheat oven to 350 degrees. With sharp knife slice dough ⅛ to ¼ inch thick. Place 1 inch apart on ungreased cookie sheets. Bake 8 to 12 minutes or until edges are very lightly browned. Let stand 1 minute on sheets. Remove from sheets. Roll in sugar while still warm and again when cool.

God the Harvester, gather us up. Amen.

~~~

Come back to me, and I will come back to you, says the Lord of Hosts.
<div align="right">Zechariah 1:3b NEB</div>

Soft Sugar Cutouts
Dough:
2 c. firmly packed brown sugar
1 c. butter-flavored shortening
2 eggs
1 tsp. vanilla

6 c. flour
2 tsp. baking soda
2 tsp. ground nutmeg
1 tsp. baking powder
1 tsp. salt
1 c. sour milk

Note: to make sour milk mix 1 tablespoon vinegar with 1 cup minus 1 tablespoon whole or 2% milk. Let milk stand a few minutes before using.

Glaze:
About 1 lb. powdered sugar
2 T. margarine, softened
½ tsp. vanilla
Milk
Food coloring (optional)

To make dough, in large mixer bowl beat brown sugar, shortening, eggs and vanilla until creamy. In another large bowl combine flour, baking soda, nutmeg, baking powder and salt. Add alternately to shortening mixture with sour milk, mixing well after each addition. Chill dough overnight.

Preheat oven to 350 degrees. Roll dough ⅛ to ¼ inch thick and place 1 inch apart on ungreased cookie sheets. Bake 8 to 10 minutes or until center of cookie is firm to the touch. Do not overbake. Cool on wire racks. In large bowl beat glaze ingredients until smooth. Drizzle over cooled cookies.

Your patience touches me, Captain of Salvation. Amen.

I am coming, I will make my dwelling among you, says the Lord.
Zechariah 2:10 NEB

Special Cookies
1 c. sugar
1 c. light corn syrup
1 c. peanut butter
5 c. flaky rice cereal
12 oz. butterscotch chips
12 oz. chocolate chips

Grease 9 by 13-inch pan. In large saucepan bring sugar, corn syrup and peanut butter to boil. Add rice cereal and mix well. Pour into prepared pan. Melt butterscotch chips and pour over cereal mixture. Melt chocolate chips and pour over mixture. Let toppings dry before cutting.

Most High God, what a magnificent neighbor you are; I want to be worthy. Amen.

~~~

Silence, all mankind, in the presence of the Lord!
Zechariah 2:13a NEB

Stone Jar Cookies
1 c. shortening
1 tsp. salt
1 tsp. vanilla
1 tsp. ground nutmeg
2 c. firmly packed light brown sugar
2 eggs, well beaten
3 c. flour, divided
1 tsp. baking soda
¼ c. milk
1 c. ground nuts

Preheat oven to 375 degrees. Grease cookie sheets or line baking sheets with parchment paper. In large mixer bowl combine shortening, salt, vanilla and nutmeg. Mix well. Add brown sugar gradually and cream well. Add eggs and mix well. Add 1½ cups of the flour and baking soda. Mix well. Stir in milk. Add remaining 1½ cups flour and nuts. Mix well. Drop by teaspoonfuls onto prepared sheets. Bake 8 to 10 minutes.

God of My Praise, I have insufficient words to describe all your goodness. Amen.

~~~

Neither by force of arms nor by brute strength, but by my spirit! Says the Lord of Hosts.
<div style="text-align: right;">Zechariah 4:6b NEB</div>

Sugar-Free Oatmeal Cookies
1 c. whole wheat flour
1 c. rolled oats, quick-cooking or regular
1 tsp. ground cinnamon
1 tsp. baking powder
½ tsp. baking soda
¼ tsp. ground nutmeg
¼ tsp. ground allspice
¼ tsp. ground cloves
½ c. raisins
1 c. unsweetened applesauce
¼ c. water
⅓ c. vegetable oil
2 eggs
1 tsp. vanilla
¼ c. finely chopped nuts

Preheat oven to 375 degrees. Lightly coat cookie sheets. In large mixer bowl beat all ingredients until well blended. Drop by tablespoonfuls onto prepared sheets. Bake 10 to 15 minutes or until lightly browned.

We err with our guns and missiles, bombs and swords, God of Peace. Amen.

Rejoice, rejoice, daughter of Zion,
shout aloud, daughter of Jerusalem;
for see, your king is coming to you,
his cause won, his victory gained,
humble and mounted on an ass,
on a foal, the young of a she-ass.

Zechariah 9:9 NEB

Texas-Size Almond Church Cookies

1 c. granulated sugar
1 c. powdered sugar
1 c. margarine or butter
1 c. oil
1 tsp. almond extract
2 eggs
3½ c. all-purpose flour
1 c. whole wheat flour
1 tsp. baking soda
1 tsp. cream of tartar
1 tsp. salt
6 oz. almond brickle baking chips
2 c. coarsely chopped almonds
Sugar

Preheat oven to 350 degrees. In large bowl combine sugars, margarine and oil. Mix well. Add almond extract and eggs and mix well. In another large bowl combine all-purpose flour, whole wheat flour, baking soda, cream of tartar and salt. Mix well. Add flour mixture to sugar mixture and mix well at low speed. Stir in almond brickle chips and almonds. Shape heaping tablespoonfuls of dough into balls. Roll in sugar. Place 5 inches apart on ungreased cookie sheets. With fork dipped in sugar flatten each cookie in crisscross pattern. Bake 12 to 18 minutes or until light brown around edges. Cool 1 minute. Remove from cookie sheets.

Living God, your royalty is unmatched in all the universe. Amen.

He shall speak peaceably to every nation,
and his rule shall extend from sea to sea,
from the River to the ends of the earth.

Zechariah 9:10b NEB

Thick and Chewy Chocolate Chip Cookies
2 c. plus 2 T. unbleached flour
½ tsp. baking soda
½ tsp. salt
12 T. unsalted butter, melted and cooled until wam
1 c. firmly packed brown sugar
½ c. granulated sugar
1 large egg
1 egg yolk
2 tsp. vanilla
1½ c. semisweet chocolate chips

Preheat oven to 325 degrees. Line baking sheets with parchment paper or coat lightly with cooking spray. In large bowl whisk flour, baking soda and salt. In large mixer bowl beat butter, brown sugar and granulated sugar until well blended. Beat in egg, egg yolk and vanilla. Add flour mixture and beat on low speed until combined. Stir in chocolate chips. Roll dough by scant ¼ cupfuls into balls. Place 2½ inches apart on prepared sheets. Bake 15 to 18 minutes or until outer edges start to harden but centers remain soft and puffy. Cool on baking sheets.

Really, Sun of Righteousness? Do you mean that you reign everywhere we look? Amen.

EGGS AND QUICHES

The Lord shall appear above them,
and his arrow shall flash like lightning;
the Lord God shall blow a blast on the horn
and march with the storm-winds of the south.
          Zechariah 9:14 NEB

Arlington Brunch
12 slices bread, crust removed
1 lb. shaved or chipped ham
½ lb. sharp cheddar cheese, grated
3 c. milk
5 eggs
½ tsp. salt
½ tsp. dry mustard
½ tsp. salt-based seasoning
½ tsp. Worcestershire sauce
½ tsp. ground nutmeg
½ c. butter
½ c. corn flake crumbs

Grease 9 by 12-inch baking pan. Line prepared pan with 6 slices of the bread. Sprinkle ham over bread. Sprinkle cheese over ham. Add remaining 6 slices of bread. In bowl mix milk and eggs. Add salt, dry mustard, salt-based seasoning, Worcestershire sauce and nutmeg. Pour milk-egg mixture over bread. Dot top with butter and corn flake crumbs. Refrigerate 8 hours. Bake 1 hour or more at 325 degrees.

I heed your warning, Lord Who Is Present, and turn from my sins. Amen.

But as he was thinking this over, behold, an angel of the Lord appeared to him in a dream, saying, Joseph, descendant of David, do not be afraid to take Mary as your wife, for that which is conceived in her is of the Holy Spirit.

Matthew 1:20 ANT

Bacon and Egg Pizza
1 (8 oz.) can refrigerated biscuits or 1 recipe
    homemade biscuit dough
3 eggs, beaten
1 T. milk
Dash salt
5 slices crisp bacon, crumbled
1 tsp. chopped chives or onion
1 c. shredded cheddar cheese

Preheat oven to 350 degrees. Flatten biscuit dough on pizza pan. In small bowl combine eggs, milk and salt. Pour into biscuit shell. Sprinkle with bacon, chives and cheese. Bake 20 minutes. Top with more bacon crumbles if desired.

Thank you, Elohim, for talking us out of our bad ideas. Amen.

~~~

She will bear a Son, and you shall call His name Jesus [in Hebrew means Savior], for He will save His people from their sins . . . .

Matthew 1:21 ANT

Breadless Egg Casserole
8 eggs
1 c. milk
1 tsp. salt
¼ tsp. garlic salt
¼ tsp. dry mustard
Dash paprika
Dash onion powder
Dash pepper

3 T. chopped onion
3 oz. shaved ham
1 c. shredded mozzarella cheese

Preheat oven to 325 degrees. Grease 9-inch square baking dish. In large bowl beat eggs and milk. Add salt, garlic salt, dry mustard, paprika, onion powder and pepper. Beat well. Stir in onion, ham and cheese. Pour into prepared dish. Bake, uncovered, 45 minutes.

It isn't that you hide your work, God the Comforter; it's that I don't pay attention. Amen.

~~~

When they had listened to the king they went their way, and lo, the star which had been seen in the East in its rising went before them, until it came and stood over the place where the young Child was.   Matthew 2:9 ANT

Breakfast Casserole
6 eggs, lightly beaten
6 slices bread, cubed
1 c. shredded cheddar cheese
1 tsp. salt
1 tsp. dry mustard
12 oz. cooked sausage, drained
2 c. milk

In large bowl mix all ingredients. Place in a 1½-quart casserole dish. Cover. Refrigerate overnight or at least 4 hours. Cover and bake 1 hour at 350 degrees.

You send us signs every day, O Lord Our Banner. Amen.

When they saw the star, they were thrilled with ecstatic joy.
Matthew 2:10 ANT

Breakfast Pizza
1 lb. sausage
1 onion, diced
1 tube refrigerated crescent rolls
1 c. frozen hash brown potatoes
1 c. shredded cheese
5 eggs, beaten
¼ c. milk
¼ tsp. pepper
2 T. Parmesan cheese

Preheat oven to 375 degrees. Saute sausage and onion in large skillet. Drain fat. Press crescent rolls out to sides of 9-inch square pan. Spoon sausage mixture over dough. Sprinkle potatoes on sausage. Spread cheese on potatoes. In small bowl stir eggs, milk and pepper. Pour over pizza. Sprinkle with Parmesan cheese. Bake 25 to 30 minutes.

You haven't asked us to do more than look up, Lord of the Heavens. Amen.

~~~

I baptize you with water to show that you have repented; but the one who will come after me will baptize you with the Holy Spirit and fire.
<div align="right">Matthew 3:11a TEV</div>

Creamed Eggs
6 eggs, hard boiled
2 T. butter
2 T. flour
1 tsp. salt
Dash pepper
2 c. milk
6 to 8 slices toast

Peel and chop eggs. Melt butter in medium saucepan over low heat. Add flour, salt and pepper. Blend well. Add milk, stirring constantly. Cook until smooth. Add eggs to hot mixture. Serve on toast.

I accept the baptisms of water, Spirit and fire, Everlasting Father, to receive forgiveness, power and purity of purpose. Amen.

~~~

Jesus said to them, "Come with me and I will teach you to catch men." Matthew 4:19 TEV

Egg and Cheese Bake
1 c. baking mix
1½ c. cottage cheese
8 oz. grated cheddar cheese
1 tsp. dried onion or 2 tsp. fresh chopped onion
1 tsp. dried parsley flakes or 1 T. fresh minced parsley
¼ tsp. salt
6 eggs, lightly beaten
1 c. milk
¾ c. butter

Preheat oven to 350 degrees. In large bowl mix all ingredients except butter in order given. Melt butter in 9 by 13-inch baking pan. Pour mixture into pan, spreading evenly. Bake 40 minutes or until tester inserted in center comes out clean.

I want to be teachable all my days, Bright Morning Star. Amen.

Jesus went all over Galilee, teaching in the synagogues, preaching the Good News of the Kingdom, and healing people from every kind of disease and sickness.

Matthew 4:24 TEV

Frittata with Veggies

3 T. olive oil, divided
1 onion, diced
1 red bell pepper, diced
1 zucchini, thinly sliced
2 c. sliced mushrooms
¼ c. water or broth
Salt and pepper
12 large eggs
1 c. part-skim ricotta cheese
8 oz. mozzarella cheese, sliced
¼ c. grated Parmesan cheese

Preheat oven to 400 degrees. Grease 9 by 13-inch baking pan with 1 tablespoon of the olive oil. In large skillet heat remaining 2 tablespoons olive oil over medium heat. Add onion and red pepper and cook 5 minutes until onion is soft and lightly browned. Add zucchini, mushrooms and water and saute until zucchini is soft. Add salt and pepper. In large bowl whisk eggs and ricotta cheese until smooth. Stir in vegetable mixture. Pour into prepared pan. Top with mozzarella cheese slices and sprinkle with Parmesan cheese. Bake 20 minutes or until set.

Christ, Son of the Living God, when you walked on earth you used your time to teach, encourage and heal. You call us to do the same. Amen.

"Happy are those who mourn: God will comfort them."
Matthew 5:4 TEV

Eggs Creole with Sausage

½ lb. sausage links, cut in ½-inch pieces
16 oz. canned tomato sauce
½ c. minced green pepper
2 T. instant minced onion
8 eggs
⅓ c. milk
½ tsp. salt
Dash pepper
1 T. butter
4 to 6 slices buttered toast
½ c. sour cream

Brown sausage in skillet. Drain. Add tomato sauce, green pepper and onion. Simmer 5 minutes. In medium bowl beat eggs, milk, salt and pepper. Melt butter in another skillet. Add egg mixture and scramble. Place buttered toast on serving platter or individual plates. Spoon egg mixture onto toast. Spoon sausage-tomato mixture on top. Top with dollops of sour cream.

It is a blessing to know that one day my tears will be dried, Light of the World. Amen.

"Happy are those whose greatest desire is to do what God requires: God will satisfy them fully!"
Matthew 5:6 TEV

Egg Souffle
8 slices bread, broken into pieces
6 eggs
2 c. milk
1 lb. sausage
2 c. cheddar cheese, shredded
1 can condensed cream of mushroom soup
½ c. milk

Butter 8-inch baking dish. Place bread in dish. Brown sausage in skillet, drain and sprinkle over bread. In medium bowl beat eggs and 2 cups milk. Pour over bread and sausage. Sprinkle cheese on top. Refrigerate 8 hours or overnight. Just before baking, in small bowl mix mushroom soup and ½ cup milk. Pour on top of casserole. Bake 50 minutes at 350 degrees.

God Almighty, I want you in my beginning, my middle and my end. Amen.

~~~

"Happy are those who show mercy to others: God will show mercy to them!"
<div align="right">Matthew 5:7 TEV</div>

Holiday Breakfast Casserole
10 eggs, lightly beaten
3 c. milk
2 tsp. dry mustard
1 tsp. salt
6 c. cubed bread, divided
8 oz. shredded sharp cheddar cheese, about 2 c.
1 lb. pork sausage, cooked, drained, crumbled
½ c. sliced mushrooms
1 medium tomato, chopped
½ c. sliced green onions
½ tsp. pepper

Preheat oven to 325 degrees. Butter 9 by 13-inch baking pan. In large bowl combine eggs, milk, dry mustard and salt. Spread half the bread in prepared pan. Sprinkle with half each of cheese, sausage, mushrooms, tomato, green onions and pepper. Repeat layers, starting with bread. Pour egg mixture evenly on top. Bake 55 to 60 minutes or until eggs are set. Tent with foil if top browns too quickly. May be refrigerated overnight before baking.

May I return your mercy a hundred times, My Shepherd. Amen.

~~~

"Happy are the pure in heart: They will see God!"
Matthew 5:8 TEV

Make Ahead Breakfast Casserole

2½ c. seasoned croutons
1 lb. pork sausage
4 eggs or equivalent substitute
2¼ c. milk
1 can condensed cream of mushroom soup
10 oz. frozen chopped spinach, thawed, squeezed dry
1 can mushrooms, drained, chopped, about 4 oz.
1 c. shredded cheddar cheese
1 c. shredded Monterey Jack cheese
¼ tsp. dry mustard

Grease 9 by 13-inch pan. Spread croutons in pan. Crumble sausage into medium skillet and cook over medium heat, stirring occasionally. Drain. Spread over croutons. In large bowl whisk eggs and milk. Stir in soup, spinach, mushrooms, cheddar cheese, Monterey Jack cheese and dry mustard. Pour over sausage and croutons. Cover and refrigerate overnight. Bake at 325 degrees 50 to 55 minutes or until set and lightly browned.

I want to see you, Lord of Glory! Amen.

"Happy are those who work for peace among men: God will call them his sons!"
Matthew 5:9 TEV

Mediterranean Frittata
2 T. vegetable oil or olive oil, divided
3 green onions or ½ zucchini, chopped
1 medium tomato, chopped
¼ c. chopped fresh basil or 1 tsp. dried basil
1 medium potato, sliced
8 oz. egg substitute
1 T. grated Parmesan cheese

Heat 1 tablespoon of the oil in 9-inch nonstick skillet over medium heat. Cook onions, tomato and basil 2 minutes. Transfer to plate. In remaining 1 tablespoon oil, cook potato slices and spread evenly in skillet. In small bowl mix egg substitute and Parmesan cheese. Pour over potatoes. Sprinkle onion-tomato mixture on top. Cook over medium heat 3 to 4 minutes or until eggs are thickened but still moist.

What a gracious inheritance you have provided, True Light. Amen.

~~~

Happy are those who suffer persecution because they do what God requires: the Kingdom of heaven belongs to them!"
Matthew 5:10 TEV

Omelet Sandwiches
16 slices bread, buttered
8 slices cheese
1 lb. shaved ham
6 eggs
3 c. milk
½ tsp. dry mustard
½ tsp. salt
1 c. crushed corn flakes
½ c. margarine, melted

Grease large baking pan. Make 8 sandwiches with the bread, cheese and ham. Place in prepared pan. In medium bowl mix eggs, milk, dry mustard and salt. Pour over sandwiches. Refrigerate overnight. In small bowl blend corn flakes and margarine. Sprinkle on sandwiches. Bake 1 hour at 350 degrees.

I lost my health, Son of God, but I did not lose you. Amen.

~~~

"You are like light for the whole world."
<div style="text-align: right;">Matthew 5:14a TEV</div>

Poached Eggs
Water
Salt
Eggs

Fill frying pan two-thirds full of water. Add ½ teaspoon salt for each quart of water. Bring to boil. Break eggs and drop carefully onto saucer. Transfer to water without breaking yolk. Do not let water boil after eggs are in it. Cook until white is firm and film forms over yolk. Drain before serving.

Nothing is worth seeing, and nothing can be truly seen, without your Light. Amen.

"You have heard that it was said, 'Love your friends, hate your enemies.' But now I tell you: love your enemies, and pray for those who mistreat you, so that you will become the sons of your Father in heaven."

Matthew 5:43-45a TEV

Potato Egg Casserole
4 c. cooked, diced potatoes
4 strips bacon, fried crisp and crumbled
3 eggs, hard boiled and chopped
1 can condensed cream of chicken soup
1 c. milk
½ c. minced onion
Salt and pepper
½ c. shredded cheese

Preheat oven to 350 degrees. Layer potatoes, bacon and eggs in casserole dish. In small bowl blend soup, milk, onion, salt and pepper. Pour over potatoes, bacon and eggs. Sprinkle cheese on top. Bake 30 minutes.

I have failed to pray for my enemies, and I repent, Rose of Sharon. Amen.

~~~

"You cannot serve both God and money."

<div align="right">Matthew 6:24b TEV</div>

Potato Omelet
2 T. margarine
1½ c. diced potatoes
½ c. chopped green pepper
⅓ c. chopped onion
1 tsp. salt, divided
8 eggs
Dash pepper
6 to 8 slices Swiss or other cheese

Preheat oven to 350 degrees. Coat 6 by 10-inch baking pan. Melt margarine in skillet. Add potatoes, green pepper, onion and ½ teaspoon of the salt. Cover and cook 10 minutes or until tender. Spoon into prepared pan. In medium bowl beat eggs with pepper and remaining ½ teaspoon salt. Pour over vegetable mixture. Bake 20 to 25 minutes. Top with cheese and continue baking until cheese melts.

Mighty One, the money belongs to you. Amen.

~~~

"God will judge you in the same way you judge others . . . ."
Matthew 7:2a TEV

Potluck Casserole
3 c. frozen shredded potatoes
3 T. vegetable oil
1 c. diced ham or ground sausage
1 c. grated cheddar cheese
4 eggs
½ c. skim evaporated milk
¼ c. chopped onion
½ tsp. salt
⅛ tsp. pepper
1 T. chopped parsley

Preheat oven to 425 degrees. In large bowl combine potatoes and oil. Press like crust into 9-inch pie pan. Bake 15 minutes or until lightly browned. Layer ham, then cheese on crust. In medium bowl blend eggs, milk, onion, salt and pepper. Pour over ham and cheese. Sprinkle with parsley. Bake 25 to 30 minutes. Cool 5 to 10 minutes before cutting into squares.

None but you, Lord Jesus Christ, can judge our hearts. Amen.

"Ask, and you will receive; seek, and you will find; knock, and the door will be opened to you."
Matthew 7:7 TEV

Quiche Lorraine
12 slices crisp bacon, drained
Pastry for one-crust 9-inch pie
4 eggs
1 T. butter, melted
1 c. grated Swiss cheese
Dash ground nutmeg
¼ tsp. sugar
¾ tsp. salt
⅛ tsp. pepper
2 c. light half-and-half

Preheat oven to 425 degrees. Crumble bacon and spread on unbaked pie shell. In medium bowl blend eggs, butter, cheese, nutmeg, sugar, salt, pepper and half-and-half. Pour evenly over bacon. Bake 15 minutes or until knife inserted in center comes out clean. Allow to set 10 minutes before serving.

Other doors are closed and locked, but not yours, Chiefest Among Ten Thousand. Amen.

"Watch out for false prophets; they come to you looking like sheep on the outside, but they are really like wild wolves on the inside." Matthew 7:15 TEV

Sausage and Sun-Dried Tomato Strata

½ c. sun-dried tomatoes (not oil packed)
3½ c. milk
5 large eggs
2 tsp. minced fresh thyme or ¾ tsp. dried thyme
1½ tsp. salt
¼ tsp. pepper
12 oz. sausage, cooked, drained, crumbled
1 lb. or 11 slices bread, cut in 1-inch pieces
½ c. chopped onion
½ c. grated Parmesan cheese
1 c. grated mozzarella cheese
Chopped fresh parsley

Coat 9 by 13-inch baking pan. Place tomatoes in medium bowl. Cover with boiling water. Let stand until softened, about 15 minutes. Drain and chop. In large bowl whisk milk, eggs, thyme, salt and pepper. Add tomatoes, sausage, bread, onion, Parmesan cheese and stir. Transfer to prepared pan. Cover and refrigerate at least 4 hours. Preheat oven to 375 degrees. Bake uncovered until puffed and golden brown, about 45 minutes. Sprinkle with mozzarella cheese and bake until cheese melts. Cool 5 to 10 minutes. Sprinkle with parsley.

So many people pretend to be your prophet, Arm of the Lord, that sometimes I want to close my eyes and ears. Help me to listen when I should. Amen.

"Even the winds and the waves obey him!"
Matthew 8:27b TEV

Skinny Spinach Cheddar Squares

1½ c. egg substitute
¾ c. skim milk
1 T. dried onion flakes
1 T. grated Parmesan cheese
¼ tsp. garlic powder
⅛ tsp. pepper
¼ c. dry bread crumbs
¾ c. shredded fat-free cheddar cheese, divided
10 oz. frozen chopped spinach, thawed and drained
¼ c. diced pimientos (optional)

Preheat oven to 350 degrees. Lightly coat 8-inch square baking pan. In medium bowl combine egg substitute, milk, onion flakes, Parmesan cheese, garlic powder and pepper. Set aside. Sprinkle bread crumbs evenly on bottom of prepared pan. Top with ½ cup of the cheddar cheese and spinach. Pour egg mixture evenly over spinach. Top with remaining ¼ cup cheddar cheese and pimientos. Bake 35 to 40 minutes or until set. Let stand 10 minutes. Cut into 2-inch squares. About 40 calories per square.

Nothing can deny your power, Author and Finisher of Faith. Amen.

"Nor does anyone pour new wine into used wineskins."
> Matthew 9:17a TEV

Sour Cream Quiche
1 pie shell, unbaked
2 T. butter
⅓ c. finely chopped onion
3 T. diced green bell pepper
½ c. diced mushrooms
3 large eggs, beaten
16 oz. sour cream, divided
5 slices bacon, cooked and crumbled
1½ c. Swiss cheese, grated
1 c. mild cheddar cheese, grated
Dash salt
Dash pepper
Sour cream for topping

Line pie shell with foil and bake 8 minutes at 450 degrees. Remove foil and bake 5 minutes or until crust is set and dry. Remove shell from oven and reduce temperature to 350 degrees. Heat butter in small skillet. Add onion, green pepper and mushrooms and saute until softened. In large bowl blend onion mixture, eggs, 8 ounces of the sour cream, bacon, Swiss cheese, cheddar cheese, salt and pepper. Pour mixture into crust. Bake 40 minutes or until center is set. Let stand 10 minutes before cutting. Top each piece with spoonful of sour cream.

How refreshed I feel, Friend of Sinners, because you've made me new all over. Amen.

Jesus called his twelve disciples together and gave them authority to drive out the evil spirits and to heal every disease and every sickness. Matthew 10:1 TEV

Springtime Egg Skillet
1 T. oil
2 c. frozen shredded hash brown potatoes
6 eggs, beaten
5 slices bacon, cut in ½-inch pieces, cooked crisp
½ c. sliced green onions, divided
Salt and pepper
⅓ c. shredded cheddar cheese
Chopped tomatoes (optional)

Heat oil in medium nonstick skillet over medium-high heat. Add potatoes. Cook 8 to 10 minutes or until potatoes are brown, stirring occasionally. Spread potatoes evenly in skillet. In small bowl mix eggs, bacon, ¼ cup of the green onions, salt and pepper. Pour evenly over potatoes in skillet. Reduce heat to medium low. Cover skillet. Cook 10 minutes or until eggs are set. Remove from heat. Sprinkle with cheese. Garnish with tomatoes and remaining ¼ cup green onions. Cut into wedges.

How awesome it is to be your emissary, Faithful and True. Amen.

~~~

"Whoever declares publicly that he belongs to me, I will do the same for him before my Father in heaven."
 Matthew 10:32 TEV

Super Easy Quiche
8 eggs
2 cans condensed cheddar cheese soup
1 c. half-and-half
2 (9-inch) pie crusts, unbaked
2 c. shredded cheddar cheese
1 c. cooked ham, chopped
1 c. broccoli, cooked, drained, chopped

Preheat oven to 350 degrees. In large bowl beat eggs until foamy. Gradually add soup and half-and-half, mixing well. Press pie crusts onto bottom of 9 by 13-inch baking pan. Sprinkle cheese, ham and broccoli evenly over crust. Pour egg mixture over all. Bake 50 minutes or until center is set. Let stand 10 minutes before serving.

What joy I feel when I meet another Christian, O Consolation of Israel. Amen.

~~~

"Whoever welcomes you, welcomes me . . . ."
<div style="text-align: right">Matthew 10:40a TEV</div>

Tomato Egg Scramble
4 T. butter, divided
1 small onion, chopped
1 T. flour
1 c. chopped tomatoes
1 tsp. Worcestershire sauce
½ tsp. salt
Dash pepper
6 eggs
½ c. milk

Heat 2 tablespoons of the butter in skillet. Add onion and cook until browned. Blend in flour. Stir in tomatoes, Worcestershire sauce, salt and pepper. Simmer until thick, 5 to 10 minutes. In small bowl beat eggs and milk. Heat remaining 2 tablespoons butter in separate skillet. Add egg mixture and cook over low heat, stirring frequently, until firm. Fold in tomato mixture. Pour into serving dish.

The honor of walking with you, Foundation of Life, is this life's greatest. Amen.

FISH AND SEAFOOD

He did not perform many miracles there because they did not have faith. Matthew 13:58 TEV

Baked Fish
1 medium onion, sliced thin
¼ lb. mushrooms, sliced thin
1½ lb. perch, whiting or other fish filets
1 c. soft whole-wheat bread crumbs
1 T. chopped parsley
¼ c. chicken broth

Preheat oven to 350 degrees. Cover bottom of baking dish with onion slices. Spread mushrooms evenly over onions. Top with fish filets. Cover with bread crumbs. Sprinkle parsley on top. Pour broth over all. Bake 15 to 20 minutes or just until fish flakes with fork.

I believe in you, God Who Knows All, with all my heart. Amen.

Everyone ate and had enough. Then the disciples took up twelve baskets full of what was left over.

                                          Matthew 14:20 TEV

Baked Tuna and Cheese Swirls
3 T. butter
3 T. finely chopped onion
⅓ c. finely chopped green pepper
1 tsp. salt
6 T. flour
1 can condensed cream of chicken soup
1½ c. milk
1 can tuna, about 7 oz.
1 T. lemon juice
1 can refrigerated biscuit dough or 1 recipe
      homemade biscuit dough
½ c. grated American cheese

Preheat oven to 450 degrees. Coat casserole dish. Heat butter in medium saucepan. Add onion and green pepper and saute until soft. Blend in salt and flour. Add soup and milk. Mix well. Cook, stirring constantly, until thick. Add tuna and lemon juice. Stir gently. Pour into prepared dish. On floured surface, roll dough into rectangle. Sprinkle cheese on top. Roll up, jellyroll style, starting with shorter end. Slice ¾ inch thick with knife dipped in flour. Place pinwheels on top of tuna mixture. Bake 15 minutes at 450 degrees, then 15 minutes at 425 degrees.

You, Faithful and True Witness, always provide enough. Amen.

The disciples in the boat worshiped Jesus. "Truly you are the Son of God!" they exclaimed.

Matthew 14:33 TEV

Broiled Lake Trout

1 fresh trout
2 T. salt or more
1 c. water or more
1 T. olive oil
¼ c. olive oil
¼ tsp. pepper
1 T. butter

Preheat broiler and broiler pan at least 10 minutes. Split trout into two filets, removing backbone. Wash thoroughly, removing all traces of blood and membrane. Soak filets 10 minutes in solution made in proportion of 2 tablespoons salt to 1 cup water. Brush or spread 1 tablespoon olive oil on heated broiler pan. Brush filets with mixture of ¼ cup olive oil and pepper. Place seasoned filets on heated broiler pan, skin side up, about 2 inches from heat. After skin turns brown, about 5 minutes, baste with oil mixture. Continue broiling until skin is well browned. Turn filets flesh side up and baste with oil mixture again. Broil until flesh side is also well browned. Transfer to hot platter. Butter tops of filets. May be garnished with crisp lettuce leaves, lemon slices or parsley.

It's wondrous to know that you are Christ, Son of the Blessed. Amen.

> As they looked on, a change came over him; his face became as bright as the sun, and his clothes as white as light.
>
> Matthew 17:2 TEV

Chinese Egg Lobster

4 T. vegetable oil
1 c. fresh or canned bean sprouts
½ c. fresh or canned bamboo shoots, sliced thin
½ c. canned water chestnuts, sliced thin
2 cups boiled lobster
6 eggs
1 tsp. salt

Heat oil in skillet. Add bean sprouts, bamboo shoots, water chestnuts and lobster. Cook 3 minutes. Remove from pan and drain water off top of oil. Reheat oil in pan. Break eggs and drop whole into skillet. Immediately spread lobster mixture over eggs. Stir constantly but gently until eggs are cooked.

I cannot comprehend your power to make new, Banner Over the Church. Amen.

~~~

> "If you have faith as big as a mustard seed, you can say to this hill, 'Go from here to there!' and it will go. You could do anything."
>
> Matthew 17:20b TEV

Cod Sandwiches

12 oz. codfish, cooked and drained
¼ c. celery, finely chopped
¼ c. zesty creamy salad dressing
2 T. onion, minced
1 T. horseradish mustard (optional)
1 T. lemon juice
¼ tsp. black pepper
Dash red pepper (optional)
Buns
Lettuce for garnish
Tomatoes for garnish

Flake fish in large bowl. Add celery, salad dressing, onion, horseradish mustard, lemon juice, black pepper and red pepper. Mix well. Cover and chill 1 hour. Serve on toasted buns with lettuce and tomato slices.

A mustard seed is small, Lord of Righteousness, but you are big. Amen.

~~~

"The Son of Man is about to be handed over to men who will kill him; but on the third day he will be raised to life."
<div style="text-align: right;">Matthew 17:22b-23a TEV</div>

Fish and Chips
Vegetable oil for frying
5 potatoes, cut in ½-inch strips
1 lb. fish filets
⅔ c. flour
½ tsp. salt
½ tsp. baking soda
1 T. cider vinegar
⅔ c. water
Vinegar and salt (optional)

Cook potatoes in skillet or deep fryer 5 to 7 minutes. Place on cookie sheet in single layer and keep warm in oven. Reserve oil. Pat fish dry. In medium bowl blend flour and salt. In small bowl combine baking soda and vinegar. Add water and mix. Add vinegar mixture to flour mixture. Beat until smooth. Dip fish in batter and fry in reserved oil until brown, turning once after about 3 minutes. Broil potatoes 6 inches from heat until crisp, 2 to 3 minutes. Sprinkle with vinegar and salt.

You were handed over to unspeakable cruelty because of me, Jesus. Amen.

"Let the little children come to me, and do not stop them, because the Kingdom of heaven belongs to such as these."
Matthew 19:14 TEV

Fish Batter for Frying
1 c. flour
½ tsp. baking soda
2 heaping T. baking powder
½ tsp salt
½ tsp. pepper
1 T. vinegar
1 c. water

In medium bowl combine flour, baking soda, baking powder, salt and pepper. In small bowl mix vinegar and water. Add vinegar mixture to flour mixture and mix well. Mixture will foam. Thicken with flour or thin with water if needed. Batter coats 1½ to 2 pounds fish or chicken. Very crunchy.

Pat food dry on paper towels. For deep frying, heat oil in fryer, dip food in batter, let stand 1 minute, and place filets in hot oil for several minutes until golden brown. For pan frying, heat 1 to 1½ inches of canola oil in skillet. Dip food in batter and drop into hot oil. Turn after several minutes and cook until golden brown on both sides.

How precious is our faith that you open it to people of all ages, Lord Our Maker. Amen.

A great crowd of people spread their cloaks on the road, while others cut branches from the trees and spread them on the road. The crowds walking in front of Jesus and the crowds walking behind began to shout, "Praise to David's Son! God bless him who comes in the name of the Lord! Praise be to God!" Matthew 21:8, 9 TEV

Fish with Butter Sauce
3 lbs. haddock or white fish filets
Boiling salt water to cover
2 T. butter

Butter sauce:
⅓ c. butter
3 T. flour
½ tsp. salt
1½ c. hot water
1 tsp. lemon juice

Cut fish into serving pieces. In skillet combine boiling water and 2 tablespoons butter. Poach fish in water 10 minutes or until fish flakes easily. To make sauce, melt ⅓ cup butter in small saucepan. Add flour and salt. Blend well. Add water gradually, stirring constantly. Bring to boil and boil about 2 minutes. Stir in lemon juice. Serve with fish.

We see that you have come to us in humility and gone ahead of us in love, Christ the Lord. Amen.

"You must love the Lord your God with all your heart, and with all your soul, and with all your mind. This is the greatest and most important commandment."
                                        Matthew 22:37, 38 TEV

Hearty Nicoise Salad
5 potatoes (about 3 c.), cooked and diced
½ lb. green beans, cut up and cooked
3 tomatoes, cut in eighths
⅔ c. canola oil
½ c. cider vinegar
3 cloves garlic, crushed
2 tsp. dry mustard
1 T. chopped parsley
1 tsp. minced onion
⅛ tsp. pepper
Leaves of 1 medium head lettuce
1 cucumber, sliced thin
1 red onion, sliced thin
1 egg, hard cooked and sliced
2 cans chunk or solid tuna, drained, about 6 oz. each
12 pitted black olives, sliced

In large bowl combine potatoes, green beans and tomatoes. In small bowl mix oil, vinegar, garlic, dry mustard, parsley, onion and pepper. Pour ½ cup of the oil mixture over potato mixture. Let stand 1 hour. Layer lettuce over potato mixture. Layer cucumber, red onion and egg on lettuce. Arrange tuna chunks on top. Garnish with olives. Pour remaining oil mixture over salad. Toss and serve.

God Who Leads with Love, help me when I struggle to love you best, for I am weak. Amen.

"When the Son of Man comes as King, and all the angels with him, he will sit on the royal throne, and all the earth's people will be gathered before him. Then he will divide them into two groups, just as a shepherd separates the sheep from the goats: he will put the sheep at his right and the goats at his left."

Matthew 25:31-33 TEV

Hot Tuna Sandwiches

1 can tuna, drained, about 6 oz.
2 hard-boiled eggs
½ c. mayonnaise
¼ lb. cheese slices or chunks
2 T. minced green pepper
2 T. minced onion
2 T. minced sweet pickle
2 T. minced olives
8 hamburger buns

Preheat oven to 250 degrees. Mix all ingredients except buns in medium bowl. Spread mixture on buns and wrap in aluminum foil. Bake 30 minutes.

Great Shepherd, we are foolish to think that we can escape your judgment. Amen.

And so John came, baptizing in the desert region and preaching a baptism of repentance for the forgiveness of sins.

Mark 1:4 NIV

Poached Italian Cod
1 lb. cod filets
½ c. water, divided
2 tsp. cornstarch
2 T. vegetable oil
2 cloves garlic, minced
2 large tomatoes, chopped
1 onion, cut into wedges
1 green pepper, sliced thin
1 tsp. fresh basil, chopped
¼ tsp. salt
¼ tsp. pepper
¼ c. ripe olives, sliced
2 c. hot cooked pasta
Grated Parmesan cheese (optional)

Cut cod into 1-inch pieces. In small bowl stir ¼ cup of the water and cornstarch. Set aside. In large skillet heat oil and saute garlic 15 seconds. Add tomatoes, onion, green pepper, remaining ¼ cup water, basil, salt and pepper. Cook and stir until onion and green pepper are tender. Add fish. Bring to boil. Reduce heat. Cover and simmer until fish flakes with fork, 8 to 12 minutes. Add cornstarch mixture. Cook and stir until thick and bubbly. Cook and stir 2 minutes. Stir in olives and serve immediately over hot pasta. Top with Parmesan cheese.

Everything happens according to your plan, Holy One of Israel. Amen.

And a voice came from heaven: "You are my Son, whom I love; with you I am well pleased." Mark 1:11 NIV

Salmon Baked in Potato Shells
1 lb. canned salmon
8 medium potatoes, baked and cooled
½ c. milk
1 onion, chopped
Salt and pepper
1 c. bread crumbs
2 T. butter or margarine

Preheat oven to 400 degrees. Flake salmon, removing skin and bones. Slice tops off potatoes and scoop out contents. Place potato pulp in large bowl and mash thoroughly. Stir in milk, onion, salt and pepper. Add salmon and mix lightly. Stuff mixture into potato shells. Cover with crumbs. Dot with butter. Bake 25 minutes.

The only approval that counts is yours, Jesus Who Will Judge. Amen.

At once the Spirit sent him out into the desert, and he was in the desert forty days, being tempted by Satan.

Mark 1:12, 13a NIV

Salmon Cakes with Creamed Peas

Salmon cakes:
1 can salmon, about 16 oz.
1 c. dry mashed potato flakes
¼ c. finely chopped onion
2 T. lemon juice
¼ tsp. pepper
2 eggs, lightly beaten

Creamed peas:
2 T. butter or margarine
2 T. flour
½ tsp. dill weed
¼ tsp. salt
Dash pepper
¾ c. milk
1 can sweet peas, drained, about 17 oz.

To make salmon cakes, heat oven to 350 degrees. Coat 8 muffin cups. Drain, debone and deskin salmon, reserving ¼ cup liquid. In large bowl combine salmon, potato flakes, onion, lemon juice, pepper and eggs. Mix well. Press firmly into muffin cups. Bake 30 to 35 minutes.

To make creamed peas, melt margarine in medium saucepan. Stir in flour, dill weed, salt and pepper. Cook until smooth and bubbly. Gradually add milk and reserved salmon liquid. Cook until mixture boils and thickens, stirring constantly. Stir in peas and heat until hot. Serve over salmon cakes.

When you ask us to serve in your name, you get us ready first, Desire of All Nations. Amen.

After John was put in prison, Jesus went into Galilee, proclaiming the good news of God.

Mark 1:14 NIV

Salmon Croquettes
2 c. canned salmon
3 T. parsley, chopped
1 T. lemon juice
1 tsp. Worcestershire sauce
¼ tsp. salt
Few grains pepper
1 c. thick white sauce (see recipe below)
1 c. bread crumbs
1 egg, lightly beaten
1 T. water
Oil for frying

In medium bowl drain salmon. Flake salmon, removing skin and bones. Add parsley, lemon juice, Worcestershire sauce, salt, pepper and white sauce. Blend well. Chill. Shape into croquettes or patties and roll in bread crumbs. In small bowl combine egg and water. Roll patties in egg mixture. Roll again in crumbs. Fry in hot oil 3 to 5 minutes. Drain on absorbent paper.

White Sauce:
2 to 3 T. butter or other fat
3 T. flour
1 c. milk

Soften and melt butter at very low temperature in saucepan. Blend flour in thoroughly. Add milk and heat slowly, stirring constantly, until mixture thickens and flour is cooked.

Let me be sensitive to your time, Day Star. Amen.

"The Kingdom of God is near. Repent and believe the good news!" Mark 1:15a NIV

Salmon Loaf
2 c. salmon
2 eggs, beaten
2 T. melted butter
½ c. cornmeal
¼ c. bread crumbs or cracker crumbs
1 c. buttermilk
⅛ tsp. pepper
½ tsp. salt

Preheat oven to 425 degrees. Coat baking dish. Flake salmon, removing skin and bones. In large bowl combine salmon with eggs, butter, cornmeal and crumbs. Mix well. Add buttermilk, pepper and salt. Mix well. Pour into prepared dish. Bake 20 minutes.

Our kingdoms come and go, Lord God Almighty, but yours is forever. Amen.

~~~

The people were amazed at his teaching, because he taught them as one who had authority . . . . Mark 1:22a NIV

Salmon Easy Patties
1 lb. canned salmon
2 eggs, lightly beaten
¼ c. milk
½ tsp. salt
⅛ tsp. pepper
½ c. cracker crumbs
1 tsp. lemon juice
Oil for frying

Drain salmon. Remove any skin and bones. In bowl combine salmon and remaining ingredients. Shape into patties, using ⅓ cup mixture per patty. Saute in small amount of vegetable or olive oil.

Yes, King of Zion, you have empowered your people to speak your truth. Amen.

~~~

Very early in the morning, while it was still dark, Jesus got up, left the house and went off to a solitary place, where he prayed.
Mark 1:35 NIV

Shrimp and Rice
2 c. cooked shrimp
2 c. steamed rice
2 T. parsley, chopped
⅛ tsp. black pepper
Few grains cayenne pepper
2 c. medium white sauce (see recipe below)
½ c. dried bread crumbs

Preheat oven to 400 degrees. Coat baking dish. In large bowl mix shrimp, rice, parsley, black pepper, cayenne pepper and white sauce. Pour into prepared dish. Sprinkle crumbs on top. Bake 20 to 25 minutes or until crumbs are brown.

White Sauce:
2 T. butter or other fat
2 T. flour
1 c. milk

Soften and melt butter at very low temperature in saucepan. Blend flour in thoroughly. Add milk and heat slowly, stirring constantly until mixture thickens and flour is cooked.

Prayer soaks up my fears and fatigue, King of Kings. Amen.

So many gathered that there was no room left, not even outside the door, and he preached the word to them.

Mark 2:2 NIV

Shrimp Salad
1 c. cold cooked rice
1 c. cooked shrimp
¼ c. diced green pepper
¾ c. diced celery
1 T. chopped onion
1 T. chopped olives
½ tsp. salt
1 T. lemon juice
2 T. French dressing
⅓ c. mayonnaise

In large bowl mix rice, shrimp, green pepper, celery, onion and olives. In small bowl mix salt, lemon juice, French dressing and mayonnaise. Pour dressing mixture over shrimp mixture. Mix lightly. Chill at least 1 hour.

When the Gospel comes out, the people do, too, Jesus of Nazareth. Amen.

Jesus withdrew with his disciples to the lake, and a large crowd from Galilee followed.
Mark 2:7 NIV

Shrimp Scampi Four Ways

1½ to 2 lbs. shrimp
6 T. butter or margarine, melted
3 T. lemon juice
3 T. chicken broth
3 cloves garlic, minced or pressed
2 T. finely chopped fresh parsley
½ tsp. salt, or to taste
¼ tsp. pepper, or to taste

Method 1
Peel and devein shrimp. Place in single layer in heatproof pan. In small bowl combine butter, lemon juice, broth, garlic, parsley, salt and pepper. Drizzle over shrimp. Broil 5 to 7 minutes or until shrimp turn pink.

Method 2
Peel and devein shrimp. Place butter in large skillet. Add garlic and shrimp. Saute until shrimp turn pink. Add lemon juice, broth, parsley, salt and pepper. Cook until heated through.

Method 3
Preheat oven to 400 degrees. Peel and devein shrimp. Place all ingredients in baking dish and bake 8 to 10 minutes or until shrimp turn pink.

Method 4
Heat grill. Thread shrimp on skewers and place on hot grill. In small bowl combine remaining ingredients and brush on shrimp before and several times during grilling. Cook until shrimp turn pink.

You lead us to sweet places to hear your word, Light Everlasting. Amen.

He appointed twelve—designating them apostles—that they might be with him and that he might send them out to preach and to have authority to drive out demons.

Mark 3:14, 15 NIV

South Pacific Filets

1½ lbs. flounder, perch or halibut filets
1 can pineapple chunks packed in juice, about 20 oz.
3 carrots, sliced diagonally into ½-inch pieces
1 tsp. sugar
1 tsp. cider vinegar
2 tsp. cornstarch
½ tsp. soy sauce
1 small green pepper, cut into thin strips
½ onion, sliced into thin rings

Preheat oven to 425 degrees. Coat baking dish and place filets in dish. Bake 20 minutes. Drain pineapple juice into medium saucepan. Add carrots, cover and cook about 15 minutes until barely tender. In small bowl mix sugar, vinegar, cornstarch and soy sauce. When carrots are just tender, add pineapple, green pepper, onion rings and sugar/vinegar mixture. Cook about 5 minutes, stirring constantly. Spread mixture over cooked fish. May be served with rice and fresh strawberries and banana slices dipped in orange juice.

I am a descendant of the first twelve, and I follow your lead, Lord and Savior. Amen.

"Others, like seed sown on good soil, hear the word, accept it, and produce a crop—thirty, sixty or even a hundred times what was sown." Mark 4:20 NIV

Stuffed Filet of Sole

2 lbs. boiled or frozen spinach
1 tsp. salt
⅛ tsp. pepper
½ c. chicken broth, divided
¼ c. bread crumbs
2 lbs. filets of sole or flounder
½ c. onion, finely chopped
2 T. parsley, finely chopped
2 T. butter, cut into pieces
1 c. mushrooms, sliced
2 medium tomatoes, peeled and quartered
2 T. flour
¼ c. whipped cream
1 T. lemon juice

Oil baking pan thoroughly. Drain and chop spinach. Add salt, pepper, ¼ cup of the broth and bread crumbs. Place a mound of mixture on one end of each filet and fold other end over it. Place in prepared pan. Sprinkle top with onion and parsley and dot with butter. Drizzle with remaining ¼ cup broth. Arrange mushrooms and tomatoes on top. Cover with parchment paper and bake 15 minutes at 500 degrees. Remove filets to heatproof platter. Mix flour with a little cold water. Add mixture to juice in baking pan and simmer 2 or 3 minutes, stirring constantly. Remove from heat. Add whipped cream and lemon juice. Pour over filets. Brown in broiler.

It's hard for me to understand, Lord from Heaven, that the crop is yours. Amen.

He got up, rebuked the wind and said to the waves, "Quiet! Be still!" Then the wind died down and it was completely calm.
Mark 4:39 NIV

Sweet and Sour Shrimp
1 T. shortening
1 medium onion, chopped
1 medium green pepper, diced
1 c. ketchup
2 T. cider vinegar
2 T. soy sauce
⅓ c. sugar
1 can pineapple chunks, about 8 oz.
1½ T. cornstarch
2 c. cooked shrimp

In large skillet heat shortening and saute onion and green pepper until crisp-tender. Add ketchup, vinegar, soy sauce and sugar. Heat through. Drain pineapple chunks, reserving liquid. Add water to juice to make 1 cup. Mix 6 tablespoons of juice mixture with cornstarch to form thin paste. Add remaining pineapple juice to skillet with vegetable mixture. Add pineapple paste and cook about 3 minutes until liquid becomes clear and thick. Add pineapple chunks and shrimp. Heat through.

Why do I sometimes doubt the calming power of your will, Lamb of God? Amen.

~~~

They ran throughout that whole region and carried the sick on mats to wherever they heard he was.
<div align="right">Mark 6:55 NIV</div>

Tuna Burgers
6 eggs, hard boiled and chopped
1 can solid white tuna, drained and flaked, about 6 oz.
1 c. shredded sharp cheddar cheese
½ c. green pepper, chopped
½ c. onion, chopped

½ tsp. garlic salt
½ tsp. pepper
1 c. zesty creamy salad dressing or mayonnaise
8 Kaiser rolls, split

Preheat oven to 400 degrees. In medium bowl mix eggs and tuna. Add cheese, green pepper, onion, garlic salt and pepper. Mix well. Stir in salad dressing. Divide among rolls. Wrap each in heavy-duty foil. Bake 15 minutes or until heated through.

Cure us, Just One, of going anywhere but to you when we hurt. Amen.

~~~

"I tell you the truth, anyone who gives you a cup of water in my name because you belong to Christ will certainly not lose his reward." Mark 9:41 NIV

Tuna Noodle Casserole
8 oz. medium noodles
3 T. margarine or butter
1 medium onion
½ c. celery, minced
1 can condensed cream of celery or cream of mushroom soup
1 soup can of milk
1 can tuna, about 6 oz.
1 T. minced pimientos (optional)
½ c. shredded cheddar cheese

Cook noodles as directed on package and drain. Preheat oven to 350 degrees. Generously butter baking dish. Melt margarine in large saucepan. Add onion and celery. Simmer until tender. Stir in soup and milk. Add tuna and pimientos. Mix well. Add noodles and mix well. Place mixture in prepared baking dish. Bake 25 minutes. Remove from oven and sprinkle cheese on top. Bake 5 minutes.

I thought I was doing those things to please you, but doing them made only me happy, Lord of All. Amen.

"But many who are first will be last, and the last first."
Mark 10:31 NIV

Tuna-Potato Chip Casserole
1 large can tuna, about 10 oz.
3 oz. potato chips (about 60 chips)
1 can condensed cream of mushroom soup
⅔ soup can milk

Preheat oven to 325 degrees. Spray 1½-quart casserole dish. Drain tuna. Place tuna in small bowl and flake with fork. Set aside. Place potato chips in plastic bag and crush. In medium bowl combine soup and milk. Place one-third of potato chips in casserole dish, then one-half of tuna and one-half of soup mixture. Add another one-third of chips, followed by another one-half of tuna and one-half of soup mixture. Top with remaining one-third of chips. Bake 25 minutes.

All our competitions are useless, aren't they, Lord and Redeemer? Amen.

FROZEN TREATS AND TOPPINGS

"For even the Son of Man did not come to be served, but to serve, and to give his life as a ransom for many."
                                                              Mark 10:45 NIV

Blender Peach Sherbet
6 ripe peaches, peeled and pitted
½ c. sugar
Juice of 1 lemon
Pinch of salt
½ tsp. almond extract
1 pt. whipping cream

Place peaches, sugar, lemon juice, salt and almond extract in blender. Blend 2 seconds. In separate bowl whip cream until stiff. Fold peach mixture into whipped cream. Pour into loaf pans and freeze. Beat with whisk when sherbet has frozen 1 inch from sides of pans. Freeze 2 hours.

God of Heaven, Satan took me for ransom but Jesus bought me back. Amen.

"At that time men will see the Son of Man coming in clouds with great power and glory." Mark 13:26 NIV

Butter Pecan Topping
½ c. butter
1 c. chopped pecans or walnuts
1 c. firmly packed brown sugar
⅓ c. cream
¼ c. corn syrup

Melt butter in heavy saucepan. Add nuts and heat over medium heat until nuts are lightly toasted and butter is lightly browned. Stir in brown sugar, cream and corn syrup. Cook over low heat until sugar dissolves completely. Do not overcook. Serve warm or cold. Makes 2 cups.

I want to be ready when you come again, Lord, Mighty in Battle. Amen.

~~~

"Heaven and earth will pass away, but my words will never pass away." Mark 13:31 NIV

Butterscotch Topping
1 c. light corn syrup
1 c. firmly packed brown sugar
1 tsp. vanilla
½ tsp. salt
1 T. butter
½ c. milk

In medium saucepan combine all ingredients. Cook 5 minutes over low heat, stirring constantly. Store in cool place.

You, My God, are the center and cause of the cosmos. Amen.

"No one knows about that day or hour, not even the angels in heaven, nor the Son, but only the Father."

Mark 13:32 NIV

Chocolate Marble Freeze
1 c. vanilla wafer crumbs
2 T. butter or margarine, melted
½ c. butter or margarine
4 oz. German sweet chocolate or 4 oz. milk chocolate candy
4 egg yolks, beaten
¼ c. sifted powdered sugar
½ c. slivered almonds, toasted, divided
4 egg whites
1 pt. vanilla or coffee ice cream, softened

In small bowl combine wafer crumbs and 2 tablespoons melted butter. Press into bottom of 9-inch square pan. In saucepan melt ½ cup butter and chocolate over low heat, stirring constantly, until well blended. Place egg yolks in bowl. Stir small amount of chocolate mixture into yolks. Add mixture to saucepan. Cook over low heat, stirring constantly, until thick. Remove from heat. Add powdered sugar. Beat until smooth. Stir in ¼ cup of the almonds. Cool. Beat egg whites in large bowl until stiff. Fold chocolate mixture gently into egg whites. Spoon over crust alternately with ice cream. Gently cut through to marble. Freeze 6 hours or until firm. Cut into squares. Sprinkle with remaining ¼ cup almonds.

I cannot fear a future where you are, God of Salvation. Amen.

"Therefore keep watch because you do not know when the owner of the house will come back—whether in the evening, or at midnight, or when the rooster crows, or at dawn."
Mark 14:15 NIV

Cocoa Syrup
1 c. cocoa
2 to 2½ c. sugar
1½ c. hot water
Dash salt
1 tsp. vanilla

In 4-quart saucepan combine cocoa, sugar, hot water and salt. Mix well. Bring to full boil over moderate heat, stirring constantly. Boil 3 to 5 minutes, stirring constantly. Remove from heat. Add vanilla. Refrigerate in squeeze bottle or covered jar.

We cannot outplan you, Jehovah. Amen.

~~~

While they were reclining at the table eating, he said, "I tell you the truth, one of you will betray me—one who is eating with me."
Mark 14:18 NIV

Freezer Ice Cream
2 c. milk
2 eggs, separated
¾ c. sugar
1 T. vanilla
¼ tsp. salt
1 c. heavy whipping cream

In top of double boiler combine milk, 2 egg yolks and sugar. Cook over boiling water about 6 minutes or until mixture thickens. In large bowl beat 2 egg whites until stiff. Pour hot mixture over egg whites. Mix well. Blend in vanilla and salt.

Chill. Add whipping cream and mix well. Pour into ice cream freezer and follow machine directions to finish.

Variation: Add 2 cups chopped peaches or strawberries.

We cannot outsmart you, Adonai. Amen.

~~~

"This is my blood of the covenant, which is poured out for many . . . ." Mark 14:24 NIV

Frozen Pineapple Dessert
1 can crushed pineapple, about 9 oz.
2 c. sour cream
2 T. lemon juice
¾ c. sugar
⅛ tsp. salt
¼ c. chopped maraschino cherries
¼ c. chopped walnuts
1 banana, sliced

Drain pineapple and place in medium bowl. Set pineapple juice aside for another use. To the drained pineapple add sour cream, lemon juice, sugar and salt. Mix well. Add cherries, walnuts and banana. Mix. Pour into 9-inch square dish or muffin tins and freeze until firm. Cut in squares.

I weep in sorrow—and joy—over the blood you shed, Elohim. Amen.

They went to a place called Gethsemane, and Jesus said to his disciples, "Sit here while I pray." Mark 14:32 NIV

Frozen Pumpkin Dessert

3 c. crushed graham crackers
⅔ c. melted margarine
½ c. granulated sugar
2 c. canned pumpkin
1 c. firmly packed brown sugar
½ tsp. salt
½ tsp. ground nutmeg
2 tsp. ground cinnamon
2 qts. soft vanilla ice cream

In large bowl mix graham cracker crumbs, margarine and granulated sugar. Press into greased 9 by 13-inch pan. In large bowl blend pumpkin, brown sugar, salt, nutmeg and cinnamon. Stir in ice cream. Pour into crust. Freeze. Cut into squares. Serve plain or with whipped topping.

Sometimes you ask us only to abide; help us to do so, God of My Strength. Amen.

~~~

Going at once to Jesus, Judas said, "Rabbi!" and kissed him. Mark 14:45 NIV

Frozen Strawberry Dessert

10 oz. frozen strawberries
1 c. sugar
1 pt. sour cream

Thaw berries thoroughly. Mix all ingredients in bowl. Pour into loaf pans. Freeze at least 2 hours, stirring at 25-minute intervals.

I can't blame everything on Judas, God of Justice, because I am also weak. Amen.

They took Jesus to the high priest, and all the chief priests, elders and teachers of the law came together.
Mark 14:53 NIV

Fruit Slush
3 c. water
2 c. sugar
6 bananas, sliced or cubed
8 oz. crushed pineapple with juice
1 (6 oz.) can orange juice concentrate

In large saucepan boil water and sugar. Cool. Add bananas, pineapple and orange juice concentrate. Freeze. Serve partially thawed. Can be frozen in small plastic bottles for lunchboxes.

How unrighteous we are to trust our councils who speak against you, Elah. Amen.

~~~

"And you will see the Son of Man sitting at the right hand of the Mighty One and coming on the clouds of heaven."
<p align="right">Mark 14:62b NIV</p>

Hot Fudge Topping
1½ c. sugar
2 T. cornstarch
3 T. cocoa
3 T. butter
¼ tsp. salt
¼ tsp. vanilla
1½ c. milk

In medium saucepan combine all ingredients. Cook over moderate heat, stirring constantly, until thick. Serve warm over ice cream. Makes 2 cups.

I notice that we won't look down to see you coming, Lord Who Sees. Amen.

Immediately the rooster crowed the second time. Then Peter remembered the word Jesus had spoken to him: "Before the rooster crows twice you will disown me three times." And he broke down and wept.   Mark 14:72 NIV

Ice Cream Pie

Crust:
½ c. crunchy peanut butter
½ c. light corn syrup
3 c. puffed rice cereal

Filling:
1 qt. ice cream
Whipped topping (optional)
Nuts (optional)

Butter 9-inch pie pan. In large saucepan warm peanut butter with corn syrup until melted. Stir in cereal. Spread mixture into prepared pan. Freeze. Soften ice cream to spreading consistency. Remove crust from freezer and fill with ice cream. Top with whipped topping and nuts.

Help me to remember what you tell me, Jehovah-Shalom. Amen.

~~~

The chief priests accused him of many things.
                                                           Mark 15:3 NIV

Italian Sorbet

2 c. sugar
2 c. water
2 T. gelatin
1 c. orange juice
½ c. lemon juice
1½ c. orange carbonated beverage
1½ c. grape carbonated beverage
1 c. lemon carbonated beverage

Boil sugar and water gently 20 minutes. Add gelatin. Cool. Add fruit juices, followed by beverages. Freeze.

Note: Ginger ale may be substituted for part or all of the carbonated beverages.

What did you feel, Messiah, when they pointed at you? Amen.

~~~

"Crucify him!" they shouted. Mark 15:13 NIV

Lemon Freeze
3 c. graham cracker crumbs
⅓ c. sugar
⅔ c. melted butter
1 can lemon pie filling, about 21 oz.
1 can sweetened condensed milk
½ c. bottled lemon juice
1 can fruit cocktail, well drained
8 oz. whipped topping, thawed

Butter 9 by 13-inch pan. In bowl mix graham cracker crumbs, sugar and butter. Reserve ⅓ cup of mixture. Press remaining mixture into prepared pan. In large bowl mix pie filling, sweetened condensed milk, lemon juice and fruit cocktail. Pour into crust. Top with whipped topping, then reserved crumbs. Freeze. Cut into squares.

How bittersweet it is, Lord of Lords, that our words would bring death while yours bring life. Amen.

They put a purple robe on him, then wove a crown of thorns and set it on him. Mark 15:17 NIV

Lemon Milk Sherbet
4 c. milk
1½ c. sugar
Grated rind of 1 lemon
Juice of 2 lemons

Mix milk and sugar until sugar dissolves. Pour into loaf pans and freeze until mixture begins to thicken. Add lemon rind and juice. Freeze at least 2 hours, stirring often.

You deserve a crown of emeralds, diamonds and rubies, Lord Christ. Amen.

~~~

And they began to call out to him, "Hail, King of the Jews!" Mark 15:18 NIV

Lemon Topping
1 T. cornstarch
½ c. sugar
⅛ tsp. salt
1 c. cold water
2 T. lemon juice
1 T. butter

In small saucepan mix cornstarch, sugar, salt, water and lemon juice. Bring to full boil. Remove from heat. Add butter. Good over cake, especially pineapple upside-down cake.

It is impossible to deny your holiness, Son of the Highest One. Amen.

The curtain of the temple was torn in two from top to bottom.
>   Mark 15:38 NIV

Lime Delight
1 can evaporated milk, about 14 oz.
1 small pkg. lime gelatin
1¾ c. hot water
1 c. sugar
¼ c. lime juice
2 tsp. lemon juice
2 c. chocolate wafer crumbs
½ c. melted butter
Shaved chocolate for garnish (optional)

Chill evaporated milk in freezer. In small bowl dissolve gelatin in hot water. Chill until partially set. Whip gelatin until fluffy. Stir in sugar, lime juice and lemon juice. In separate bowl whip chilled milk. Fold into gelatin mixture. In small bowl combine wafer crumbs and melted margarine. Press into bottom of 9 by 13-inch pan. Pour gelatin mixture over crumbs. Shave chocolate over top. Freeze. Cut into squares. Can be kept frozen several weeks.

Thank you, Lord Who Provides, for showing our eyes what our hearts see. Amen.

And when the centurion, who stood there in front of Jesus, heard his cry and saw how he died, he said, "Surely this man was the Son of God!" Mark 15:39 NIV

Milky Way Dessert
12 oz. sugar-free, fat-free vanilla ice cream
1 c. fat-free whipped topping, thawed
¼ c. fat-free caramel ice cream topping
1 small box sugar-free, fat-free instant chocolate pudding mix

Soften ice cream and spread in 9-inch square or round pan. In large bowl combine whipped topping, caramel topping and pudding mix. Spread over ice cream. Freeze 4 hours.

No enemy can stand before you, Alpha and Omega. Amen.

~~~

So Joseph bought some linen cloth, took down the body, wrapped it in the linen, and placed it in a tomb cut out of rock. Then he rolled a stone against the entrance of the tomb.
Mark 15:46 NIV

Orange Ice
2 c. sugar
4 c. water
2 c. orange juice
½ c. lemon juice

In saucepan mix sugar and water. Bring to boil. Boil 5 minutes. Cool. Add juices. Mix well. Pour into pan. Freeze until solid. Remove from freezer and break into chunks. Place chunks in blender and blend until slushy. Place in plastic or paper cups and cover tops with plastic wrap. Freeze to sherbet consistency.

Thank you, Ancient of Days, for your servant Joseph who honored your earthly body. Amen.

But when they looked up, they saw that the stone, which was very large, had been rolled away.

Mark 16:4 NIV

Orangy Chocolate Pops
1 pt. chocolate ice cream
1 c. chocolate milk
⅓ c. frozen orange juice concentrate (half of 6 oz. can)
¼ c. powdered sugar
10 wooden sticks
Ten 3-oz. waxed-paper drink cups

In blender combine ice cream, chocolate milk, orange juice concentrate and powdered sugar. Cover. Blend until smooth. Pour into drink cups. Partially freeze. Insert wooden stocks. Freeze firm. To serve, peel off paper wrappings.

You are the King of Glory and the King of Surprises, God. Amen.

~~~

"He has risen!"

Mark 16:6b NIV

Pineapple Delight
10 oz. miniature marshmallows
1 c. milk
1 can crushed pineapple, with juice, about 15 oz.
2 c. whipped topping, thawed
1 c. pecan pieces
⅓ lb. graham cracker crumbs

In medium saucepan melt marshmallows with milk. Cool. Add pineapple, whipped topping and pecans. Place half of graham cracker crumbs in 9 by 13-inch pan. Pour in pineapple mixture. Sprinkle with remaining crumbs and freeze. Cut into squares to serve.

Hallelujah! Amen.

"He is going ahead of you into Galilee. There you will see him, just as he told you." Mark 16:6d NIV

Pistachio Ice Cream Dessert
½ c. powdered sugar
¼ c. margarine
50 round buttery crackers, crushed
1 small pkg. instant pistachio pudding mix
2 c. milk
5 c. softened vanilla ice cream
1 c. frozen whipped topping

In large bowl mix powdered sugar, margarine and cracker crumbs. Press into bottom of 8 by 12-inch or 9 by 13-inch pan, reserving ½ cup of mixture. In large bowl combine pudding mix and milk. Stir in ice cream. Pour into crumb crust. Freeze. Remove from freezer up to 15 minutes before serving. Top with whipped topping and sprinkle with reserved crumbs.

Sometimes I have to go home to be with you, Author of Faith. Amen.

~~~

When Jesus rose early on the first day of the week, he appeared first to Mary Magdalene . . . .
 Mark 16:9a NIV

Pumpkin Ice Cream Squares
1½ c. graham cracker crumbs
¼ c. granulated sugar
¼ c. melted butter
16 oz. canned pumpkin
½ c. firmly packed brown sugar
½ tsp. salt
1 tsp. ground cinnamon
¼ tsp. ground ginger
⅛ tsp. ground cloves
1 qt. vanilla ice cream, softened
Whipped cream and pecans for garnish

In small bowl mix crumbs, granulated sugar and butter. Press into bottom of 9-inch square pan. In large bowl combine pumpkin with brown sugar, salt, cinnamon, ginger and cloves. Fold in ice cream. Pour over crumbs. Cover and freeze solid. About 20 minutes before serving, cut into 3-inch squares. Top with whipped cream and pecans.

Thank you, Christ the Lord, for staying on Earth to show us yourself. Amen.

~~~

Now in the sixth month the angel Gabriel was sent by God to a city of Galilee named Nazareth, to a virgin betrothed to a man whose name was Joseph, of the house of David. The virgin's name was Mary.   Luke 1:26 NKJV

Three Fruit Sherbet
1 ripe banana
Juice of 1 orange
Juice of 1 lemon
1 tsp. grated orange rind
1 tsp. grated lemon rind
1 c. sugar
1 c. water
1 egg white, beaten stiff

In medium bowl mash banana. Cover with orange juice, lemon juice, orange rind and lemon rind. Mix well. Add sugar and stir to dissolve. Add water and blend well. Pour into loaf pan and freeze until mushy. Turn out into cold bowl and beat until smooth to break up ice crystals. Fold in stiffly beaten egg white, by hand, until completely blended. Pour mixture back into pan and freeze.

You have it all thought out, don't you, Creator? Amen.

"He will be great, and will be called the Son of the Highest; and the Lord God will give Him the throne of His father David."
Luke 1:32 NKJV

Strawberry Ice
3 packages frozen strawberries, about 10 oz.
2 c. sugar
4 c. water
Juice of 4 lemons

Thaw strawberries. Place strawberries in blender and puree. In saucepan bring sugar and water to boil. Add strawberries to sugar mixture and mix well. Blend in lemon juice. Pour into loaf pan. Freeze until mushy. Whip to remove crystals. Freeze until solid.

I rest, rise and stand on your promises, Foundation of All. Amen.

PASTA AND RICE

So it was, that while they were there, the days were completed for her to be delivered. And she brought forth her firstborn Son, and wrapped him in swaddling cloths, and laid Him in a manger, because there was no room for them in the inn.

Luke 2:6,7 NKJV

Baked Macaroni and Cheese
1 lb. dry macaroni
½ c. margarine
4 c. milk, divided
1 tsp. salt
½ c. flour
1½ lb. Colby cheese, grated

Cook macaroni according to package directions. Drain and set aside. In large saucepan melt margarine. Add 3 cups of the milk and salt. In small bowl mix remaining 1 cup of milk with flour. Stir flour mixture into hot mixture. Boil 1 minute. Add most of cheese. Stir to melt. Add macaroni and mix well. Bake uncovered 30 minutes at 300 degrees. Sprinkle remaining cheese on top. Bake 15 minutes. Can be made a day ahead.

God, you gave us your Son, and you wrapped the gift in straw—and grace. Amen.

Now there were in the same country shepherds living out in the fields, keeping watch over their flock by night.
Luke 2:8 NKJV

Cajun Chicken Fettuccine
2 T. flour
2 c. vegetable or tomato juice
2 tsp. Cajun seasoning
2 T. vegetable oil, divided
4 skinless boneless chicken breasts
1 green pepper, chopped
1 onion, chopped
4 c. fettuccine, cooked and drained

In small bowl combine flour, tomato juice and Cajun seasoning. Set aside. In large skillet heat 1 tablespoon of the oil. Brown chicken on both sides. Remove chicken and set aside. In same skillet heat remaining 1 tablespoon oil. Add green pepper and onion. Cook until tender-crisp. Add flour mixture and cook until thickened. Return chicken to skillet. Cover and cook through, about 10 to 12 minutes. Place chicken on fettuccine to serve.

Your wonder is never hidden from us, Lily of the Valley. Amen.

~~~

And behold, an angel of the Lord stood before them, and the glory of the Lord shone around them, and they were greatly afraid.
Luke 2:9 NKJV

Cheesy Rice
1 c. uncooked long-grain rice
1 pt. sour cream
4 oz. diced green chili peppers (optional)
Salt, pepper and garlic
10 to 12 oz. Jack or sharp cheddar cheese,
    half sliced, half finely shredded

Grease 2-quart casserole dish. Cook rice according to package directions. Stir in sour cream, chili peppers, salt, pepper and garlic. In prepared dish layer half of rice mixture, cheese slices, remaining half of rice mixture and shredded cheese. Bake 30 to 35 minutes at 350 degrees.

Variation: For milder flavor, substitute banana peppers for chili peppers.

I believe you send angels, and I know I've seen a few of them, Merciful God. Amen.

~~~

Then the angel said to them, "Do not be afraid, for behold, I bring you good tidings of great joy which will be to all people."
<div style="text-align:right">Luke 2:10 NKJV</div>

Chicken Noodle Stew
3 cans condensed cream of chicken soup, undiluted
7 c. boiling water
1 tsp. salt
1 tsp. dried dill weed
4 c. dry fine egg noodles (8 oz.)

In large saucepan combine soup, water, salt and dill weed. Bring to boil. Gradually add noodles so that mixture continues to boil. Cook uncovered, stirring frequently, until noodles are tender.

The angel's good news is as awesome today as it was two thousand years ago, Lord of Lords. Amen.

"For there is born to you this day in the city of David a Savior, who is Christ the Lord." Luke 2:11 NKJV

Deluxe Macaroni Salad
1¼ lb. dry macaroni
2 dozen eggs, hard boiled, shelled and chopped
4 c. sweet pickles, chopped
1½ lbs. boxed processed cheese, cut into small cubes
½ large bunch celery, chopped
Carrots, radishes and onions, chopped
3 c. zesty creamy salad dressing
2 c. sugar
1¼ c. cider vinegar
2 tsp. celery salt
1 tsp. pepper
1 tsp. dried oregano
4 shakes seasoning salt
3 shakes paprika
2 shakes sage
3 T. prepared mustard

Cook macaroni in salted water. Drain and cool. Dice or shred if desired. In very large bowl combine macaroni, eggs, pickles, cheese, celery and equal parts carrots, radishes and onions. In separate bowl combine salad dressing and sugar and mix well. Add dressing to macaroni mixture and mix well. Add cider vinegar, celery salt, pepper, oregano, seasoning salt, paprika, sage and mustard. Mix gently and thoroughly. Chill before serving.

Variation: Use approximately 5 pounds cooked and salted potatoes instead of macaroni.

Everything is just as you promised, Our Peace. Amen.

"And this will be the sign to you: You will find a Babe wrapped in swaddling cloths, lying in a manger."

Luke 2:12 NKJV

Easy Baked Manicotti
1 lb. ground beef
1 jar spaghetti sauce, about 28 oz.
1 carton ricotta cheese, about 15 oz.
1 c. shredded Monterey Jack or provolone cheese
½ c. grated Parmesan cheese, divided
12 to 16 uncooked manicotti shells
2 T. minced onion
¼ c. chopped parsley

Preheat oven to 350 degrees. In skillet brown ground beef. Drain fat. Spoon enough spaghetti sauce into 9 by 13-inch baking pan to cover bottom. In large bowl mix beef, ricotta, Monterey Jack cheese and ¼ cup of the Parmesan cheese. Stuff uncooked manicotti with mixture and place in baking dish. Cover with remaining sauce. Top with remaining ¼ cup Parmesan cheese. Cover with foil. Bake 1¼ hours. Uncover and bake 5 minutes.

Sent by God, born of peasants, adored by shepherds, a Savior for all humankind. Thank you, Lion of the Tribe of Judah. Amen.

And suddenly there was with the angel a multitude of the heavenly host praising God and saying:
"Glory to God in the highest,
And on earth peace, goodwill
   toward men!" Luke 2:13,14 NKJV

Fettuccine Alfredo

½ c. soft butter
¼ c. heavy cream
½ c. freshly grated Parmesan cheese
1 lb. dry fettuccine pasta
Salt and pepper

In small bowl cream butter until light and fluffy. Beat in cream a little at a time. Stir in cheese by the tablespoonful, beating well after each addition. Cook fettuccine as directed on package. Drain well immediately. Transfer at once to hot serving bowl. Add butter-cheese mixture and toss until pasta is well coated. Season with salt and pepper. Serve hot with additional cheese.

We've all forgotten that good will is your goal, Holy Mediator. Amen.

And they came with haste and found Mary and Joseph, and the Babe lying in a manger. Luke 2:16 NKJV

Fried Rice with Ham, Onion and Peas
3 T. oil
3 cloves garlic, minced
¾ c. chopped onion
¾ c. chopped ham
¾ c. green peas
3 eggs, beaten
4 c. cold cooked white rice
2 tsp. soy sauce or ½ tsp. salt
¼ c. minced flat leaf parsley or cilantro (optional)

Have all ingredients ready before starting. Heat oil in skillet. Add garlic. Cook until golden, about 1 minute. Add onion and ham. Cook until ham is slightly crisp and onion is soft, about 5 minutes. Stir in peas. Cook until heated through, about 1 minute. Pour beaten eggs into pan. Toss vigorously, breaking up any large clumps that begin to form, about 1 minute. Cook until eggs are just firm but not dry, about 2 minutes. Stir in cold rice, breaking apart any clumps. Toss rice rapidly, allowing grains to heat through, about 2 minutes. Season with soy sauce or, for "white" fried rice, sprinkle with ½ teaspoon salt. Garnish with parsley.

It was the holiest night of all history, and it was all about you, Only Begotten Son. Amen.

And all those who heard it marveled at those things which were told them by the shepherds.

Luke 2:18 NKJV

Lasagna
1 lb. pork sausage or ground beef
½ c. chopped onion
1 clove garlic, minced
16 oz. canned diced tomatoes, including juice
8 oz. tomato sauce
6 oz. tomato paste
2 tsp. dried basil, crushed
2 tsp. salt, divided
¾ tsp. pepper, divided
1 T. vegetable oil
8 oz. dry lasagna noodles
2 eggs
2½ c. ricotta or cottage cheese
¾ c. grated Parmesan or Romano cheese, divided
2 T. dried parsley flakes
1 lb. mozzarella cheese, shredded

In large skillet saute meat, onion and garlic until meat is browned. Drain. Stir in tomatoes with juice, tomato sauce, tomato paste, basil, 1 teaspoon of the salt and ¼ teaspoon of the pepper. Simmer over medium-low heat 15 minutes, stirring often. In large pot of boiling salted water to which oil has been added, cook noodles until tender. Drain pot and rinse noodles. In small bowl beat eggs. Add ricotta, ½ cup of the Parmesan cheese, parsley, remaining 1 teaspoon salt and remaining ½ teaspoon pepper. Layer half the noodles in 9 by 13-inch baking pan. Spread half the ricotta mixture on noodles. Add layers of half the mozzarella cheese and half the meat sauce. Repeat layers. Sprinkle remaining ¼ cup Parmesan cheese on top. Bake at 375 degrees 30 to 35 minutes or until cooked through. Let stand 10 minutes before cutting.

I love to tell your story, Holy Child. Amen.

And the Child grew and became strong in spirit, filled with wisdom; and the grace of God was upon Him.

Luke 2:40 NKJV

Macaroni Salad

Salad:
2 c. dry macaroni
½ c. chopped celery
1 onion, chopped
1 tsp. dried parsley
1 carrot, grated
6 eggs, hard boiled, peeled and chopped
Celery seed

Dressing:
1½ c. sugar
¼ c. flour
¼ tsp. salt
1½ c. water
Scant ½ c. cider vinegar
¼ c. prepared mustard
1 c. zesty creamy salad dressing

Cook macaroni in salted water as directed on package and drain. In large bowl combine cooked macaroni with remaining salad ingredients. To make dressing, in medium saucepan combine sugar, flour, salt, water and vinegar. Cook, stirring constantly, until thickened. Cool. Add mustard and salad dressing. Stir into macaroni mixture. Chill.

Without your grace, Lord Our Righteousness, the world spins for nothing. Amen.

Now when the devil had ended every temptation, he departed from Him until an opportune time.   Luke 4:13 NKJV

Mexican Rice
1½ c. uncooked long-grain rice
1 can tomatoes, about 16 oz.
2 T. taco seasoning
3⅓ c. water

Stir ingredients together in large skillet or saucepan that has lid. Bring to boil over medium-high heat. Cover with lid. Continue cooking, over low heat, until rice is tender, 20 to 30 minutes.

I kneel before you, Living Bread, knowing that I cannot resist temptation without your help. Amen.

~~~

"The spirit of the Lord is upon Me,
Because He has anointed Me
To preach the gospel to the poor;
He has sent Me to heal the brokenhearted,
To proclaim liberty to the captives
And recovery of sight to the blind,
To set at liberty those who are oppressed;
To proclaim the acceptable year of the Lord."   Luke 4:18, 19 NKJV

Nutty Vegetable Pilaf
1 T. vegetable oil
2 c. coarsely chopped broccoli
2 medium carrots, julienned
1 medium onion, chopped
1 c. sliced fresh mushrooms
2 cloves garlic, minced
½ tsp. dried thyme
½ tsp. dried basil
½ tsp. salt
¼ tsp. pepper
3 c. cooked brown rice (cooked in low-sodium chicken broth)

½ c. chopped pecans, toasted
½ c. shredded Parmesan cheese (optional)

Heat oil in large skillet over medium-high heat. Add broccoli, carrots and onion. Cook and stir 5 to 7 minutes or until broccoli and carrots are tender and onion begins to brown. Add mushrooms, garlic, thyme, basil, salt and pepper. Cook and stir 2 to 3 minutes or until mushrooms are tender. Add rice and pecans. Cook 1 to 2 minutes, stirring, until well blended and thoroughly heated. Just before serving, sprinkle with cheese.

All that oppressed us is lifted, Jehovah Jireh. Amen.

~~~

He said to Simon, "Launch out into the deep and let down your nets for a catch." Luke 5:4b NKJV

One Skillet Spaghetti
1 lb. ground beef
2 medium onions, chopped
7 oz. uncooked spaghetti, broken
1 can diced tomatoes, about 28 oz.
⅓ c. chopped green pepper
½ c. water
1 can sliced mushrooms, drained, about 8 oz.
1 tsp. chili powder
1 tsp. oregano
1 tsp. sugar
1 tsp. salt
1 c. shredded cheese, 4 oz.

In large skillet brown beef and onions. Drain. Stir in spaghetti and all remaining ingredients except cheese. Bring to boil. Reduce heat and simmer 30 minutes or until spaghetti is tender. Sprinkle with cheese. Cover and heat until melted.

You've sent me into the deep many times, Almighty One, but you swam there beside me. Amen.

"But I say to you who hear: Love your enemies, do good to those who hate you, bless those who curse you, and pray for those who spitefully use you." Luke 5:27 NKJV

Orzo Salad
1 c. uncooked orzo pasta
1 can sliced ripe olives, drained and rinsed, about 2¼ oz.
1 c. diced red bell pepper
¼ c. feta cheese, crumbled
1 packet dry ranch dressing mix (1 oz.)
3 T. olive oil
3 T. red wine vinegar
1 tsp. sugar
½ tsp. dried basil

Cook orzo according to box directions, omitting salt. Drain and rinse in cold water. In large bowl mix orzo, olives, red pepper and feta. In small bowl whisk ranch mix, oil, vinegar, sugar and basil. Add to orzo mixture. Cover and refrigerate at least 2 hours.

Sometimes I want to argue with you, Jehovah Rapha, because there's no fun in praying for my enemies. Amen.

~~~

"Judge not, and you shall not be judged."
Luke 6:37a NKJV

Pasta Salad
1 lb. thin spaghetti, cooked, drained, rinsed
1 medium cucumber, diced
1 medium red or purple onion, diced
1⅓ c. prepared slaw dressing
3 c. mozzarella cheese, shredded medium

Combine all ingredients in large bowl and refrigerate.

It saves a lot of time, Holy Advocate, to leave the judging to you. Amen.

"Condemn not, and you shall not be condemned."
Luke 6:37b NKJV

Pasta Salad with Sweet Vinaigrette
1 lb. pasta
⅔ c. white vinegar
2 tsp. Worcestershire sauce
¼ c. mustard
½ c. extra virgin olive oil
⅓ c. sugar
4 c. chopped vegetables

Cook pasta according to package directions. Drain and set aside to cool. In large bowl whisk vinegar, Worcestershire sauce, mustard, olive oil and sugar. Add pasta and vegetables. Toss until well coated. Cover and refrigerate until ready to serve. Toss lightly before serving. Can be made a day ahead.

Holy Branch, I know I may not condemn, but may I at least criticize? Amen.

"Forgive, and you will be forgiven."

Luke 6:37c NKJV

Rice and Mushroom Bake
4 T. margarine
1 medium onion, minced
1 medium green pepper, minced
1 clove garlic, minced
1 c. uncooked long-grain rice
2 T. soy sauce
1 tsp. oregano
1 can chicken broth, about 12 oz.
1 can mushroom stems and pieces, about 4 oz.
¾ c. water

Preheat oven to 350 degrees. Butter 1½-quart casserole dish. In medium skillet melt margarine over medium heat. Add onion, green pepper and garlic and saute until tender. Stir in rice and cook over moderate heat until lightly browned, stirring occasionally. Add soy sauce and oregano. Reduce heat and simmer 20 minutes, stirring occasionally. Pour rice mixture into prepared dish. Add broth, mushrooms and water. Cover and bake 1¼ hours. May be made ahead to prebaking stage; if so, cut baking time in half. Good with chicken, beef or pork.

Holy Spirit, if I forgive only twice, will I be forgiven only twice? Amen.

"Give, and it will be given to you: good measure, pressed down, shaken together, and running over will be put into your bosom."
Luke 6:38a NKJV

Rice Creole
1 lb. ground beef
1 medium onion, sliced thin
1 medium clove garlic, minced
1 can diced tomatoes, including juice, about 16 oz.
1 c. converted long-grain rice
2 T. steak sauce
3 T. diced green pepper
1 tsp. salt
1 c. thinly sliced celery

In large skillet brown beef until crumbly. Drain. Add onion and garlic. Cook until onion is soft. Measure tomatoes with liquid. Add enough water to make 2¼ cups. Stir tomatoes, rice, steak sauce, green pepper, salt and celery into meat mixture. Simmer, covered, 20 to 25 minutes or until rice is tender and liquid is absorbed.

Your math is amazing, Christ My Lord. Amen.

"And why do you look at the speck that is in your brother's eye, but do not perceive the plank in your own eye?"

Luke 6:41 NKJV

Rice Pilaf

½ c. uncooked very fine noodles
¼ c. margarine or butter
3 c. chicken broth
1 c. uncooked long-grain rice
Salt and pepper

In small saucepan saute noodles in margarine, stirring constantly, until noodles are golden brown. Set aside. In another saucepan bring chicken broth to rolling boil. Add rice, noodles, salt and pepper. Cover, reduce heat and simmer 30 minutes or just until moisture is absorbed. Do not stir.

That's not a plank in my eye, Refiner's Fire, but a platform for my opinion. Amen.

"Go and tell John the things you have seen and heard: that the blind see, the lame walk, the lepers are cleansed, the deaf hear, the dead are raised, the poor have the gospel preached to them."   Luke 7:22 NKJV

Sesame Noodles
Marinade:
¼ c. sesame oil
7 T. soy sauce
3 T. balsamic vinegar
3½ T. brown sugar
2 tsp. salt
2 tsp. hot sauce
1 T. minced fresh ginger
1 clove garlic, minced
¼ c. chopped fresh cilantro

Noodles:
1 lb. uncooked pasta (spaghetti or other small shape)
2 lbs. chopped fresh vegetables such as broccoli, asparagus, green beans
10 scallions, sliced thin
¼ c. toasted sesame seeds

In medium bowl combine all marinade ingredients and set aside. Cook pasta according to package directions. Drain and set aside. Steam or boil vegetables briefly just until crisp-tender. Rinse in cold water and drain. In large bowl combine pasta, vegetables, marinade, scallions and sesame seeds. Cover tightly and refrigerate 3 hours or overnight, tossing occasionally to blend flavors.

When I take a breath and look around me, all is just as you said it would be, Lord God Almighty. Amen.

"Your faith has saved you. Go in peace."

Luke 7:50b NKJV

Skillet Spaghetti

1 lb. ground beef
¼ c. chopped celery (optional)
¼ to ¾ c. chopped onion
5 c. tomato juice
¾ c. ketchup or 6 oz. tomato paste
1½ tsp. chili powder (optional)
1 tsp. garlic salt
1 tsp. salt
1½ tsp. dried oregano
½ tsp. pepper
1 bay leaf
¼ c. firmly packed brown sugar
8 oz. uncooked spaghetti
Parmesan cheese

In large skillet cook ground beef, celery and onion until browned. Drain fat. Add all remaining ingredients except spaghetti and Parmesan cheese. Simmer, uncovered, 30 minutes. Remove bay leaf. Add spaghetti and simmer, covered, until pasta is tender, about 20 minutes. Serve with Parmesan cheese.

Christ the Mediator, there is no weight on my soul because of you. Amen.

"No one, when he has lit a lamp, covers it with a vessel or puts it under a bed, but sets it on a lampstand, that those who enter may see the light." Luke 8:16 NKJV

Souper Macaroni

2 T. margarine
½ c. cooked ham, finely chopped
¼ c. chopped onion
1 can condensed cream of mushroom soup
½ c. milk or water
1 c. shredded cheddar cheese, divided
2 c. cooked macaroni, about 4 oz. uncooked
1 T. margarine
¼ c. bread crumbs

Butter 1½-quart casserole dish. In large skillet melt 2 tablespoons margarine and lightly brown ham and onion. Stir in soup, milk and ¾ cup of the cheese. Heat until cheese melts, stirring often. Pour sauce over macaroni in large bowl and mix. Pour into prepared dish. Melt 1 tablespoon margarine and bread crumbs together, stirring but not browning. Sprinkle crumb mixture and remaining ¼ cup cheese over macaroni. Bake at 350 degrees 30 minutes or until brown and bubbling.

The wick in my candle fluttered today, Lord of All, and I ask forgiveness. Amen.

"If anyone desires to come after Me, let him deny himself, and take up his cross daily, and follow Me."

Luke 8:23 NKJV

Stir Fried Rice Confetti
6 T. butter
½ c. minced green onions with tops
4 c. cooked rice
8 slices bacon, fried and crumbled
½ tsp. sugar
½ tsp. salt
½ to 1 c. leftover vegetables (peas, carrots, etc.)
Roasted salted sunflower seeds (optional)

Melt butter in large skillet. Saute onion 5 minutes. Add all remaining ingredients except sunflower seeds. Heat, uncovered, over medium heat about 10 minutes or until rice is golden. Sprinkle sunflower seeds over top before serving.

I want to follow you, Jesus the Nazarene, but why must the cross be so heavy? Amen.

"For whoever desires to save his life will lose it, but whoever loses his life for My sake will save it."

Luke 8:24 NKJV

Tuna and Bowtie Salad

8 oz. uncooked whole grain or regular bowtie pasta
6 T. regular or light mayonnaise
2 T. red wine vinegar
2 T. chopped fresh basil or 1 tsp. dried basil leaves, crushed
1 clove garlic, finely chopped
¼ tsp. pepper
2 cans tuna, drained and flaked, about 5 oz. each
1 pkg. frozen green beans, thawed, about 9 oz.
2 c. cherry tomatoes, quartered, or grape tomatoes, halved
⅓ c. chopped red onion

Cook bowtie pasta according to package directions. Drain and rinse with cold water until completely cool. In large bowl combine mayonnaise, vinegar, basil, garlic and pepper. Mix well. Add pasta, tuna, green beans, tomatoes and onion. Toss well. Chill if desired.

But I decided to follow, Son of Man, and you gave me strength and courage to carry the cross. Amen.

"Life is more than food, and the body is more than clothing."
Luke 12:23 NKJV

Vegetable Lasagna
8 oz. uncooked whole wheat or spinach lasagna noodles
1 can whole tomatoes, chopped, about 28 oz.
12 oz. tomato paste
2 small zucchini, sliced
2 small carrots, grated or sliced
1 large onion, chopped
2 c. mushrooms, sliced
1 T. basil
2 T. oregano
2 tsp. sugar
2 tsp. pepper
8 oz. low-fat ricotta cheese
1 pkg. frozen chopped spinach, about 10 oz.
8 oz. shredded low-fat mozzarella cheese
3 T. grated Parmesan cheese

Cook noodles according to package directions and drain. In large saucepan blend tomatoes, tomato paste, zucchini, carrots, onion, mushrooms, basil, oregano, sugar and pepper. Simmer about 1 hour. In small bowl blend ricotta cheese and spinach. Set aside. In 9 by 13-inch baking pan, layer one-third of tomato sauce, one-third of noodles, one-half of ricotta mixture, one-half of mozzarella cheese, one-third of tomato sauce, one-third of noodles, one-half of ricotta mixture, one-half of mozzarella cheese, one-third of noodles and one-third of tomato sauce. Sprinkle with Parmesan cheese. Bake uncovered at 350 degrees about 50 minutes.

Did you know, Holy Carpenter, that it would be so confusing for us to see beyond material things? Amen.

PIES, COBBLERS AND DUMPLINGS

"And which of you by worrying can add one cubit to his stature?"
Luke 13:25 NKJV

Apple Dumplings
3 c. flour
1 tsp. salt
1¼ c. shortening
1 egg, beaten
5 T. water
1 T. cider vinegar
About 5 c. apple slices
Brown sugar for sprinkling
Cinnamon for sprinkling
¼ c. butter, cut in small pieces
½ c. firmly packed brown sugar
½ c. granulated sugar
1 T. cornstarch
¾ c. water
1 T. butter or margarine

Preheat oven to 400 degrees. Mix flour and salt in large bowl and cut in shortening. In small bowl mix egg, 5 tablespoons water and vinegar. Pour into flour mixture. Blend with fork just until flour is moistened. Divide into small balls and roll into 5 by 5-inch squares. Place 3 or 4 tablespoonfuls of apple slices in middle of each square. Top with sprinkle of brown sugar, dash of cinnamon and dot of butter. Pull sides of dough around apples and pinch seams to secure. Place dumplings 1 inch apart in 9 by 13-inch pan. In saucepan mix ½ cup brown sugar, granulated sugar and cornstarch. Add ¾ cup water and 1 T. butter. Bring mixture to boil. Pour half over dumplings. Bake 20 minutes, pour remaining syrup over dumplings, and bake 30 to 40 minutes or until crust is golden brown and fruit is tender.

Why can I fret but not pray, Spirit of God? Amen.

"Consider the lilies, how they grow: they neither toil nor spin.... If then God so clothes the grass, which today is in the field and tomorrow is thrown into the oven, how much more will He clothe you, O you of little faith?" Luke 13:27,28 NKJV

Banana Cream Pie
1½ c. graham cracker crumbs
2 T. sugar
4 T. butter, melted
5 c. milk
3 small pkg. instant vanilla pudding mix
8 oz. sour cream
12 oz. whipped topping, thawed, divided
3 or 4 bananas, sliced

In bowl mix graham cracker crumbs, sugar and butter until well moistened. Press into 9-inch glass or ceramic pie plate. Place in refrigerator. In large bowl whisk milk and pudding mix. Add sour cream and blend. Add about three-fourths of the whipped topping. Blend. Place banana slices on prepared crust. Pour pudding mixture on top. Cover with remaining whipped topping.

Blessed are you, Water of Life, for caring about even me. Amen.

~~~

"Do not fear, little flock, for it is your Father's good pleasure to give you the kingdom." Luke 13:32 NKJV

Blini
3 eggs
¾ c. buttermilk
1 c. milk
1 c. all-purpose flour
¾ c. buckwheat or whole wheat flour
¼ tsp. salt
½ c. butter

In medium bowl whisk eggs, buttermilk and milk. In separate bowl combine all-purpose flour, buckwheat flour and salt. Add flour mixture to egg mixture and whisk again. Heat nonstick skillet over medium heat until hot. Thoroughly butter bottom of skillet. Using 1 tablespoon batter per blini, pour batter into skillet and cook until golden brown, about 90 seconds, on the first side. Turn when blini is dry and slightly bubbly around edges. Cook about 30 seconds on second side. Four to 5 blini may be cooked at a time in a large skillet. Rebutter skillet for each batch. Serve with favorite filling.

Blini may be prepared up to 2 days ahead, refrigerated and warmed to room temperature before serving.

Your kingdom is founded on grace, Emmanuel. Amen.

~~~

"For where your treasure is, there your heart will be also."
Luke 13:34 NKJV

Butterscotch Pie
3 T. melted butter
2 c. firmly packed brown sugar
4 T. flour
3 egg yolks
2 c. milk
½ tsp. vanilla
One baked 9-inch pie shell
Topping of choice

Heat butter in medium saucepan. Stir in brown sugar and flour and cook on low heat until dissolved. In small bowl mix yolks and milk. Stir egg mixture into brown sugar mixture in saucepan. Cook over low heat until thick. Stir in vanilla. Pour into baked shell. Cool and top with meringue, whipped cream or whipped topping.

I want kingdom things to be my important things, God of Eternity. Amen.

"Therefore you also be ready, for the Son of Man is coming at an hour you do not expect." Luke 13:40b NKJV

Caramel Crunch Peach Pie

½ c. flour
1½ c. oatmeal
⅔ c. firmly packed brown sugar
1 tsp. ground cinnamon
½ tsp. salt
½ c. melted butter
4 to 8 c. peaches, sliced, drained

Preheat oven to 375 degrees. In large bowl mix flour, oatmeal, brown sugar, cinnamon and salt. Stir in melted butter. Press into 9-inch pie pan, reserving ½ cup. Arrange peach slices on top. Sprinkle with reserved crumbs. Bake 30 minutes.

I need not worry about your timing, Lamb of God. Amen.

~~~

"Strive to enter through the narrow gate, for many, I say to you, will seek to enter and will not be able." Luke 13:24 NKJV

Caramel Pecan Pie

3 eggs
⅔ c. sugar
1 jar caramel topping, about 12 oz.
¼ c. butter, melted
1½ c. pecan halves
1 unbaked 9-inch pie shell

Preheat oven to 350 degrees. In bowl beat eggs lightly with fork. Add sugar and stir until dissolved. Stir in caramel topping and butter. Mix well. Stir in pecan halves. Pour filling into pie shell. Bake 45 minutes or until knife inserted in center comes out clean. Cool thoroughly on rack.

Only with your help, Redeemer God, can I walk the way of righteousness. Amen.

"For whoever exalts himself will be humbled, and he who humbles himself will be exalted." Luke 14:11 NKJV

Carrot Pie
Pastry for two-crust pie
1 c. grated raw carrot
⅔ c. sugar
1½ c. milk
1 egg, well beaten
¼ tsp. ginger
¼ tsp. ground cinnamon
¼ tsp. salt

Line pie pan with pastry. Mix other ingredients and place in pan. Wet edges of pastry. Top with crust. Prick top. Bake at 425 degrees 10 minutes, then at 325 degrees 45 to 50 minutes.

Only you decide whom to lift high, Plant of Renown. Amen.

~~~

"I say to you that likewise there will be more joy in heaven over one sinner who repents than over ninety-nine just persons who need no repentance." Luke 15:7 NKJV

Cherry Pie
Pastry for double-crust pie
4 c. cherries
1¾ c. sugar
¼ c. cherry juice or water
3 T. cornstarch
½ tsp. ground cinnamon

Preheat oven to 400 degrees. Line pie pan wih pastry. In saucepan over medium heat cook and stir other ingredients. Pour into shell. Cover with crust. Prick top. Bake 30 minutes or until top is golden brown.

May heaven ring with joy, Mighty to Save. Amen.

"He who is faithful in what is least is faithful also in much . . . ."
Luke 16:10a NKJV

Chocolate Pie
2¼ c. sugar
4 T. cocoa
½ tsp. salt
10 T. flour
3 c. milk, divided
4 egg yolks, lightly beaten
1 T. margarine
2 tsp. vanilla
2 baked 9-inch pie shells
Topping of choice

In medium saucepan mix sugar, cocoa, salt and flour. Add 1 cup milk. Stir well. In small bowl mix small amount of cocoa mixture with egg yolks. Add egg mixture to cocoa mixture. Add remaining 2 cups milk. Stir well. Cook over medium heat, stirring constantly, until thick. Remove from heat. Add margarine and vanilla. Pour into baked shells. Top with meringue, whipped cream or whipped topping.

Would you give me more to bear than I can carry, O Resurrection and Life? Amen.

So the Lord said, "If you have faith as a mustard seed, you can say to this mulberry tree, 'Be pulled up by the roots and be planted in the sea,' and it would obey you."

Luke 16:6 NKJV

Chuck's Never Fail Meringue

1 T. cornstarch
2 T. cold water
½ c. water
3 egg whites
6 T. sugar
1 tsp. vanilla

In small cup blend cornstarch and 2 tablespoons cold water. In saucepan boil ½ cup water. Add cornstarch mixture and cook over moderate heat, stirring constantly, until clear and thick. Cool in sink by setting saucepan in cold water. In large glass or metal bowl (not plastic) beat egg whites at high speed until foamy. Gradually add sugar and beat until stiff but not dry. On low speed add vanilla. Add cornstarch mixture. Beat well on high speed. Spread on pies or puddings. Does not stick to utensils.

You've given us power beyond our understanding, Rock of Ages. Amen.

"The things which are impossible with men are possible with God." Luke 18:27 NKJV

Coconut Crème Pie

Pastry for 9-inch pie shell
⅓ c. sugar
2 T. cornstarch
¼ tsp. salt
3 egg yolks, beaten
1½ c. scalded milk
1 T. butter
½ c. shredded coconut
½ tsp. vanilla
Topping of choice

Line pie pan with pastry and set aside. In top part of double boiler mix sugar, cornstarch, salt and beaten egg yolks. Pour scalded milk into egg mixture and cook over hot water until thickened, stirring constantly. Add butter, coconut and vanilla. Pour into pastry-lined pan. Bake at 450 degrees until crust is set, then at 325 degrees until crust is lightly browned. Pie may be covered with meringue or whipped cream.

I cannot, she cannot, he cannot, but you can, Son of the Father. Amen.

"Then they will see the Son of Man coming in a cloud with power and great glory."   Luke 21:27 NKJV

Decadent Peanut Butter Pie

1 c. creamy peanut butter
8 oz. cream cheese, at room temperature
½ c. sugar
12 oz. whipped topping, thawed, divided
1 prepared chocolate cookie pie crust
12 oz. hot fudge ice cream topping, divided
2 T. creamy peanut butter

In large bowl beat 1 cup peanut butter, cream cheese and sugar. Gently fold in 3 cups of the whipped topping. Spoon mixture into crust. Spread filling to edge of crust.

Reserving 2 tablespoons of the hot fudge, place remaining hot fudge in microwavable bowl or glass measuring cup. Microwave 1 minute. Stir. Spread over peanut butter layer in crust. Refrigerate until serving time.

Just before serving, spread remaining whipped topping over hot fudge layer, being careful not to mix the two parts. Place the 2 tablespoons reserved hot fudge in small plastic bag and knead for a few seconds. Cut tiny hole in corner of bag and drizzle hot fudge over pie. Do the same with 2 tablespoons peanut butter, drizzling in opposite direction.

We eagerly await the day of your return, Righteous One. Amen.

"Heaven and earth will pass away, but My words will by no means pass away." Luke 21:33 NKJV

Easy Fruit Cobbler
1 can fruit pie filling, such as apple, peach or cherry
1 small yellow cake mix
½ c. butter or margarine, melted

Preheat oven to 325 degrees. In 9 by 9-inch baking dish place pie filling, then cake mix, then melted butter. Bake 1 hour or until golden brown.

I worried about the future until I read your word, Jesus My Future. Amen.

~~~

And He took bread, gave thanks and broke it, and gave it to them, saying, "This is My body, which is given for you; do this in remembrance of Me." Luke 22:19 NKJV

Frozen Lime Pie
1 can frozen limeade, about 6 oz.
1 can sweetened condensed milk, about 14 oz.
1 carton whipped topping, thawed, about 12 oz.
1 prepared 9-inch crumb crust

In large bowl combine limeade with condensed milk. Stir in whipped topping. Spoon into crumb crust and freeze. Serve frozen or semi-frozen.

Thank you, Savior of the World, for becoming like us so that we might realize the gift of your suffering. Amen.

Likewise He also took the cup after supper, saying, "This cup is the new covenant in My blood, which is shed for you."
Luke 22:20 NKJV

Key Lime Pie

8 oz. cream cheese, softened
½ c. Key lime or lime juice
1 can sweetened condensed milk, about 14 oz.
1 tsp. vanilla
1 prepared 9-inch crumb crust
Whipped cream or whipped topping
Lime zest

In large bowl combine cream cheese with lime juice and condensed milk. Mix well. Stir in vanilla. Pour into crust and chill several hours. Top with whipped cream and garnish with lemon zest.

You did it all for me, Jesus Who Reigns, and I want to give my all for you. Amen.

> While He had said this, He had showed them His hands and His feet.
> Luke 24:40 NKJV

Lemon Velvet Pie

1⅓ c. sugar
6 T. cornstarch
½ tsp. salt
1½ c. cold water
2 egg yolks, lightly beaten
2 T. butter
⅓ c. lemon juice
1 tsp. grated lemon peel
1 tsp. vanilla
1 T. unflavored gelatin
¼ c. cold water
1 c. light cream or whole milk
2 egg whites, stiffly beaten
One 9-inch baked pie shell
1 c. heavy cream, sweetened and whipped

In large saucepan combine sugar, cornstarch and salt. Gradually stir in 1½ cups water. Cook over medium heat, stirring constantly, until smooth and thick enough to mound. Slowly blend in egg yolks and butter. Cook 2 minutes. Remove from heat and add lemon juice, lemon peel and vanilla. Set aside 1¼ cups to cool. To remainder add gelatin softened in ¼ cup cold water. When dissolved, stir in light cream. Cool. When mixture begins to thicken, fold in egg whites and pour into crust. Chill 15 minutes. Top with reserved 1¼ cups filling. Chill well and top with whipped cream.

These hands and feet belong to you, Chief Shepherd. Amen.

In the beginning was the Word, and the Word was with God, and the Word was God. John 1:1 NRSV

No-Crust Pecan Pie
Whites of 3 large eggs, at room temperature
1 tsp. baking powder
1 c. sugar
1 c. chopped pecans
20 round buttery crackers, crushed
1 tsp. vanilla
½ pt. heavy cream, whipped

Preheat oven to 300 degrees. Grease 8-inch or 9-inch pie pan. In large metal bowl beat egg whites until frothy. Stir in baking powder. Add sugar gradually, beating until stiff. Fold in pecans, cracker crumbs and vanilla. Pour into prepared pan. Bake 40 minutes. Cool. Cover with whipped cream. May be prepared and refrigerated 24 hours before serving.

Let your word be the root of all my words, Blessed Savior. Amen.

He was in the beginning with God. John 1:2 NRSV

Oatmeal Pie
¼ c. butter
½ c. sugar
½ tsp. ground cinnamon
½ tsp. ground cloves
¼ tsp. salt
1 c. dark corn syrup
3 eggs
1 c. quick-cooking rolled oats
1 unbaked 8-inch or 9-inch pie shell

Preheat oven to 350 degrees. In large bowl cream butter and sugar. Add cinnamon, cloves and salt. Mix well. Stir in corn syrup. Add eggs, one at a time, stirring after each addition until well blended. Stir in oats. Pour into pie shell. Bake 1 hour or until knife inserted in center comes out clean.

Variation: For lighter pie, use only ½ cup oats.

It's a blessing to live in a world begun and ordered by you, God Manifest in the Flesh. Amen.

~~~

All things came into being through him, and without him not one thing came into being. John 1:3a NRSV

Old Fashioned Cobbler
½ c. butter
1 c. flour
1 c. sugar
1 T. baking powder
½ c. milk
12 c. berries with juice

Preheat oven to 350 degrees. Melt butter in bottom of 9 by 13-inch pan. In large bowl mix flour, sugar, baking powder and milk.

Pour mixture into pan. Pour berries and juice on top. Bake 1 hour.

I give thanks that you are my heavenly parent, God Who Rules. Amen.

~~~

What has come into being in him was life, and the life was the light of all people. John 1:3b NRSV

Perfect Pumpkin Pie
1 can pumpkin, about 15 oz.
1 can sweetened condensed milk, about 14 oz.
2 eggs
1 tsp. ground cinnamon
½ tsp. ground ginger
½ tsp. ground nutmeg
½ tsp. salt
1 unbaked pie shell, pastry or crumb

Preheat oven to 425 degrees. In large mixer bowl beat pumpkin, sweetened condensed milk, eggs, cinnamon, ginger, nutmeg and salt. Pour into crust. Bake 15 minutes. Reduce temperature to 350 degrees. Bake 35 to 40 minutes or until knife inserted in center comes out clean. Cool. Refrigerate leftovers.

Sometimes I forget that you care about everyone, Everlasting Father. Amen.

The light shines in the darkness, and the darkness did not overcome it.
John 1:4 NRSV

Pie Crust for Prebaking

1½ c. flour
½ tsp. salt
2 T. sugar
2 T. cold milk
½ c. vegetable oil

Preheat oven to 375 degrees. In large bowl stir ingredients until dough forms ball. Place in 10-inch pie pan and pat to make crust in pan and over edge. Press edge with fork. Prick bottom with fork. Bake until light brown. Cool and fill.

The evil one will never conquer you, True Light of the World. Amen.

~~~

"Very truly, I tell you, no one can see the kingdom of God without being born from above."
John 2:3 NRSV

Pie Crust with Buttery Shortening

1⅓ c. flour
½ tsp. salt
½ c. butter-flavored shortening
3 T. ice water

In large bowl combine flour and salt. Cut in shortening. Add water, a little at a time, mixing constantly with fork. Roll out on floured surface. Makes 2 crusts.

Two births are mine through the grace of God and the blood of Christ. Amen.

"For God so loved the world that he gave his only Son, so that everyone who believes in him may not perish but have eternal life."
John 3:16 NRSV

Pie Crust with Egg
4 c. flour
1 T. sugar
2 tsp. salt
2 c. shortening
1 egg, beaten
1 T. cider vinegar
½ c. cold water

In large bowl mix flour, sugar and salt. Cut in shortening until mixture forms crumbs the size of peas. Add egg, vinegar and water. Handle lightly; dough will be soft. Refrigerate and use as needed. Keeps 1 week. Makes 3 or 4 crusts.

If you could love the world, Holy One, why can't I love my neighbor? Amen.

~~~

"Indeed, God did not send the Son into the world to condemn the world, but in order that the world might be saved through him."
John 3:17 NRSV

Pie Crust with Graham Crumbs
1⅓ c. graham cracker crumbs
¼ c. sugar
¼ c. melted butter

Preheat oven to 375 degrees. Mix all ingredients well and press firmly on bottom and sides of 9-inch pie pan. For baked shell, bake 5 to 8 minutes. For unbaked shell, chill 1 hour.

Lamb of God, why are we so eager to condemn each other? Amen.

Many Samaritans from that city believed in him because of the woman's testimony.   John 4:39a NRSV

Pie Crust with Lard and Shortening
3 c. flour
⅔ c. lard plus ⅓ c. shortening
2 tsp. cider vinegar plus enough water to make ¼ c.
¼ c. cold milk
¼ c. vegetable oil
Pinch of salt

Place flour in large bowl. Cut in shortening and lard. In separate bowl blend vinegar, water, milk, oil and salt. Blend into flour mixture. Roll out on floured surface. Makes 3 crusts.

Let me speak of you today, Living Stone. Amen.

~~~

"The Father loves the Son and shows him all that he himself is doing; and he will show him greater works than these, so that you will be astonished."   John 5:20 NRSV

Pie Crust with Oatmeal
1 c. quick-cooking rolled oats
⅓ c. sifted flour
⅓ c. firmly packed brown sugar
½ tsp. salt
⅓ c. cold butter or margarine

Preheat oven to 375 degrees. In medium bowl mix oats, flour, brown sugar and salt. Cut in butter until mixture becomes crumbly. Press firmly on bottom and sides of 9-inch pie pan. Bake about 15 minutes. Shell may need reshaping after baking; if so, reshape while still warm. Cool thoroughly before filling. Good with cream or chiffon filling. May be used instead of graham crust.

A universe of surprise, a history of wonder, a world of creation—all from you, King Over All the Earth. Amen.

"I am the bread of life." John 6:48 NRSV

Pie Crust with Puffed Rice
⅓ c. light corn syrup
⅓ c. peanut butter
2 c. puffed rice cereal

Mix all ingredients in pie pan and press into place. Fill with ice cream or other filling.

Variation: In bowl melt 10 ounces semisweet chocolate chips and 3 tablespoons butter. Add 2 cups puffed rice cereal. Press into bottom and sides of pie pan. Chill and add mint ice cream or other ice cream.

Thank you, Bread of Life, for nourishing my spirit every day. Amen.

~~~

"Let anyone who is thirsty come to me." John 7:37 NRSV

Pie Crust with Shortening
1½ c. pastry flour
1 tsp. baking powder
½ tsp. salt
½ c. shortening
About 4 T. cold milk

In large bowl mix pastry flour, baking powder and salt. Cut in shortening. Add milk a little at a time, mixing constantly with fork, until dough forms ball. Roll out on floured surface. Makes 2 crusts.

I was parched, dry, uninspired—until you watered my soul, Living Water. Amen.

"Neither do I condemn you. Go your way, and from now on do not sin again."
John 8:11b NRSV

Pie Crust with Vegetable Oil
1 c. vegetable oil
½ c. cold water
3 c. flour
2 tsp. baking powder
1 tsp. salt

In large bowl combine oil and water. In separate bowl mix flour, baking powder and salt. Add to oil mixture. Roll out on floured surface. Makes 3 crusts.

You revolutionized everyone's life, even mine, Most Mighty. Amen.

~~~

"I am the light of the world. Whoever follows me will never walk in darkness but will have the light of life."
John 8:12 NRSV

Pie Crust with Vegetable Oil and Sugar
1½ c. flour
½ tsp. salt
1½ T. sugar
½ c. vegetable oil
2 T. milk

Preheat oven to 375 degrees. Mix all ingredients in pie pan. Pat into bottom and sides of pan. Prick or crimp edge of crust. Bake about 15 minutes until golden but not brown.

From your Light, there is warmth, welcome and wattage. Amen.

If you continue in my word, you are truly my disciples; and you will know the truth, and the truth will make you free."

John 8:31b,32 NRSV

Pie Crust with Whole Wheat Flour
2 c. whole wheat flour
1 c. all-purpose flour
1 tsp. salt
1 c. lard, softened
1 egg
½ c. cold water
1 T. cider vinegar

In big bowl combine whole wheat flour, all-purpose flour and salt. Mix well. Cut in lard until mixture becomes crumbly. In separate bowl beat egg, water and vinegar. Mix with flour mixture only until flour is moistened. Refrigerate up to 2 weeks.

I grow only as I grow in your word, Christ the Lord. Amen.

~~~

"He calls his own sheep by name and leads them out."

John 10:3b NRSV

Pineapple Sour Cream Pie
2 c. sour cream
1 large box instant vanilla pudding mix
1 can crushed pineapple, drained, about 20 oz.
1 T. sugar (optional)
1 graham cracker crust
Whipped cream (optional)

In large bowl mix sour cream and pudding mix. Stir in pineapple. Add sugar if unsweetened pineapple is used. Mix 1 minute. Pour into crust. Chill 3 hours. Garnish with whipped cream.

You knew my name when nobody else remembered it, Great I Am. Amen.

"I am the good shepherd. The good shepherd lays down his life for the sheep."
John 10:11 NRSV

Raisin Pie
2 c. water
1½ c. raisins
¾ c. sugar
⅛ tsp. salt
2 T. cornstarch
¼ c. water
1 T. lemon juice (optional)
1 baked pie shell
Sweetened whipped cream

In medium saucepan combine 2 cups water, raisins, sugar and salt. Mix well. Bring to boil, stirring constantly. Reduce heat and simmer 5 minutes. In small cup dissolve cornstarch with ¼ cup water. Add to raisin mixture. Boil 1 minute. Remove from heat. Add lemon juice if desired. Pour into baked pie shell. Cool and top with sweetened whipped cream.

I want to relax more and let you lead me, Christ the Shepherd. Amen.

~~~

"Lazarus, come out!"
John 11:43b NRSV

Russian Apple Pie
4 large Granny Smith apples, cored,
    peeled, cut in 2-inch chunks
3 large eggs, at room temperature
½ c. sugar
1 c. flour

Preheat oven to 375 degrees. Line bottom of springform pan with parchment paper. Lay apples on parchment paper. In medium bowl beat eggs until light yellow and foamy. Add sugar in small portions, letting sugar dissolve after each addition. Add flour. Mix until air bubbles appear. Pour mixture over apples.

Mixture will soak through apples. Do not mix apples with batter. Bake 55 minutes. Remove from oven and invert pan on serving dish. Apples will be on top.

By the time you speak it, it is done, Holy Word. Amen.

~~~

"Whoever serves me, the Father will honor."
<div style="text-align:right">John 12:36b NRSV</div>

Shoo Fly Pie
1 c. flour
⅔ c. firmly packed brown sugar
1 T. butter
1 c. dark molasses or dark corn syrup
¾ c. boiling water
1 tsp. baking soda
1 egg, beaten
1 unbaked 8-inch or 9-inch pie shell

Preheat oven to 375 degrees. In medium bowl mix flour, brown sugar and butter until crumbly. Divide mixture in half. In separate bowl combine molasses and boiling water. Add baking soda and mix. Add egg and mix. Fold in half of flour mixture. Mix but do not beat. Pour into pie shell and cover with remaining half of flour mixture. Bake 10 minutes at 375 degrees. Reduce heat to 350 degrees and bake 30 minutes.

I praise you, Savior Mine, for providing purpose to my days. Amen.

"I give you a new commandment, that you love one another. Just as I have loved you, you also should love one another. By this everyone will know that you are my disciples, if you have love for one another." John 13:34,35 NRSV

Slow Cooker Cobbler

16 oz. mixed berries, fresh, canned or frozen
¾ c. sugar
2 T. quick-cooking tapioca
2 tsp. grated lemon peel
1½ c. flour
½ c. firmly packed brown sugar
2¼ tsp. baking powder
¼ tsp. ground nutmeg
¾ c. milk
⅓ c. melted butter
Vanilla ice cream (optional)

In slow cooker stir berries, sugar, tapioca and lemon peel. In bowl combine flour, brown sugar, baking powder and nutmeg. Add milk and butter. Stir just until blended. Drop by spoonfuls into berry mixture. Cover and cook on low 4 hours. Turn cooker off. Uncover and let stand 30 minutes before serving. Spoon cobbler into bowls. Top with ice cream if desired.

My neighbors never had a harder challenge than loving me, God of Harmony. Amen.

"Do not let your hearts be troubled. Believe in God, believe also in me."   John 14:1 NRSV

Sour Cream Apple Pie

Filling:
2 T. flour
⅛ tsp. salt
¾ c. sugar
1 egg
1 c. sour cream
1 tsp. vanilla
¼ tsp. ground nutmeg
2 c. diced apples
1 unbaked 8-inch or 9-inch pie shell

Topping:
⅓ c. sugar
⅓ c. flour
1 tsp. ground cinnamon
¼ c. hard butter

Preheat oven to 400 degrees. For filling, in large bowl mix flour, salt, sugar, egg, sour cream, vanilla, nutmeg and apples. Pour into pie shell. Bake 12 minutes. Reduce heat to 350 degrees and bake 15 to 17 minutes. For topping, in small bowl combine sugar, flour and cinnamon. Mix well. Cut in butter until crumbles are pea size. Sprinkle topping evenly on pie hot from oven. Return to oven and bake 10 minutes at 350 degrees.

I know I shouldn't worry, Wise God. Amen.

"In my Father's house there are many dwelling places. If it were not so, would I have told you that I go to prepare a place for you?" John 14:2 NRSV

Walnut Cream Pie
¾ c. butter
1½ c. sugar
2 eggs
¼ c. light cream
1½ tsp. ground cloves
½ c. raisins
1½ c. walnut pieces
2 T. flour
2 tsp. vanilla
1 unbaked 9-inch pie shell
1 c. heavy cream, sweetened and whipped

Preheat oven to 450 degrees. In medium bowl cream butter and sugar. Beat in eggs one at a time. Slowly blend in light cream. Add cloves and mix well. In small bowl dredge raisins and walnuts in flour. Add to creamed mixture with vanilla. Mix well. Spoon mixture into pie shell. Bake 10 minutes at 450 degrees. Reduce heat to 350 degrees and bake 40 minutes. Cool. Serve with sweetened whipped cream.

God of the Future, help me not to worry about my dwelling place for today or tomorrow. Amen.

POTATOES

"Very truly, I tell you, the one who believes in me will also do the works that I do and, in fact, will do greater works than these, because I am going to the Father."

John 14:12 NRSV

Baked Sliced Potatoes
4 large baking potatoes, unpeeled
¼ c. butter or margarine, melted
¼ c. vegetable oil
2 cloves garlic, minced or pressed
½ to 1 tsp. salt
½ tsp. dried thyme

Preheat oven to 400 degrees. Butter 9 by 13-inch baking pan. Cut potatoes into ¼-inch slices. Overlap slices in prepared pan. In small bowl mix butter and oil. Brush slices with mixture. Pour remaining mixture over potatoes. Sprinkle with garlic, salt and thyme. Bake 35 to 30 minutes or until potatoes are tender and brown at edges. Serve immediately.

Forgive us, Christ Jesus, for not doing the works that you empowered us to do. Amen.

"I will do whatever you ask in my name, so that the Father may be glorified in the Son." John 14:13 NRSV

Breakfast Potatoes
4 medium potatoes, peeled, sliced thin
1 tsp. vegetable flakes
4 beef bouillon cubes

Place potato slices in large saucepan. Add water just to cover. Add vegetable flakes and bouillon cubes. Bring to boil. Cook until potatoes are tender and liquid is nearly cooked off.

Yes, we err when we seek glory for ourselves. Amen.

~~~

"If you love me, you will keep my commandments. And I will ask the Father, and he will give you another Advocate, to be with you forever. This is the Spirit of truth, whom the world cannot receive, because it neither sees him nor knows him. You know him, because he abides with you, and he will be in you." John 14:15-17 NRSV

Candied Sweet Potatoes
4 to 6 medium sweet potatoes
⅔ c. sugar
⅓ c. water
1½ T. butter or margarine.

Scrub potatoes and boil until tender. Drain water and remove skins. Cut in halves lengthwise and place in greased baking pan. Boil sugar, water and butter 5 minutes. Pour over potatoes. Bake at 400 degrees 20 minutes or until delicate brown, basting occasionally with syrup.

Microwaved Candied Sweet Potatoes
About 2 lbs. canned sweet potatoes or 2 lbs.
    fresh sweet potatoes, cooked and peeled
2 tsp. vanilla
⅔ c. firmly packed brown sugar

1½ c. maple syrup
2 T. butter (not margarine)

Drain potatoes and place in large microwavable dish. Sprinkle with vanilla and brown sugar. Pour syrup on top. Dot with butter. Cover lightly to avoid splatter. Microwave on high, in 2-minute intervals, until potatoes are heated through and butter is melted.

This gift of your Holy Spirit, Precious Lord, is with me every day. Amen.

~~~

"I will not leave you orphaned; I am coming to you."
John 14:18 NRSV

Caramel Sweet Potatoes
2 lbs. cooked whole sweet potatoes, drained, peeled
¾ c. firmly packed brown sugar
½ c. light corn syrup
¾ c. butter
1 tsp. ground cinnamon
¼ tsp. salt

Preheat oven to 350 degrees. Slice sweet potatoes and arrange in 9 by 13-inch baking ban. In medium saucepan bring brown sugar, corn syrup, butter, cinnamon and salt to boil. Reduce heat and simmer 5 minutes. Pour over sweet potatoes. Bake 20 to 25 minutes, basting often. To serve, spoon syrup over potatoes.

Nobody can take away my salvation except myself, Abba. Amen.

"But the Advocate, the Holy Spirit, whom the Father will send in my name, will teach you everything, and remind you of all that I have said to you." John 14:26 NRSV

Company Potatoes
1 bag hash brown potatoes, cubed or sliced, about 32 oz.
1 c. butter or margarine, divided
2 c. shredded cheddar cheese
½ c. chopped onion
16 oz. sour cream
½ tsp. pepper
1 can condensed cream of chicken soup
2 c. crushed corn flakes or bread crumbs

Preheat oven to 350 degrees. Place potatoes in 9 by 13-inch pan. Melt ½ cup of the butter and pour over potatoes. In medium bowl mix cheese, onion, sour cream, pepper and soup. Pour evenly over potatoes. In small bowl melt remaining ½ cup butter and stir in corn flakes. Sprinkle on potatoes. Bake 1 hour. Good as leftover. May be frozen and reheated. Good for quick freezer-to-oven meals.

You remind me that you are my protector, Gentle Whisper. Amen.

~~~

"Peace I leave with you; my peace I give to you. I do not give to you as the world gives. Do not let your hearts be troubled, and do not let them be afraid." John 14:27 NRSV

Crumb Topped Potatoes
⅓ c. butter
3 or 4 large potatoes
¾ c. dry bread crumbs
2 tsp. salt
1½ c. shredded cheese
1½ tsp. paprika

Melt butter in jellyroll pan in 375-degree oven. Cut potatoes lengthwise into ½-inch slices. Place in melted butter. Turn once to butter other side. In small bowl mix crumbs, salt, cheese and paprika. Sprinkle over potatoes. Bake at 375 degrees 30 minutes or until potatoes are tender and tops are crisp.

Peace, courage and calm are mine because of your Holy Spirit. Amen.

~~~

"I am the vine, and my Father is the vinegrower."
<div align="right">John 15:1 NRSV</div>

Decadent Mashed Potatoes
2 lbs. russet potatoes, peeled and cut in eighths
2 lbs. Yukon Gold potatoes, peeled and cut in eighths
1 tsp. plus 1 T. sea salt
¾ c. butter
1¼ c. heavy cream or whole milk
Pinch of white pepper
Thinly sliced fresh chives or basil for garnish (optional)

Place potato pieces in 6-quart saucepan and cover with cold water. Add 1 teaspoon sea salt, place lid on saucepan and bring to simmer. Cook 20 minutes. In small saucepan over low heat, melt butter with cream, 1 tablespoon sea salt and white pepper. When potatoes are cooked thoroughly, drain and pass through potato ricer or food mill with medium sieve attachment. Place sieved potatoes back into hot saucepan. Slowly pour butter-cream mixture into potatoes. Incorporate gently with wooden spoon. Adjust seasoning. Garnish with chives or basil. Serve hot.

Sometimes those pruning shears smart, God the Purifier. Amen.

"He removes every branch in me that bears no fruit."
John 15:2a NRSV

Golden Parmesan Potatoes
⅓ to ½ c. margarine
3 lbs. potatoes (about 6 large)
¼ c. flour
¼ c. Parmesan cheese, grated
¾ tsp. salt
⅛ tsp. pepper
Chopped parsley (optional)

Preheat oven to 375 degrees. Melt margarine in 9 by 13-inch pan. Peel potatoes and cut into large chunks. Mix flour, cheese, salt and pepper in large plastic bag and shake well. Toss potatoes in bag, in small batches, until well coated. Place potatoes in single layer in prepared pan. Bake 1 to 1½ hours, turning once. Sprinkle with parsley before serving.

I want to produce big, thriving fruits for you, Root of David. Amen.

~~~

"Abide in me as I abide in you."
<div align="right">John 15:4a NRSV</div>

Gourmet Cheese Potatoes
¼ c. butter
⅓ c. onion, chopped
¼ c. flour
1 to 1½ tsp. salt
¼ tsp. pepper
1½ c. milk
2 c. grated American or boxed processed cheese
4 c. cooked cubed potatoes
1 T. butter
¼ c. dry bread crumbs

Preheat oven to 350 degrees. Melt ¼ cup butter in large skillet and saute onion until soft. Add flour, salt and pepper. Gradually add milk and cook until thickened. Add cheese and stir until melted. Alternately layer potatoes and cheese mixture in 1½-quart casserole dish. In small saucepan melt 1 tablespoon butter. Add bread crumbs. Top potatoes with buttered bread crumbs. Bake about 25 minutes or until potatoes are tender.

I depend, wait, rest and count on you, my God. Amen.

~~~

"As the Father has loved me, so I have loved you; abide in my love." John 15:9 NRSV

Grated Potatoes
6 medium potatoes
¼ c. margarine
1 can condensed cream of chicken soup
1 pint sour cream
⅓ c. chopped green onions, including tops
¾ c. grated cheddar cheese
¼ c. crushed corn flakes

Preheat oven to 350 degrees. Butter 2½-quart baking dish. Boil potatoes in skins. Cool, peel and grate. In medium saucepan heat margarine with soup. Blend in sour cream, onions and cheese until cheese melts. Stir in potatoes. Pour into prepared dish. Top with corn flakes and bake 45 minutes.

Jesus, you teach me every day what it means to love another. Amen.

"I have said these things to you so that my joy may be in you, and that your joy may be complete."

John 15:11 NRSV

Hash Brown Cheese Potato Casserole

1 to 2 lbs. frozen hash brown potatoes
1 can condensed cream of chicken soup
4 T. butter, melted
1 small onion, chopped
1 c. sour cream
1 T. lemon juice
1½ c. shredded cheese, divided
1 c. crushed potato chips

Preheat oven to 350 degrees. Coat 9 by 13-inch baking pan. In large bowl mix potatoes, soup, butter, onion, sour cream, lemon juice and ¾ cup of the cheese. Pour into prepared pan. Bake 1 hour. Remove from oven. Sprinkle on remaining ¾ cup cheese and potato chips. Bake 15 minutes.

Your Good News is like a soft cloud under me, around me and over me, God My Shield. Amen.

~~~

"When the Advocate comes, whom I will send to you from the Father, the Spirit of truth who comes from the Father, he will testify on my behalf. You are also to testify because you have been with me from the beginning."

<div align="right">John 15:26, 27 NRSV</div>

Honey Mustard Potato Salad

1 lb. red potatoes, cut in quarters
1 red bell pepper, diced
3 stalks celery, diced
1 medium red onion, diced
½ tsp. salt
8 oz. honey mustard salad dressing

Boil potatoes until tender, about 15 minutes. Drain potatoes, cut into smaller pieces and place in large bowl. Add pepper, celery, onion and salt. Mix in honey mustard dressing. Stir until well mixed. Serve warm.

In all of time there was never a minute when you abandoned us, Triune God. Amen.

~~~

"So you have pain now; but I will see you again, and your hearts will rejoice, and no one will take your joy from you."
<div style="text-align: right;">John 16:22 NRSV</div>

Hot German Potato Salad with Bacon
5 strips bacon
¾ c. onion, chopped fine
2 stalks celery, chopped fine
2 heaping T. flour
⅔ c. cider vinegar
1⅓ c. water
¼ c. sugar
1 tsp. salt
⅛ tsp. pepper
8 c. sliced cooked potatoes

In large skillet or saucepan fry bacon until crisp. Remove bacon and cut or break into small pieces. Cook onion and celery in drippings over moderate heat. Slowly stir in flour. Add vinegar and water and cook, stirring constantly, until thick. Stir in sugar, salt and pepper. Simmer 10 minutes. Add potatoes and bacon. Stir well. Cook until heated through.

Your promise is as reliable as the sunrise, Living Stone. Amen.

"And this is eternal life, that they may know you, the one true God, and Jesus Christ whom you have sent."
John 17:3 NRSV

No-Fry Spicy Potato Skins
4 large russet potatoes
¼ c. olive oil
1 tsp. salt
½ tsp. pepper
1½ tsp. chili powder
1½ tsp. curry powder
1½ tsp. ground coriander

Preheat oven to 400 degrees. Bake potatoes 1 hour. Remove from oven but keep oven on. Slice potatoes in half lengthwise and cool 10 minutes. Scoop out most of the potato flesh, leaving about ¼ inch of flesh against the skin. Save potato flesh for mashed potatoes or another use. Cut each potato in half crosswise into 3 pieces. Place olive oil in small cup. Dip each potato piece in oil and place on baking sheet. In small bowl combine salt, pepper, chili powder, curry powder and coriander. Sprinkle mixture over potatoes. Bake skins 15 minutes or until crispy and brown. Serve hot.

All is ephemeral but you, Lord Our Righteousness. Amen.

When he had said this, he breathed on them and said to them, "Receive the Holy Spirit. If you forgive the sins of any, they are forgiven them; if you retain the sins of any, they are retained."
John 20:22,23 NRSV

Old Fashioned Potato Salad

5 lbs. white potatoes
2 T. oil
2 T. salt
2 tsp. pepper
1 T. garlic powder
2 T. celery seed
1 T. paprika
10 T. zesty creamy salad dressing
½ c. yellow mustard
5 hard-boiled eggs, chopped
10 sweet pickles, chopped
6 celery ribs, chopped
1 large onion, chopped

Boil potatoes with skin on until fork-tender. Drain. Refrigerate overnight. Peel potatoes. Cut into bite-size pieces and place in large bowl. Toss with oil. Add salt, pepper, garlic powder, celery seed and paprika. Toss gently. In small bowl mix salad dressing and mustard. Add to potatoes and toss gently. Add eggs, pickles, celery and onion and toss gently. Refrigerate until cold.

Breathe on me, Friend of Sinners, for I am lost without you. Amen.

"Blessed are those who have not seen and yet have come to believe." John 20:29b NRSV

Orange Pecan Sweet Potatoes

3 lbs. sweet potatoes (about 4 large), peeled, chunked, cooked
½ c. chopped pecans, toasted
1 c. firmly packed brown sugar
2 T. cornstarch
1 c. orange juice
2 T. butter
1 tsp. vanilla

Preheat oven to 350 degrees. Coat 9 by 13-inch baking dish. Add sweet potatoes and pecans. In small saucepan combine brown sugar and cornstarch. Gradually add orange juice, whisking to blend. Cook over high heat, stirring constantly, until mixture boils. Reduce heat and simmer 2 to 3 minutes. Remove from heat. Add butter and vanilla. Pour over sweet potatoes. Bake 45 minutes or until edges are browned and bubbly.

What's this I read, God? It is impossible to be alive and not see you at work. Amen.

Jesus said to him, "Feed my sheep."

John 21:17c NRSV

Oven Fries

4 or 5 russet potatoes, about 2 lbs.
3 T. olive oil
½ tsp. garlic powder
½ tsp. onion powder
½ tsp. dried marjoram
½ tsp. dried thyme
½ tsp. cayenne powder
½ tsp. paprika
Salt and pepper

Preheat broiler on low setting. Set rack in top third of oven. Scrub and rinse potatoes in cold water. Dry on paper towels. Slice potatoes in half lengthwise and into strips about ½ inch thick. If potatoes are long, cut in half again to handle fries more easily. In large bowl toss potatoes with oil and remaining ingredients. Arrange potato strips in single layer on large rimmed baking sheet. Cook under broiler 15 to 20 minutes until golden on all sides and tender when pierced with fork. Turn with spatula halfway through cooking time. Serve with ketchup, salsa or cocktail sauce if desired.

Help us, Head of the Church, to understand what food your sheep need. Amen.

During the forty days after his crucifixion he appeared to the apostles from time to time, actually alive, and proved to them in many ways that it was really he himself they were seeing. And on these occasions he talked to them about the Kingdom of God.   Acts 1:3 LB

Potato Stuffing
1 c. hot mashed potatoes (leftovers okay)
1 egg, well beaten
2 c. bread cubes
1 small onion, minced
¼ c. diced celery
1 T. minced parsley
2 T. melted butter
1 tsp. salt
½ tsp. poultry seasoning
⅛ tsp. pepper

Preheat oven to 375 degrees. In large bowl mix potatoes and beaten egg. In separate bowl soak bread in cold water. Squeeze dry. Add to potato mixture. Add remaining ingredients and mix well. Bake 25 minutes.

Variations:
1. In green peppers that have been parboiled 5 minutes; bake about 25 minutes.
2. As stuffing for chicken or turkey; bake as for bird filled with bread stuffing.
3. As stuffing or layering in meatloaf; bake according to directions for meatloaf.

Sometimes I sit on the fence about you, Head of the Body, but you have always been on my side. Amen.

"But when the Holy Spirit has come upon you, you will receive power to testify about me with great effect . . . ."

Acts 1:8a LB

Refrigerator Mashed Potatoes

9 large potatoes, boiled and mashed
15 oz. sour cream
8 oz. cream cheese
2 tsp. onion salt
1 tsp. salt
¼ tsp. pepper
2 T. butter or margarine
1 c. grated cheese

In large bowl combine all ingredients. Beat until light and fluffy. Add milk if too stiff. Spread into 9 by 13-inch baking pan. Cool. Keeps 2 weeks in refrigerator. Freezes well. Bake about 30 minutes at 350 degrees.

This power you have granted is my strength and my purpose, Lord. Amen.

"Jesus has gone away to heaven, and some day, just as he went, he will return!" Acts 1:11b LB

Scalloped Potatoes
9 c. cooked and shredded potatoes
1 tsp. salt
1 can condensed cream of mushroom soup
1 c. shredded cheese
2 c. milk
¼ c. margarine
½ medium onion, chopped
Black pepper

Preheat oven to 350 degrees. Mix all ingredients except pepper in 9 by 13-inch pan. Spread evenly in pan. Sprinkle with pepper. Bake 1½ hours.

Your days on Earth, Our Lord, were a season of wonder. Amen.

~~~

They were at the Mount of Olives when this happened, so now they walked the half mile back to Jerusalem and held a prayer meeting in an upstairs room . . . . Acts 2:12, 13 LB

Supper Potatoes
2 to 3 c. mashed potatoes (leftovers okay)
3 T. grated onion
½ tsp. minced garlic or garlic powder
1 tsp. fresh or dried parsley
½ tsp. celery flakes
1 T. vegetable oil

Drain any liquid off potatoes. In bowl mix potatoes, onion, garlic, parsley and celery flakes. Heat oil in large skillet. Drop potatoes by tablespoonfuls into oil. Fry both sides till golden.

Yes, My Redeemer, prayer is the right response when questions abound. Amen.

Suddenly there was a sound like the roaring of a mighty windstorm in the skies above them and it filled the house where they were meeting. Then, what looked like flames or tongues of fire appeared and settled on their heads. And everyone present was filled with the Holy Spirit and began speaking in languages they didn't know, for the Holy Spirit gave them this ability.

Acts 2:2-4 LB

Sweet Potato Balls
2 c. hot mashed sweet potatoes
2 T. melted butter
½ tsp. salt
1 egg, beaten
Bread crumbs or crushed corn flakes
Deep fat for frying

Combine sweet potatoes, butter, salt and egg. Beat well. Shape into balls. Roll in bread crumbs or corn flakes. Fry in deep fat at 365 to 380 degrees until golden brown. Drain on unglazed paper.

God of Truth, my tongue is afire, too, when I speak of your glory. Amen.

And Peter replied, "Each one of you must turn from sin, return to God, and be baptized in the name of Jesus Christ for the forgiveness of your sins; then you also shall receive this gift, the Holy Spirit." Acts 2:38 LB

Sweet Potato Casserole
¾ c. granulated sugar
4 c. sweet potatoes, cooked, peeled, mashed
2 eggs, beaten
¼ c. plus ⅓ c. melted margarine, divided
⅔ c. evaporated milk
1½ tsp. pumpkin pie spice
2 tsp. vanilla
¾ c. firmly packed brown sugar
1 c. chopped nuts
½ c. flour
1 c. flaked coconut (optional)

Preheat oven to 350 degrees. Butter large casserole dish. In large bowl blend granulated sugar, sweet potatoes, eggs, ¼ cup melted margarine, evaporated milk, pumpkin pie spice and vanilla. Place in prepared dish. In small bowl blend brown sugar, nuts, remaining ⅓ cup melted margarine, flour and coconut. Sprinkle over sweet potatoes. Bake 45 minutes.

God the Potter, you mold humankind with your Holy Spirit, and we are better for it. Amen.

"Faith in Jesus' name—faith given us from God—has caused this perfect healing." Acts 4:16b LB

Twice Baked Potatoes

2 large baking potatoes
4 strips bacon, cut in fourths
¼ c. chopped green onion
2 T. grated Parmesan ceese
½ c. sour cream
½ tsp. salt
½ tsp. white pepper
2 T. melted butter or margarine
Paprika

Preheat oven to 400 degrees. Scrub potatoes. Dry and prick with fork. Bake 1 hour. Let potatoes cool slightly for easy handling. In small skillet fry bacon until crisp. Drain off all fat except 3 tablespoons. Add onion and saute until tender but not brown. Remove from heat. Cut potatoes in half lengthwise. Scoop out potato skins carefully and add removed portion to skillet. Add cheese, sour cream, salt and white pepper, mixing and mashing thoroughly. Return skillet to low heat until mixture is heated through. Spoon mixture into potato shells. Drizzle with melted butter and sprinkle with paprika. Bake at 350 degrees 15 to 20 minutes or until lightly browned. Can be made ahead and heated just before serving.

I am ashamed, God My Rock, for the times I accepted congratulations for what you had brought about. Amen.

"And now, O Lord, hear their threats, and grant to your servants great boldness in their preaching, and send your healing power, and may miracles and wonders be done by the name of your holy servant Jesus." Acts 4:29,30 LB

Zesty Sweet Potato Sticks
2 large sweet potatoes, cut lengthwise in ½-inch sticks
1 tsp. chili powder
½ c. grated Parmesan cheese
¼ tsp. pepper
Salt

Preheat oven to 450 degrees. Coat baking sheet and large bowl. Place potato sticks in bowl. Add chili powder, cheese and pepper and toss to coat well. Arrange potato sticks on baking sheet in single layer. Bake 20 minutes, turn over and bake 10 minutes or until golden. Salt to taste.

We err, God of Resurrection, when we don't ask in the name of Jesus. Amen.

SALADS AND DRESSINGS

After this prayer, the building where they were meeting shook and they were all filled with the Holy Spirit and boldly preached God's message.　　　　　　　　　　　　　　　　　Acts 4:31 LB

Amish Cole Slaw
1 small head cabbage, about 2 lbs.
1 small red onion
¼ green pepper
1 medium carrot
¾ c. mayonnaise
¾ c. sugar
1 tsp. celery salt
1 tsp. mustard seed
½ tsp. salt
¼ tsp. pepper

In large bowl shred cabbage, onion, green pepper and carrot. In small bowl combine mayonnaise, sugar, celery salt, mustard seed, salt and pepper. Pour over cabbage mixture. Stir well. Refrigerate at least 2 hours before serving.

Master of Souls, give us power anew to speak of you. Amen.

All the believers were of one heart and one mind . . . .
Acts 4:32a LB

Bacon Dressing
1½ c. zesty creamy salad dressing
¼ c. light corn syrup
¼ c. milk
6 slices bacon, cooked, drained, crumbled (about ¼ c.)
1 T. finely chopped onion
¼ tsp. pepper
1 T. dried parsley (optional)

Blend all ingredients in jar or bowl. Cover and chill. Makes 2½ cups.

May all who believe, throughout the world, agree in min an heart. Amen.

~~~

But an angel of the Lord came at night, opened the gates of the jail and brought them out.
Acts 5:19 LB

Bean Salad Dressing
2 eggs
½ c. sugar
1 tsp. dry mustard
½ tsp. salt
¼ c. cider vinegar
½ c. mayonnaise
1 c. water
1 rounded T. flour

Blend all ingredients in top of double boiler. Cook over moderate heat until thick. Refrigerate in airtight container.

Thank you, Jealous God, for the angels who attend us. Amen.

God's message was preached in ever-widening circles . . . .
Acts 6:7a LB

Blue Cheese Dressing
24 oz. blue cheese
2 c. mayonnaise
1 c. sour cream
½ tsp. pepper
2 T. vegetable oil
2 T. cider vinegar
1 tsp. garlic salt
1 tsp. onion salt

Blend all ingredients in blender. Refrigerate in airtight container up to 2 weeks. Makes 2 quarts.

I smile, God, when I think how you apply your laws of physics to the Gospel. Amen.

~~~

Soon the news reached the apostles and other brothers in Judea that Gentiles also were being converted!
Acts 11:1 LB

Caesar Dressing
1½ c. mayonnaise
½ c. grated Parmesan cheese
¼ c. light corn syrup
2 T. cider vinegar
1 clove garlic, pressed
¼ tsp. pepper

In medium bowl or jar blend all ingredients. Cover and chill. Makes 2 cups.

Yesterday I heard that Christians had fled Iraq, and I remembered your goal of spreading the Good News, God Who Is Covenant of the People. Amen.

"Everyone who trusts in him is freed from all guilt and declared righteous . . . ." Acts 13:39a LB

Chicken Salad
2 c. cooked, cubed chicken
1 c. chopped celery
1 c. seedless white grapes, halved
½ c. pecans, chopped
Mayonnaise

In bowl mix chicken, celery, grapes and pecans with enough mayonnaise to bind. Good on pineapple ring or lettuce leaf.

Your grace, Gift of God, healed my guilt sickness. Amen.

~~~

And their converts were filled with joy and with the Holy Spirit. Acts 13:52 LB

Cucumber Freezer Salad
6 to 8 cucumbers, sliced thin
2 or 3 sweet onions, sliced thin
1 or 2 bell peppers, sliced thin (optional)
2 tsp. salt
1 c. cider vinegar
1½ c. sugar
Pinch of salt
½ c. shredded carrot (optional)

In flat 2-quart plastic container with lid, alternately layer slices of cucumbers, onions and bell peppers. Fill to top of container. Sprinkle 2 teaspoons salt on top. Set aside 2 hours. Meanwhile, in medium saucepan boil vinegar, sugar, salt and carrot 1½ minutes. After cucumber mixture has "rested" 2 hours, drain liquid. Pour vinegar solution over cucumber mixture. Mix well. Freeze, either in same container or in other containers or freezable bags. Aunt Barb says this is great with fried chicken.

Holy Spirit, our joy in you constantly surprises us. Amen.

And the Lord proved their message was from him by giving them great power to do miracles. Acts 14:3b LB

Foo Yung Toss

1 head romaine, torn into pieces
16 oz. bean sprouts, rinsed and drained
5 oz. water chestnuts, drained and sliced
6 slices bacon, crisp-cooked and crumbled
2 hard-cooked eggs, sliced
Salt and pepper

Dressing:
1 c. salad oil
½ c. sugar
⅓ c. ketchup
¼ c. cider vinegar
2 T. grated onion
2 tsp. Worcestershire sauce

In a salad bowl combine romaine, sprouts, water chestnuts, bacon and eggs. Season with salt and pepper. To prepare dressing combine oil, sugar, ketchup, vinegar, onion and Worcestershire sauce in a shaker jar. Shake well and pour over salad, tossing lightly.

I rest on your promises through times good and bad, Finisher of Faith. Amen.

Paul and Barnabas also appointed elders in every church and prayed for them with fasting, turning them over to the care of the Lord in whom they trusted. Acts 14:23 LB

Frosted Cranberry Salad
13 to 15 oz. crushed pineapple, drained, juice reserved
6 oz. lemon gelatin
7 oz. ginger ale
2 c. jellied cranberry sauce
2 oz. pkg. dessert topping mix, prepared according to directions
8 oz. cream cheese, softened
½ c. chopped pecans
1 T. butter melted

Add water to reserved pineapple juice to make 1 cup. In saucepan heat to boil. Dissolve gelatin in hot liquid. Cool. Stir in ginger ale. Chill until partially set. In small bowl mix pineapple and cranberry sauce. Fold into gelatin. Place in 9 by 9-inch dish. Chill until firm. In small bowl mix topping and cream cheese. Spread on chilled gelatin. Toast pecans in butter 10 minutes at 350 degrees. Sprinkle on salad. Chill.

Help us, God Who Guides, to serve before we lead. Amen.

~~~

His unique identity as the Son of God was shown by the Spirit when Jesus was raised from the dead . . . . Romans 1:3,4 TM

Fruit Salad Dressing
1 small box instant vanilla pudding mix
1½ c. milk
3 oz. orange juice concentrate, thawed
¾ c. sour cream

Beat pudding mix, milk and concentrate in mixer bowl 2 minutes at low speed. Blend in sour cream. Pour over mixed fruit.

Only you, Jesus the One. Amen.

Through him we received both the generous gift of his life and the urgent task of passing it on to others who receive it by entering into obedient trust in Jesus.

Romans 1:5 TM

Green Salad
1 small pkg. lime gelatin
1 small pkg. lemon gelatin
2 c. boiling water
1¾ c. cold water
2 T. lemon juice
Dash salt
1 can crushed pineapple, drained, about 16 oz.
1 can white seedless grapes
½ c. nuts

Dressing:
½ c. sugar
2 T. flour
1 egg, well beaten
1 c. pineapple juice
1 T. lemon juice
2 T. butter
½ c. whipped cream
1 c. grated cheese

In large bowl prepare gelatin according to package directions. Add remaining salad ingredients. Stir well. Place in 9 by 13-inch pan. Chill until firmly set. For dressing, in medium saucepan cook sugar, flour, egg, juices and butter until thick. When cool, fold in whipped cream. Pour over chilled gelatin. Sprinkle grated cheese on top.

When we trust you, the rest follows, God Our Commander. Amen.

People knew God perfectly well, but when they didn't treat him like God, refusing to worship him, they trivialized themselves into silliness and confusion . . . . Romans 1:21 TM

Hot Bacon Dressing
4 slices bacon
½ c. sugar
½ tsp. salt (optional)
1 T. cornstarch
1 egg, beaten
¼ c. cider vinegar
1 c. water
Fresh spinach, washed, drained, chilled

Fry bacon until crisp. Drain fat, reserving drippings, and crumble bacon. In small saucepan combine sugar, salt and cornstarch. Add egg and vinegar. Mix well. Add water, bacon and drippings. Cook to desired thickness. Serve over spinach.

Oh, the trouble we cause for ourselves and others when we deny you, Christ the Wisdom of God. Amen.

They made life hell on earth with their envy, wanton killing, bickering, and cheating. Look at them: mean-spirited, venomous, fork-tongued God-bashers. Bullies, swaggerers, insufferable windbags!

Romans 1:30,31 TM

Italian Dressing

1½ c. vegetable oil
½ c. cider vinegar
¼ c. grated Parmesan cheese
Fresh parsley, minced
1 clove garlic, minced
1 T. honey
½ tsp. celery salt
½ tsp. pepper
½ tsp. dry mustard
¼ tsp. paprika
¼ tsp. dried basil

Blend all ingredients in blender until smooth. Cover and chill. Makes 1¾ cups.

God of Eternal Life, our sin distorts your design and fouls your creation. Amen.

Every time you criticize someone, you condemn yourself.
Romans 2:1b TM

Kathy's Shower Salad
2 small pkg. strawberry gelatin
1 c. boiling water
1 c. crushed pineapple
4 small bananas, mashed
1 c. chopped nuts
2 pkg. frozen strawberries, about 10 oz. each
½ pint sour cream

In bowl dissolve gelatin in boiling water. Add pineapple, bananas, nuts and strawberries. Place half of mixture in 9-inch square dish and chill until firmly set. Spread sour cream on chilled gelatin. Pour remaining gelatin mixture on top and chill until set. May be served on lettuce leaf.

Our lips can build or delay your kingdom, First Begotten, so help us to speak your truth. Amen.

God is kind, but he's not soft.   Romans 2:4b TM

Macaroni Vegetable Salad
2 c. macaroni
1 pkg. frozen mixed vegetables, about 16 oz.
2 T. margarine, melted
1 green pepper, chopped
1 small sweet onion, chopped
1 stalk celery, chopped

Dressing:
1 T. flour
¾ c. sugar
¾ c. cider vinegar
¼ tsp. salt
1 T. dry mustard

Cook macaroni according to package directions. Drain and cool. Cook mixed vegetables. Drain and place in large bowl. Add melted margarine, green pepper, onion and celery. Add cooked macaroni and mix well. For dressing, in small saucepan combine flour, sugar, vinegar, salt and dry mustard. Cook over moderate heat until thick. Cool slightly and pour over macaroni and vegetables. Chill overnight before serving.

Your care for me keeps me going, God of Glory. Amen.

Doing, not hearing, is what makes the difference with God.
Romans 2:13 TM

Navy Bean Salad
1 lb. dried navy beans
6 c. hot water
½ tsp. butter
2 tsp. salt
½ tsp. pepper
½ tsp. dry mustard

Dressing:
½ c. ketchup
½ c. vegetable oil
1 tsp. paprika
½ c. sugar
2 T. minced onion
½ c. cider vinegar
½ tsp. salt

Cold additions:
1 c. chopped ham
1 medium green pepper, chopped
1 c. chopped celery
1 small jar olives, chopped

Soak beans in hot water 1 hour. In large saucepan cook over low heat with ½ teaspoon butter until tender, about 1 hour. Add salt, pepper and dry mustard. Simmer 5 minutes. Remove from heat. Drain.

While beans are cooking, blend all seven dressing ingredients in medium bowl. Pour dressing over hot, drained beans. Blend gently with rubber spatula. Cover and refrigerate overnight. Before serving, gently fold in ham, green pepper, celery and olives. May be served in lettuce-lined bowl.

Lord Our Sanctifier, you've provided a to-do list and the power to do it. Amen.

The God-setting-things-right that we read about has become Jesus-setting-things-right for us.   Romans 3:22 TM

Romaine Orange Salad
¼ c. sugar
3 oz. slivered almonds
1 T. sherry vinegar
1 T. honey
¼ tsp. salt
⅛ tsp. pepper
1 T. vegetable oil
2 T. orange juice
1 head romaine, rinsed, dried, torn into small pieces
1 bunch green onions, thinly sliced
1 small can Mandarin oranges, drained

Lightly coat sheet of aluminum foil with cooking spray. Melt sugar in small skillet over medium heat. Add almonds and stir to coat. Pour almonds onto prepared foil. Set aside to cool. When cooled, break into pieces. In jar combine vinegar, honey, salt, pepper, oil and orange juice. Shake or whisk well just before serving. Arrange romaine pieces in bowl and sprinkle with green onions and Mandarin oranges. Toss. Pour dressing over salad and toss to coat. Garnish with sugared almonds.

Thank you, Prince of the Kings of the Earth, for sticking with us in our searching and struggling. Amen.

God sacrificed Jesus on the altar of the world to clear that world of sin. Romans 3:25 TM

Spicy Sweet Ham Salad
8 oz. cooked cured ham, trimmed of fat
1 c. minced celery
¼ c. minced sweet onion
2 hard-cooked eggs, finely chopped
¼ c. drained hot pickle relish or finely chopped hot pickles
½ c. mayonnaise, or more to taste
1 tsp. yellow mustard, or more to taste
Salt and pepper to taste

In food processor pulse ham just until finely chopped but not pasty. Transfer to bowl and stir in celery, onion, eggs and pickle relish. Add mayonnaise as needed to bind mixture. Add mustard, salt and pepper.

Jesus, you are the ransom of God for our world. Amen.

He presented himself for this sacrificial death when we were far too weak and rebellious to do anything to get ourselves ready.

Romans 5:6 TM

Spinach Salad

1 large pkg. raw spinach
Escarole or lettuce
1 can water chestnuts, sliced thin
1 can bean sprouts, drained and rinsed
3 hard-boiled eggs
6 slices bacon, fried crisp, drained, crumbled

Dressing:
1 c. oil
¾ c. sugar
⅓ c. ketchup
¼ c. cider vinegar
1 small onion, chopped
1 T. Worcestershire sauce
Dash salt

Wash spinach. Wrap in towel and refrigerate for crispness. In large bowl combine spinach and remaining salad ingredients. In small bowl combine all dressing ingredients and mix well. Toss spinach with dressing.

Thank you, Messiah, for coming, for caring, for commanding our future with your sacrifice. Amen.

When we are lowered into the water, it is like the burial of Jesus; when we are raised up out of the water, it is like the resurrection of Jesus.
Romans 6:3 TM

Strawberry Pretzel Salad
2 c. crushed pretzels
¾ c. melted margarine
3 T. sugar
8 oz. cream cheese
1 c. sugar
8 oz. whipped topping, thawed
1 (6 oz.) pkg. strawberry gelatin
4 c. frozen strawberries

Preheat oven to 400 degrees. In bowl mix pretzels, margarine and 3 tablespoons sugar. Press into 9 by 13-inch baking dish. Bake 8 minutes. Cool. In large bowl blend cream cheese and 1 cup sugar. Fold topping into mixture and spread over cooled crust. Dissolve gelatin in 2 cups boiling water. Stir in strawberries and let rest 10 minutes or until mixture starts to set and strawberries separate. Pour strawberry mixture over cream cheese mixture and refrigerate 2 hours or more.

I'm never down and out, with you, God Who Conquers. Amen.

~~~

Our old way of life was nailed to the Cross with Christ . . . .
Romans 6:6 TM

Sweet Balsamic Mayonnaise
½ c. mayonnaise
¼ c. balsamic vinegar
¼ c. firmly packed brown sugar
1 T. onion powder

Whisk ingredients together. Refrigerate in airtight container.

Because of you, Dayspring of Life, I don't have to look over my shoulder. Amen.

Embracing what God does for you is the best thing you can do for him. Romans 12:1 TM

Taco Salad

1 head lettuce, torn into small pieces
1 lb. ground beef, browned and drained
1 can kidney beans, drained, about 16 oz.
2 c. taco cheese, shredded fine
10 to 12 oz. nacho-flavored tortilla chips
10 oz. Catalina salad dressing
½ medium red onion, chopped
2 large tomatoes, diced

Toss all ingredients together in large bowl. Chill and serve.

You've never held back, Fountain of Peace, and I adore you. Amen.

~~~

Don't become so well-adjusted to your culture that you fit into it without even thinking. Instead, fix your attention on God. You'll be changed from the inside out. Romans 12:2 TM

Thousand Island Dressing

½ c. zesty creamy salad dressing
2 T. cream
3 T. ketchup
1 tsp. chili powder
¼ tsp. salt
½ tsp. paprika
Dash onion powder

Blend ingredients in bowl. Cover and refrigerate. Makes 2 cups.

How exciting it is to do things your way, Jehovah Shammah. Amen.

Love from the center of who you are; don't fake it.

Romans 12:9 TM

Three Bean Wacky Salad
1 pkg. multicolor macaroni, prepared according to box directions
1 can green beans, drained, about 14.5 oz.
1 can wax beans, drained, about 14.5 oz.
1 can kidney beans, drained, about 14.5 oz.
1 c. chopped sweet onion
½ c. canola or olive oil
¾ c. cider vinegar
⅔ c. sugar
1½ c. halved cherry tomatoes
Salt and pepper

Rinse cooked pasta in cool water and drain. In large bowl combine beans and onion. In small bowl mix oil and vinegar. Slowly add sugar to dissolve. Add pasta and oil mixture to bean mixture. Add tomatoes, salt and pepper. Toss gently.

God, I dream that you smile at me. Amen.

~~~

All governments are under God.

Romans 13:1 TM

Western Dressing
2 c. zesty creamy salad dressing
1½ c. sugar
¼ c. cider vinegar
½ c. ketchup
2 tsp. prepared mustard
1 tsp. paprika
4 tsp. water
½ c. vegetable oil
½ tsp. salt

Blend ingredients in blender. Refrigerate in airtight container.

We work under God, with God and because of God. Amen.

SOUPS AND STEWS

Welcome with open arms fellow believers who don't see things the way you do.   Romans 14:1 TM

Baked Potato Soup
2 large baking potatoes
6 T. margarine, divided
1 c. sour cream
Salt and pepper
2 T. flour
½ c. chicken stock
2 c. milk, scalded
3 green onions, chopped, tops included
3 oz. sharp cheddar cheese, shredded

Wash, pierce and bake potatoes at 350 degrees 1½ hours. Split hot potatoes in half lengthwise and scoop contents into bowl. Add 4 tablespoons of the margarine, sour cream, salt and pepper. Mix until smooth. In large saucepan melt remaining 2 tablespoons margarine. Add flour and blend into paste over medium heat. Add stock and stir over low heat until smooth. Whisk in scalded milk. Add potato mixture. Stir over medium heat until warm. Add green onions and cheese. Stir until cheese melts.

You remind me, Elohim, of the courtesies you require of believers for each other. Amen.

Those of us who are strong and able in the faith need to step in and lend a hand to those who falter; and not just do what is most convenient for us. Romans 15:1 TM

Campfire Chicken Noodle Stew
3 cans condensed cream of chicken soup, undiluted
7 c. boiling water
1 tsp. salt
1 tsp. dill weed
4 c. fine egg noodles (8 oz.)

In large pot combine soup, water, salt and dill weed. Bring to boil. Gradually add noodles so mixture continues to boil. Cook uncovered, stirring frequently, until noodles are tender.

You give us strength, Brightness of the Father's Glory, not just for ourselves but for each other, too. Amen.

~~~

Stand fast then, and do not . . . submit again to a yoke of slavery. Galatians 5:1 AB

Cheese Soup
6 c. chicken broth
1 c. finely diced carrots
1 c. finely chopped onions
1 c. finely diced celery
4 T. butter
1 c. flour
6 c. milk
Dash paprika
1 to 1½ lb. medium cheddar cheese, cut in chunks
Salt and pepper
Parsley or no-hull popcorn for garnish

Place chicken broth in large pot and cook carrots, onions and celery at slow boil until tender. In saucepan melt butter. Add flour, stirring and cooking a few minutes, until paste forms. Whisk into vegetable mixture. Add milk and paprika. Stir cheese into mixture. Cook over low heat, stirring constantly to avoid scorching, until thick. Add flour to thicken or water to thin. Add salt and pepper. Serve in bowls and garnish with chopped parsley or no-hull popped corn.

Better to be your humblest servant, Christ Jesus Our Lord, than the world's proudest ruler. Amen.

~~~

And let us not lose heart and grow weary and faint in acting nobly and doing right, for in due time and at the appointed season we shall reap, if we do not loosen and relax our courage and faint. <span>Galatians 6:9 AB</span>

Cheesy Baked Potato Soup
⅔ c. butter or margarine
⅔ c. flour
7 c. milk
4 large baking potatoes, baked, peeled, cubed
4 green onions, sliced
12 bacon strips, cooked, crumbled
1¼ c. shredded cheddar cheese
¾ tsp. salt
¾ tsp. pepper

Melt butter in large soup pot or Dutch oven. Add flour. Cook and stir until smooth. Gradually add milk, stirring constantly. Cook until thickened. Add potatoes and green onions. Bring to boil, stirring constantly. Reduce heat. Simmer 10 minutes. Add bacon, cheese, salt and pepper. Stir until cheese melts. If soup is too thick, thin with additional milk.

The only way with you, Heir of All Things, is forward. Amen.

He has let us know the mystery of his purpose.

Ephesians 1:9a NJB

Chicken Chowder with Cheese
2 c. chicken broth
2 chicken bouillon cubes
3 T. butter
1 c. celery, diced
2 c. carrots, shredded
1 medium onion, diced
2 T. flour
1 c. milk
Poultry seasoning
2 c. cooked chicken, cut in pieces
1 pkg. frozen mixed vegetables, about 10 oz.
Salt and pepper
8 oz. cheddar cheese, shredded

In saucepan heat chicken broth and dissolve bouillon cubes. Set aside. Melt butter in large pot. Add celery, carrots and onion and saute until tender. Stir in flour. Gradually add milk and stir constantly until thickened. Add poultry seasoning, chicken, broth mixture, mixed vegetables, salt and pepper. Heat thoroughly. Stir in cheese just before serving.

Let my purpose reflect yours in all that I say and do, Jesus of Nazareth. Amen.

Because it is by grace that you have been saved, through faith; not by anything of your own, but by a gift from God.
Ephesians 2:8 NJB

Clam Chowder
1 dozen clams
2 T. butter
4 T. chopped onion
3 c. boiled potatoes, cubed
1½ tsp. salt
⅛ tsp. pepper
4 c. scalded milk
2 T. flour

Strain liquor from clams and set it aside. Clean and pick over clams, straining repeatedly to remove sand and shell particles. Mince clams and place in saucepan with clam liquor. Cook 10 minutes. In separate saucepan melt butter and saute onion until delicate brown. Strain butter into clams. Add potatoes, salt, pepper and scalded milk. Bring to boil. In small bowl mix flour with a little cold water to make smooth paste. Add to chowder. Stir gently until chowder thickens. Serve immediately.

Your grace—ah, my God, 'tis the only true basis for joy. Amen.

We are God's work of art, created in Christ Jesus for the good works which God has already designated to make our way of life. Ephesians 2:10 NJB

Country Clam Chowder
2 cubic inches chopped salt pork or 6 slices bacon
¼ c. chopped green pepper
½ c. chopped onion
1½ c. water
2 c. raw potatoes, diced
½ c. diced carrot
½ c. sliced celery
2 T. chopped parsley
1 tsp. salt
¼ tsp. pepper
¼ tsp. thyme
2 c. milk
1 T. butter
1 can clams, minced, about 10 oz.
6 to 8 soda crackers, broken
⅛ c. sherry (optional)

In skillet fry salt pork or bacon. Remove cooked meat. Saute green pepper and onion in remaining fat. Place water in large saucepan and boil potatoes, water, carrot, celery, parsley, salt, pepper and thyme. Add meat mixture to potato mixture. Cook several minutes. Add milk, butter, clams and crackers. Simmer several minutes over low heat. Add sherry. Serve hot.

To think that you see us sinners as beautiful, this is yet a mystery to me, Adonai. Amen.

For I am confident of this very thing, that He who began a good work in you will perfect it until the day of Christ Jesus.
Philippians 1:6 NAS

Cream of Celery Soup
2 T. butter or margarine
½ c. chopped celery, with tops if desired
2 c. milk plus extra milk for thinning, divided
2 heaping tsp. cornstarch
Salt and pepper

In medium saucepan heat butter and saute celery until soft. In small bowl stir 1 cup of the milk and cornstarch until smooth. Add cornstarch mixture to celery mixture in saucepan. Cook on medium heat, stirring constantly, until soup begins to thicken. Add about 1 cup milk, more or less, to obtain desired consistency. Add salt and pepper. Serve hot.

I am liberated by your care of my future, King of Kings. Amen.

~~~

For to me, to live is Christ, and to die is gain.
Philippians 1:21 NAS

Cream of Pea Soup
1½ c. green peas
1 onion slice
1 c. chicken broth
1 T. butter
1 T. flour
2½ c. half-and-half or diluted evaporated milk

In medium saucepan cook peas with onion. Drain. Puree in blender with chicken broth. In same saucepan melt butter. Stir in flour and pea puree. Bring to boil. Add half-and-half. May be served hot or cold.

I do not worry, Lord of Lords, for you are my companion. Amen.

He humbled himself by becoming obedient to the point of death, even death on a cross.
Philippians 2:8b NAS

Cream of Potato Soup

5 medium potatoes, pared and cubed
1 onion, sliced thin, divided
2 tsp. salt
3 T. butter or margarine
1⅔ c. evaporated milk
1 c. water
1 T. chopped parsley

In 3-quart saucepan barely cover potatoes and most of the onion slices with water. Add salt. Bring to boil. Reduce heat and simmer 15 minutes or until potatoes are tender. Mash or strain potatoes. Add butter, milk, water and remaining onion slices. Heat about 10 minutes. Add parsley. Serve hot.

God the Lawgiver, how amazing you are to ask only obedience when you could command servitude. Amen.

~~~

Therefore also God highly exalted Him, and bestowed on Him the name which is above every name . . . .
Philippians 2:9 NAS

Cream of Tomato Soup

2 c. pulpy tomato juice
½ tsp. baking soda
4 c. whole milk
Salt
Pepper
Butter

In large saucepan boil tomato juice. Add baking soda. Stir and quickly add milk. Add salt and pepper. Heat and add butter. Serve with crackers or toast.

Variation: Use fresh tomatoes. Brown 1 tablespoon butter in large saucepan. Add 4 cups peeled, chopped tomatoes. Add salt and cook until tomatoes are soft and thin juice has evaporated. Mash tomatoes with potato masher. Add soda and milk. Heat through. Serve with crackers or toast.

Our trophies, and plaques, and citations, and medals embarrass me when I think of you, Light of the World. Amen.

~~~

That at the name of Jesus every knee should bow, of those who are in heaven, and on earth, and under the earth . . . .
<div style="text-align: right;">Philippians 2:10 NAS</div>

French Onion Soup
5 c. thinly sliced onions
¼ tsp. sugar
¼ c. butter
3 cans condensed beef broth
3 broth cans water
½ tsp. salt
Pepper
6 slices French bread, toasted, buttered, cubed
½ c. grated Swiss cheese
2 T. grated Parmesan cheese

Place onion slices in large skillet. Sprinkle with sugar. Add butter and saute slowly until golden brown. Add broth and water. Cover. Simmer gently 45 minutes. Add salt and pepper. Pour soup into bowls or tureen. Top with cubed bread. Sprinkle with cheeses. Heat in oven a few minutes at 400 degrees until cheese melts.

Jesus, thank you for being my helper, my teacher, my redeemer, my friend. Amen.

And that every tongue should confess that Jesus Christ is Lord, to the glory of God the Father. Philippians 2:11 NAS

Ham Stew
8 c. ham broth or chicken broth
4 c. cooked ham, cut in bite-size cubes
4 c. raw potatoes, cubed
4 c. green beans
4 c. carrot chunks (optional)
Salt and pepper
2 T. or more cornstarch
2 T. butter or margarine

Place broth in large pot. Add ham, potatoes, green beans and carrots and cook until tender. Add salt and pepper. Thicken with paste made of 4 tablespoons water and 2 tablespoons cornstarch, adding more paste as desired. Add butter before serving. Good with buttermilk biscuits.

Yes, Jesus, you are Christ the Lord, Son of the Most High God, Word of God incarnate, vessel of God's Holy Spirit. Amen.

~~~

Do all things without grumbling or disputing . . . .
 Philippians 2:14 NAS

Healthy Chicken Chowder
1 c. low-fat milk
6 T. flour
2 c. cooked white chicken, cut in pieces
1 can cream-style yellow corn
1 can sweet corn, undrained
2 c. frozen southern-style hash browns
1 can fat-free/low-sodium chicken broth, about 14.5 oz.
½ c. chopped yellow onion
1 c. chopped red bell pepper
Salt and pepper

In 4-quart saucepan blend milk and flour. Add chicken, corn, hash browns, broth, onion and red pepper. Stir until well blended. Heat, simmering for 15 minutes or until hot and thick. Stir occasionally. Add salt and pepper.

Heal my sickness, Great Physician, that I may glorify you. Amen.

~~~

Rejoice in the Lord.   Philippians 3:1a NAS

Hearty Bean and Frank Soup
2 frankfurters, sliced
1 tsp. butter
1 can condensed bean with bacon soup
1 can condensed pea soup
1 can milk
1 can water

Cut frankfurters in ⅛-inch slices and cook in butter in large saucepan. Add bean with bacon soup, pea soup, milk and water. Heat and serve immediately.

At the end of the day, and at the break of the morn, my soul delights in you, Jehovah's Fellow. Amen.

I count all things to be loss in view of the surpassing value of knowing Christ Jesus my Lord, for whom I have suffered the loss of all things, and count them but rubbish in order that I may gain Christ.   Philippians 3:8 NAS

High Fiber Chili
½ lb. lean ground beef
½ lb. lean ground turkey
1 c. chopped onions
½ c. chopped green pepper
1 c. total bran cereal
1 can kidney beans, drained and rinsed, about 15.5 oz.
1 can tomato sauce, about 8 oz.
1 can diced tomatoes, about 14.5 oz.
½ c. water
1 tsp. salt
2 T. chili powder
¼ tsp. garlic powder
1 bay leaf

In 4-quart saucepan over medium heat, cook ground beef, ground turkey, onions and green pepper, stirring frequently, until meat is no longer pink. Drain fat and liquid. Stir cereal and remaining ingredients into meat mixture. Bring to boil, stirring frequently. Cover and reduce heat to low. Cook 1 hour, stirring frequently. Remove bay leaf before serving.

There is no loneliness for those who know you, God Who Sanctifies. Amen.

First the Christian dead will rise, then we who are left shall join them, caught up in the clouds to meet the Lord in the air.
> 1 Thessalonians 4:17 NEB

Lentil Soup
1½ c. lentils, washed
4 T. olive oil
2 cloves garlic, minced
1 large red onion, finely chopped
1 bay leaf
2 large celery stalks, finely chopped
1 or 2 medium carrots, finely chopped
2 sprigs fresh thyme or ¼ tsp. dried thyme
½ c. fresh minced parsley
12 to 14 c. water
1 or 2 fresh tomatoes, peeled and chopped
½ c. uncooked elbow macaroni
2 T. soy sauce
Kosher sea salt
Fresh ground pepper

In large pot soak lentils overnight. Drain. In large soup pot heat oil with garlic and onion. Add bay leaf, celery and carrot and saute. Add soaked lentils and mix well. Add thyme and parsley. Cook over medium heat until vegetables are tender. Add water and tomatoes. Bring to boil. Cover and simmer 45 minutes. Stir in macaroni and soy sauce and bring to boil. Simmer uncovered 30 minutes. Add salt and pepper.

God of Truth, thank you for the second birth that holds no death. Amen.

Church helpers must also be of a good character and sincere . . . .
1 Timothy 3:8a TEV

One Nation Chicken Stew

2 T. fat, preferably chicken fat
½ c. diced onion
½ c. diced carrot
½ c. diced celery
1 to 2 T. diced green pepper
2 c. apples, peeled, cored, sliced
16 oz. canned tomatoes
2 tsp. salt
Pinch of ground black pepper
¼ tsp. curry powder
2¼ qts. plus 1 c. water
3 oz. chicken base*
⅔ c. flour
2 c. cooked diced chicken
Parsley for garnish

Heat fat in large pot or Dutch oven. Saute onion, carrot, celery, green pepper and apples until tender, about 7 minutes. Add tomatoes, salt, pepper, curry powder, 2¼ quarts water and chicken base. Mix well. In small bowl combine flour and remaining 1 cup water. Mix until smooth. Add to vegetable mixture, stirring constantly. Bring to boil. Reduce heat and simmer 1 hour. Add chicken. Heat through. Garnish with parsley.

*Chicken base can be found at some specialty stores. To substitute, use 2¼ quarts canned low-sodium chicken broth for the water and omit the base.

Many are your gifts, Holy Spirit, and many are the world's needs of them. Amen.

Their wives must also be of good character, and not gossip . . . .
1 Timothy 3:11a TEV

Onion Soup

2 T. butter
1 lb. onions
1 T. flour
1½ qts. chicken stock
2 beef broth cubes
Salt and pepper
Parmesan cheese (optional)

Heat butter in large soup pot. Slice onions and saute in butter until brown. Sprinkle with flour and stir. Slowly add chicken stock and stir until smooth. Dissolve beef broth cubes in mixture. Season with salt and pepper. Flavor improves if soup is allowed to stand several hours before serving. May be served with sliced French bread sprinkled with Parmesan cheese and oven-toasted. Additional Parmesan cheese may be sprinkled on soup at table.

The sin of gossip weighs heavily, God of Salvation. Amen.

Everything that God created is good . . . .   1 Timothy 4:4a TEV

Potato Bean Soup
2 tsp. margarine
½ c. sliced celery
2 medium carrots, shredded
1 clove garlic, minced
4 c. chicken broth
3 medium potatoes, peeled and cubed, about 3 c.
2 tsp. snipped fresh dill or 2 tsp. dried dill weed
15 oz. canned cannelloni or great northern beans, drained
½ c. lower-calorie sour cream or plain nonfat yogurt
1 T. flour
⅛ tsp. pepper
Salt (optional)

Heat margarine in large saucepan. Add celery, carrots and garlic and cook over medium heat 4 minutes or until tender. Carefully stir in broth, potatoes and dill. Heat to boiling. Reduce heat. Simmer covered 20 to 25 minutes or until potatoes are tender. With back of spoon, lightly mash about half the potatoes in the broth. Add drained beans to potato mixture. In small bowl stir sour cream, flour and pepper. Add salt. Stir into potato mixture. Cook and stir until thick and bubbly. Cook and stir 1 minute.

All the factories of the world are but a dark shadow of your bright creation, Jehovah Sabbaoth. Amen.

Do not neglect the spiritual gift that is in you . . . .
                              1 Timothy 4:14a TEV

Quick Minestrone Soup
1 can commercial minestrone soup
1 can commercial tomato-with-basil soup
1 can black beans
1 small can diced tomatoes with Italian seasoning, about 15 oz.
1 can white corn, about 16 oz.
1 can Italian green beans, cut, about 16 oz.
½ tsp. Italian seasoning
2 c. croutons
¼ c. butter, melted
Grated or shredded cheese

In large soup pot combine soups, beans, tomatoes, corn, green beans and Italian seasoning. Cook until bubbly. Pour into casserole dish and chill. In bowl or plastic bag toss croutons with melted butter until coated. Bake casserole, uncovered, at 350 degrees 30 minutes. Sprinkle with croutons, then cheese. Bake 10 minutes.

Thank you, Holy Branch, for ability and power to work for your kingdom. Amen.

For the love of money is the source of all kinds of evil.
1 Timothy 6:10a TEV

Quick Tortellini Bean Soup
1 c. sliced carrots
2 cans chicken broth, about 14.5 oz. each
1 can great northern beans, about 16 oz.
9 oz. cheese tortellini
Salt and pepper

In large pot cook carrots in broth on medium heat until tender. Add beans and bring to boil. Add tortellini and cook until pasta is tender. Add salt and pepper.

If we all loved you most, all would be well, Christ of God. Amen.

~~~

Strive for righteousness, godliness, faith, love, endurance, and gentleness.
1 Timothy 6:11 TEV

Sausage and Bean Chowder
1 lb. sausage, browned and drained
2 cans stewed tomatoes, about 30 oz. each
1 large onion, chopped
1 bay leaf
½ tsp. garlic salt
½ tsp. pepper
2 cans kidney beans, about 16 oz. each
4 c. water
½ green pepper, chopped
1 tsp. salt
¼ tsp. thyme
2 c. cubed potatoes

Mix ingredients in Dutch oven. Cook over low heat 1½ hours.

Our sins are compounded by our strivings, Rabboni. Amen.

Run your best in the race of faith, and win eternal life for yourself; for it was to this life that God called you when you made your profession of faith before many witnesses.

1 Timothy 6:12 TEV

Split Pea and Ham Soup

2 c. split peas
2 lb. ham shank
½ tsp. salt
½ tsp. dried basil
¼ tsp. pepper
2 qts. water
2 stalks celery, sliced thin
1 onion, chopped
1 carrot, finely chopped (optional)

In large saucepan or stockpot combine all ingredients. Cover and simmer 2 hours or until peas are tender. Cut meat from bone and return to soup.

I ran the race of faith until I could only walk the race, but each step is still for you, Minister of the Sanctuary. Amen.

Obey the commandment and keep it pure and faultless, until the Day of our Lord Jesus Christ will appear.

1 Timothy 6:14 TEV

Wild Rice Soup
2 T. butter or margarine
2 medium stalks celery, sliced thin
1 medium carrot, coarsely shredded
1 medium onion, chopped (about ½ c.)
1 small green pepper, chopped
3 T. flour
1 tsp. salt
¼ tsp. pepper
1½ c. cooked wild rice
1 c. water
1 can condensed chicken broth
1 c. half-and-half
⅓ c. toasted slivered almonds
¼ c. snipped parsley

Heat butter in 3-quart saucepan. Add celery, carrot, onion and green pepper and cook until celery is tender, about 5 minutes. Stir in flour, salt, pepper, wild rice, water and broth. Bring to boil. Reduce heat. Cover and simmer, stirring occasionally, 15 minutes. Stir in half-and-half, almonds and parsley. Heat just until hot.

I know your day is coming, Lord of Righteousness, because you have told us so. Amen.

SWEET BREADS AND MUFFINS

His appearing will be brought about at the right time by God, the blessed and only Ruler, the King of kings and the Lord of lords.
1 Timothy 6:15 TEV

Apple Muffins
1 c. apples, peeled, chopped fine
¼ c. sugar
1¾ c. flour
2 T. sugar
1 T. baking powder
½ tsp. salt
½ tsp. ground cinnamon
1 c. milk
¼ c. vegetable oil
1 egg, lightly beaten

Preheat oven to 425 degrees. Coat 12 muffin cups. Place apples in small bowl and sprinkle with ¼ cup sugar. Set aside. In large bowl mix flour, 2 tablespoons sugar, baking powder, salt and cinnamon. Add milk, oil and egg. Stir just enough to moisten dry ingredients. Stir in apple mixture. Drop into prepared muffin cups. Bake 20 to 25 minutes.

Offspring of David, I am eager for your return. Amen.

Command those who are rich in the things of life not to be proud, and to place their hope, not on such an uncertain thing as riches, but on God, who generously gives us everything for us to enjoy. 2 Timothy 6:17 TEV

Banana Muffins
½ c. butter, at room temperature
½ c. sugar
2 eggs, beaten
2 c. flour
1 tsp. baking powder
¾ tsp. baking soda
½ tsp. salt
¼ c. buttermilk or sour milk*
1 c. mashed ripe banana, about 2 large
1 tsp. vanilla
1 c. toasted chopped nuts (optional)

Preheat oven to 375 degrees. Coat muffin pans or line with paper or foil liners. In large mixer bowl cream butter and sugar. Add eggs and beat well. Into separate bowl sift flour, baking powder, baking soda and salt. In separate bowl stir together buttermilk, bananas and vanilla. Add dry ingredients to butter mixture alternately with banana mixture, stirring just until combined after each addition. Stir in nuts. Fill muffin cups three-fourths full. Bake 20 minutes or until tester inserted in center comes out clean.

*To make sour milk, add 1 teaspoon vinegar or lemon juice to ¼ cup milk and let stand 5 minutes.

Our pride, Holy Overseer, causes you much pain, and we have no excuse. Amen.

For the Spirit that God has given us does not make us timid; instead, his Spirit fills us with power and love and self-control.
>2 Timothy 1:7 TEV

Becky's Banana Bread
1½ c. sifted flour
½ tsp. baking soda
½ tsp. baking powder
¼ tsp. salt
½ c. butter
1 c. sugar
2 eggs
1 tsp. vanilla
Grated rind of ½ lemon
¾ c. mashed banana
2 T. sour cream
½ c. chopped pecans, walnuts or Macadamia nuts

Preheat oven to 350 degrees. Coat loaf pan. Into large bowl sift flour, baking soda, baking powder and salt. Set aside. In medium bowl cream butter until soft. Add sugar a little at a time. Beat until smooth. Beat in eggs 1 at a time. Add vanilla, lemon rind and bananas. Stir butter mixture and sour cream alternately into flour mixture. Mix in nuts. Pour into prepared pan. Bake 1 hour. Remove from pan and cool on rack. Cut in thin slices to serve.

No inheritance is larger than your power, love and self-control, Only Begotten. Amen.

Do not be ashamed, then, of witnessing for our Lord . . . .
2 Timothy 1:8a TEV

Blueberry Muffins
3 c. flour, sifted
4 tsp. baking powder
1 tsp. salt
1 c. sugar
2 eggs
1 c. milk
½ c. vegetable oil
2 c. blueberries

Preheat oven to 375 degrees. Coat muffin cups or muffin pan. In large bowl combine flour, baking powder, salt and sugar. In small bowl beat eggs, milk and oil. Add egg mixture to flour mixture. Stir only enough to moisten. Batter should be slightly lumpy. Fold in blueberries. Spoon batter into muffin cups about two-thirds full. Bake 25 minutes.

May my demeanor, my words, my appearance, my actions, my choices be pleasing unto you, Jehovah Yahweh. Amen.

~~~

He saved us and called us to be his own people, not because of what we have done, but because of his own purpose and grace.
2 Timothy 1:9a TEV

Bran Cereal Muffins
1 c. flour
⅓ c. firmly packed brown sugar
1 T. baking powder
½ tsp. salt
2½ c. bran flakes or raisin bran cereal
1 c. milk
1 egg
⅓ c. vegetable oil

Preheat oven to 400 degrees. Coat 12 muffin cups. In small bowl combine flour, brown sugar, baking powder and salt. In large bowl combine bran flakes and milk. Let stand 3 minutes. Add egg and oil to cereal mixture. Mix well. Add flour mixture to cereal mixture. Mix well. Batter will be thick. Fill prepared muffin cups about two-thirds full. Bake 25 minutes or until golden brown. Serve warm.

Variation: Nuts or fruit may be added.

This salvation on which we rest, and in which we delight, was your idea alone, Holy Shepherd. Amen.

~~~

For Christ has ended the power of death, and through the Good News he has revealed immortal life.
<div style="text-align: right;">2 Timothy 1:10b TEV</div>

Bran Muffins
2 c. whole wheat flour
1½ c. pure unprocessed bran
2 T. honey
½ tsp. salt
1¼ tsp. baking powder
2 c. buttermilk
1 egg
½ c. dark molasses
2 T. melted butter

Preheat oven to 350 degrees. Coat 24 muffin cups. In large bowl combine flour, bran, honey, salt and baking powder. In medium bowl combine buttermilk, egg, molasses and butter. Add buttermilk mixture to flour mixture. Stir just enough to moisten. Fill prepared muffin cups with batter about two-thirds full. Bake 20 to 25 minutes until light brown.

The minute you died for us, Messiah Jesus, worry lost its power. Amen.

But I am still full of confidence, for I know whom I have trusted, and I am sure that he is able to keep safe until that Day what he has entrusted to me.   2 Timothy 1:12 b TEV

Carrot Raisin Muffins

2 c. flour
1 c. rolled oats
⅔ c. sugar
1 T. baking powder
½ tsp. ground cinnamon
½ tsp. ground nutmeg
¼ tsp. salt
⅔ c. skim milk
3 T. vegetable oil
2 egg whites
¼ c. unsweetened applesauce
⅓ c. golden raisins
1¼ c. shredded carrot

Preheat oven to 400 degrees. Line 12 muffin cups with baking liners or lightly coat with cooking spray. In large mixer bowl combine flour, oats, sugar, baking powder, cinnamon, nutmeg and salt. In smaller bowl combine milk, oil, egg whites and applesauce. Blend milk mixture into flour mixture, stirring just until moistened. Stir in raisins and carrots. Spoon batter into prepared muffin cups, filling each about three-quarters full. Bake 16 to 18 minutes or until golden.

Each morning brings a day full of your promise, Root of Jesse. Amen.

Keep the good things that have been entrusted to you, through the power of the Holy Spirit who lives in us.
2 Timothy 1:14 TEV

Cranberry Bread

2 c. flour
1 c. sugar
1 T. grated orange peel
1½ tsp. baking powder
1 tsp. salt
½ tsp. baking soda
¾ c. butter, softened
1 egg
1 c. fresh or frozen cranberries, chopped
½ to 1 c. chopped nuts

Coat 10-inch ring pan or 9-inch baking pan. Preheat oven to 325 degrees for ring pan or 350 degrees for all other pans. In large bowl combine all ingredients except cranberries and nuts. Mix well. Stir in cranberries and nuts. Pour into prepared pan. Bake 35 to 45 minutes or until tester inserted in center comes out clean. Remove from pan immediately. Serve warm or cool.

What you give me, Holy Vine of God, cannot be stolen, destroyed or imitated. Amen.

Take your part in suffering, as a loyal soldier of Christ Jesus.
2 Timothy 2:3 TEV

Easy Drop Danish
2 c. baking mix
¼ c. margarine, softened
2 T. sugar
⅔ c. milk
½ c. raspberry jam
⅔ c. powdered sugar
1 T. warm water
¼ tsp. vanilla

Preheat oven to 400 degrees. Lightly coat cookie sheet. In medium bowl stir baking mix, margarine and sugar until crumbly. Stir in milk until ball forms. Beat 12 strokes. Drop rounded tablespoonfuls 2 inches apart on prepared cookie sheet. Use back of spoon to make well in center of each. Fill with 1 heaping teaspoon jam. Bake 10 to 12 minutes until golden. While Danish are warm, drizzle with glaze made by beating powdered sugar, water and vanilla until smooth.

I chafed when you asked me to suffer for your sake, Wonderful God, but now I am glad. Amen.

~~~

An athlete who runs in a race cannot win the prize unless he obeys the rules.
2 Timothy 2:5 TEV

Fresh Apple Loaves
1 spice cake mix
2 large apples, peeled, cored, finely chopped
3 eggs
¾ c. vegetable oil
¼ c. flour
⅔ c. water
2 tsp. ground cinnamon
½ c. raisins (optional)

Preheat oven to 350 degrees. Coat two 9 by 5-inch loaf pans. In large bowl stir all ingredients until blended. Divide between prepared pans. Bake 30 to 40 minutes or until tester inserted in center comes out clean. Cool loaves in pans about 2 hours before removing.

You asked me to run the race fairly, squarely and faithfully, Jesus the Lamb of God. Amen.

~~~

The farmer who has done the hard work should have the first share of the harvest.   2 Timothy 2:6 TEV

Great Gingerbread Muffins
2 c. flour
1 T. baking powder
½ tsp. baking soda
½ c. margarine or butter
2 T. brown sugar
1 c. sour cream
½ c. light molasses
2 eggs
3 c. raisin bran or similar cereal

Preheat oven to 375 degrees. Coat 12 muffin cups and top of pan. In large mixer bowl combine flour, baking powder and baking soda. In large mixer bowl beat margarine 30 seconds. Add brown sugar. Beat until fluffy. Beat in sour cream and molasses until blended. Beat in eggs. Stir flour mixture into creamed mixture just until moistened. Fold in cereal. Fill prepared muffin cups even with top of pan. Bake about 25 minutes or until tester inserted in center of muffin comes out clean. Remove from pan. Serve warm.

The fields ripe with harvest are ready, Lord; we await your will and your glory. Amen.

This is a true saying:
"If we have died with him, we shall also live with him . . . ."
2 Timothy 2:11 TEV

Holiday Pumpkin Bread
3½ c. flour
1 tsp. baking powder
2 tsp. baking soda
1 tsp. ground cloves
1 tsp. ground cinnamon
1 tsp. ground nutmeg
½ tsp. salt
2 c. canned pumpkin
1 c. vegetable oil
3 c. sugar
3 eggs
1 c. chopped nuts
1 c. raisins

Orange glaze (optional):
1½ c. powdered sugar
1 tsp. grated orange peel
2 T. orange juice
Chopped walnuts

Preheat oven to 350 degrees. Coat 2 loaf pans. In medium bowl mix flour, baking powder, baking soda, cloves, cinnamon, nutmeg and salt. In large mixer bowl mix pumpkin, oil, sugar and eggs until well blended. Add dry ingredients and mix well. By hand, stir in nuts and raisins. Divide batter between prepared pans. Bake 50 to 55 minutes or until tester inserted in center comes out clean. Cool pans on wire racks 15 minutes. Remove from pans and cool completely.

For glaze, combine all ingredients in small bowl. Stir until blended. Spoon over tops of cooled loaves, letting excess run down over sides. Sprinkle with more nuts before glaze hardens.

I still cannot comprehend all your works and ways, Holy Stone, but I can trust and obey. Amen.

"If we continue to endure, we shall also rule with him;
 If we deny him, he also will deny us . . . ."
2 Timothy 2:12 TEV

Lemon Bread

½ c. shortening
1 c. sugar
2 eggs, lightly beaten
¼ c. flour
1 tsp. baking powder
¼ tsp. salt
½ c. milk
½ c. chopped nuts
Grated rind of 1 lemon
Juice of 1 lemon
¼ c. sugar

Preheat oven to 350 degrees. Grease and flour loaf pan. In large mixer bowl cream shortening and 1 cup sugar. Stir in eggs. In medium bowl combine flour, baking powder and salt. Mix well. Alternately add milk and flour mixture to creamed mixture, mixing well after each addition. Add nuts and lemon rind. Mix well. Pour batter into prepared pan. Bake 1 hour. Remove from oven and pierce top with small holes. Combine lemon juice and ¼ cup sugar and pour over hot bread. Cool.

You ask us to stay faithful through all circumstances, Holy Scepter, and we need new strength to do that in these troubled times. Amen.

"If we are faithful, he remains faithful,
For he cannot be false to himself." 2 Timothy 2:13 TEV

Monkey Bread
4 tubes refrigerated biscuits, 10 each
2 T. ground cinnamon, divided
1¾ c. sugar, divided
¾ c. margarine

Preheat oven to 350 degrees. Coat tube pan. Cut biscuits into pieces. Place biscuit pieces in plastic bag with 1 tablespoon of the cinnamon and 1 cup of the sugar. Shake bag to coat biscuit pieces. Place dough in prepared pan. In medium saucepan combine remaining ¾ cup sugar, margarine and remaining 1 tablespoon cinnamon. Bring to boil. Pour over dough in pan. Bake 40 to 50 minutes.

My tears today are joyful because you are faithful, God My Salvation. Amen.

~~~

Do your best to win full approval in God's sight, as a worker who is not ashamed of his work, one who correctly teaches the message of God's truth. 2 Timothy 2:15 TEV

Morning Muffins
1 c. whole wheat flour
1 c. all-purpose flour
1¼ c. sugar
2 tsp. baking soda
½ tsp. salt
2 c. grated carrots
½ c. raisins
½ c. chopped nuts
½ c. shredded coconut
1 apple, peeled, grated
3 eggs
1 c. vegetable oil
2 tsp. vanilla

Preheat oven to 350 degrees. Coat 16 muffin cups or muffin pans with 16 openings. In large bowl combine whole wheat flour, all-purpose flour, sugar, baking soda and salt. Stir in carrots, raisins, nuts, coconut and apple. In small bowl combine eggs, oil and vanilla. Add to flour mixture and stir just enough to moisten. Fill muffin cups nearly full with batter. Bake 20 minutes or until light brown.

To teach of you, God of Righteousness, is happiness. Amen.

~~~

Keep away from godless and foolish discussions, which only drive people farther away from God.
<div align="right">2 Timothy 2:16 TEV</div>

Peach Muffins
1 egg, beaten
1 c. milk
¼ c. shortening, melted
⅔ c. sugar
½ tsp. salt
¼ tsp. vanilla
1 tsp. lemon juice
¼ tsp. ground cinnamon
2 c. flour
1 T. baking powder
1 c. peaches, peeled, diced

Preheat oven to 375 degrees. Coat 15 muffin cups. In large bowl mix egg and milk. Add shortening, sugar, salt, vanilla and lemon juice. Mix well. Into medium bowl sift cinnamon, flour and baking powder. Fold dry mixture into egg mixture just enough to moisten. Gently fold in peaches. Fill prepared muffin cups two-thirds full. Bake about 15 minutes or until tester inserted in center of muffin comes out clean.

Every word I speak must reflect your grace, Redeeming God. Amen.

But the solid foundation that God has laid cannot be shaken; and these words are written on it: "The Lord knows those who are his . . . ." 2 Timothy 2:19 a TEV

Peanut Butter Bread
1½ c. flour
1 c. sugar
1 T. baking powder
½ tsp. salt
½ c. chunky peanut butter
1 c. rolled oats
1 egg
1 c. milk

Preheat oven to 350 degrees. Coat bread pan. In large bowl combine flour, sugar, baking powder and salt. Stir well. Cut in peanut butter. Add oats, egg and milk. Mix well. Pour into prepared pan. Bake about 1 hour or until brown and tester inserted in center comes out clean. May be served with jelly.

I am yours, you are mine, and all is well, Mighty One of Jacob. Amen.

~~~

Avoid the passions of youth, and strive for righteousness, faith, love, and peace . . . . 2 Timothy 2:22a TEV

Pineapple Bread
2½ c. baking mix
⅓ c. sugar
¼ c. butter or margarine, softened
2 eggs
1 can crushed pineapple, well drained, 3 T. juice reserved
½ c. chopped nuts

Preheat oven to 350 degrees. Grease and flour loaf pan. In large mixer bowl blend all ingredients on low speed 30 seconds, scraping bowl frequently. Beat 2 minutes at medium speed. Pour batter into prepared pan. Bake about 55 minutes or until tester inserted in center comes out clean. Cool 10 minutes. Remove from pan. Cool thoroughly.

No goals are better than those you have for us, Messenger of the Covenant. Amen.

~~~

The Lord's servant must not quarrel. He must be kind toward all, a good and patient teacher.   2 Timothy 2:24 TEV

Prune Bread
1½ c. pitted prunes
1½ c. water
½ c. reserved prune juice
2 T. butter, softened
½ c. sugar
1 egg
1½ c. whole wheat flour
1 tsp. baking powder
1 tsp. baking soda
¼ tsp. salt
1 c. sour milk

Preheat oven to 350 degrees. Coat loaf pan. In small saucepan bring prunes to boil in water. Lower heat and simmer 2 minutes. Remove from heat and cool. Drain prunes, reserving 1 cup prunes and ½ cup prune juice. Mince cooked prunes. In large mixer bowl cream butter and sugar on high speed. Add egg and beat well. Into medium bowl sift flour, baking powder, baking soda and salt. Add about one-quarter of flour mixture to creamed mixture. Mix only until blended. Blend in prune juice lightly. Add remaining flour mixture alternately with sour milk, beating after each addition only until blended. Lightly fold in minced prunes. Spread batter in prepared pan. Bake 50 to 55 minutes or until tester inserted in center comes out clean.

Yes, I must not quarrel but must speak fairly and patiently, Lord Jesus. Amen.

Remember this! There will be difficult times in the last days. For men will be selfish, greedy, boastful, and conceited; they will be insulting, disobedient to their parents, ungrateful, and irreligious; they will be unkind, merciless, slanderers, violent, and fierce; they will hate the good; they will be treacherous, reckless, and swollen with pride; they will love pleasure rather than God; they will hold to the outward form of our religion, but reject its real power. Keep away from these men.

2 Timothy 3:1-5 TEV

Raisin Nut Bread
2 eggs
2 c. sugar
2 c. buttermilk*
¼ c. melted margarine or butter, or vegetable oil
2 c. all-purpose flour
2 c. whole wheat (graham) flour
2 tsp. baking soda
2 tsp. salt
1 c. raisins
1 c. nuts, whole or pieces

Preheat oven to 350 degrees. Grease and flour 2 loaf pans. In large bowl beat eggs. Add sugar gradually and beat well. Add remaining ingredients, in order given, mixing after each addition. Pour into prepared pans. Bake about 1 hour or until tester inserted in center comes out clean. Remove from oven. Turn pans on sides 15 minutes. Turn bread out of pans and set top side up to cool. When cool, refrigerate in plastic bag or wrapped in foil.

*2 cups milk plust 2 tablespoons cider vinegar or lemon juice may be substituted for 2 cups buttermilk.

Evil is all around me, and sometimes I fear I will not survive, Light of the World. Amen.

But they will not go very far, because everyone will see how stupid they are . . . .   2 Timothy 3:9a TEV

Rhubarb Bread
2½ c. flour, divided
1 tsp. baking powder
1 tsp. baking soda
½ tsp. salt
½ c. granulated sugar
1 tsp. ground cinnamon
1 T. butter, melted
1½ c. firmly packed light brown sugar
⅔ c. vegetable oil
1 extra-large egg
1 tsp. vanilla extract
1 c. buttermilk
1½ c. fresh rhubarb, dried, diced ¼ inch square
½ c. broken pecans

Preheat oven to 350 degrees. Coat 2 loaf pans. Into small bowl sift 2¼ cups of the flour, baking powder, baking soda and salt. In small bowl mix granulated sugar and cinnamon. Blend in butter until crumbly. In large mixer bowl cream brown sugar and oil. Add egg and vanilla. Beat well. Alternately add flour mixture and buttermilk to creamed mixture, beating on low speed after each addition only until blended.

In small bowl combine rhubarb and pecans. Stir until evenly mixed. Sprinkle with remaining ¼ cup flour and toss to coat. Fold rhubarb mixture into batter only until fruit and nuts are distributed. Spread batter into prepared pans. Sprinkle cinnamon mixture evenly over batter. Bake 50 minutes or until tester inserted in center comes out clean. Remove from oven. Cool 10 minutes on wire racks. Remove from pans and cool completely on wire racks.

Give them eyes and ears to recognize the evil, Holy One. Amen.

"I am the Alpha and Omega, says the Lord God, who is and who was and who is to come, the Almighty."
Revelation 1:8 NRSV

Ripe Banana Bread
½ c. butter, at room temperature
¾ c. sugar
2 eggs
1 c. all-purpose flour
1 tsp. baking soda
½ tsp. salt
1 c. whole wheat flour
3 large ripe bananas, mashed
1 tsp. vanilla
½ c. walnuts, coarsely chopped

Preheat oven to 350 degrees. Coat bread pan. In large mixer bowl cream butter and sugar until light and fluffy. Add eggs 1 at a time, beating well after each addition. Into separate bowl sift all-purpose flour, baking soda and salt. Stir in whole wheat flour and add to creamed mixture, mixing well. Fold in bananas, vanilla and nuts. Pour mixture into pan. Bake 50 to 60 minutes or until tester inserted in center comes out clean. Cool in pan 10 minutes. Turn out on rack and cool completely.

I bow in awe of your sovereignty, God of All. Amen.

~~~

"I know your affliction and your poverty, even though you are rich."
<div align="right">Revelation 2:9a NRSV</div>

Sweet Cornbread
⅔ c. sugar
1 tsp. salt
⅓ c. butter, softened
1 tsp. vanilla
2 eggs, lightly beaten
2 c. flour
1 T. baking powder

¾ c. yellow cornmeal
1⅓ c. milk

Preheat oven to 400 degrees. Coat 9-inch square pan. In large bowl cream sugar, salt, butter, vanilla and eggs. In medium bowl combine flour, baking powder and cornmeal. Add flour mixture and milk alternately to creamed mixture, blending well after each addition. Bake 20 to 25 minutes or until tester inserted in center comes out clean.

To be rich in grace and joy, this is my hope in you, God of Grace. Amen.

~~~

To everyone who conquers, I will give permission to eat from the tree of life that is in the paradise of God.
<div style="text-align: right;">Revelation 2:7b NRSV</div>

Whole Wheat Banana Bread
3 c. whole wheat flour
2 c. sugar
2 c. mashed ripe bananas, about 5 medium
½ c. coarsely chopped nuts
⅔ c. vegetable oil
2 tsp. baking soda
1 tsp. salt
½ tsp. baking powder
4 eggs

Preheat oven to 350 degrees. Coat bottoms only of 2 loaf pans. In large mixer bowl at low speed, beat all ingredients 30 seconds. Beat on medium speed 45 seconds, scraping bowl frequently. Pour into prepared pans. Bake 50 to 60 minutes or until tester inserted halfway between center and edge comes out clean. Cool 10 minutes. Loosen sides of loaves from pans. Remove from pans. Cool completely before slicing.

If I conquer, Jesus, it is because you strengthen me. Amen.

Whoever conquers will not be harmed by the second death.
Revelation 2:11b NRSV

Zucchini Bread
2 c. sugar
1 c. oil
3 eggs
1 tsp. vanilla
3 c. flour
¼ tsp. baking powder
1 tsp. baking soda
½ tsp. salt
1 tsp. ground cinnamon
1 tsp. ground cloves
1 tsp. ground ginger
2 c. raw zucchini, shredded
1 c. chopped nuts

Preheat oven to 325 degrees. Grease and flour loaf pan or coat with nonstick cooking spray. In large bowl cream sugar, oil, eggs and vanilla. Into medium bowl sift flour, baking powder, baking soda, salt, cinnamon, cloves and ginger. Add to creamed mixture. Mix well. Fold in zucchini and nuts. Bake 1 hour or until tester inserted in center comes out clean.

Death brings no fear for me because of you, God Who Sanctifies. Amen.

VEGGIES AND BEANS

To everyone who conquers I will give some of the hidden
manna . . . .   Revelation 2:17b NRSV

Baked Stuffed Tomato
1 medium tomato
2 T. bread crumbs
½ tsp. Italian herb blend
¼ c. chopped broccoli, steamed
½ tsp. grated Parmesan cheese

Preheat oven to 400 degrees. Cut tomato in half. Scoop out
pulp. In small bowl combine pulp, bread crumbs, herb blend and
broccoli. Fill each tomato half with mixture. Sprinkle with
Parmesan cheese. Bake 5 minutes.

Your manna—I dared not hope it could be mine, but you have
said it will be, Precious Cornerstone. Amen.

To the one who conquers I will also give the morning star.
Revelation 2:28b NRSV

Belgian Carrots
1½ c. diced boiled carrots
2 T. butter
2 tsp. powdered sugar
1 onion, chopped
Salt and pepper
1 T. parsley, chopped

Mix all ingredients and place in greased baking dish. Bake at 350 degrees 15 to 20 minutes.

The morning star, Lord? I confess I don't understand what that is, and yet you will make it mine. Your grace is unfathomable. Amen.

~~~

If you conquer, you will be clothed like them in white robes, and I will not blot your name out of the book of life.
Revelation 3:5a NRSV

Black Bean Chili
1 T. vegetable oil
1½ c. chopped red bell pepper
¼ c. chopped green onion
1 T. chili powder
1 T. ground cumin
¾ tsp. garlic powder
2 cans black beans, about 15 oz. each
⅓ c. ketchup
¼ c. low-fat yogurt
1 c. part-skim cheddar cheese, shredded

In saucepan heat oil. Add red peppers and green onions. Saute. Stir in chili powder, cumin and garlic powder. Saute 30 seconds. Add black beans and bean liquid. Simmer 20 to 25 minutes. Add ketchup and simmer 10 minutes. Stir in yogurt and simmer until heated. Sprinkle with cheddar cheese. Simmer until cheese melts.

That white robe will be the best outfit ever, Lord from Heaven. Amen.

~~~

If you conquer, I will make you a pillar in the temple of my God, you will never go out of it. I will write on you the name of my God, and the name of the city of my God, the new Jerusalem that comes down from my God out of heaven, and my own new name. Revelation 3:12 NRSV

Caramelized Onions
2 tsp. olive oil
1 large onion, sliced or chopped
½ tsp. sugar

Heat olive oil in large skillet over medium heat. Add onion. Cook 5 minutes, stirring occasionally. Sprinkle sugar over onion. Continue cooking until onion is caramelized and golden, about 5 minutes. Yields about ¼ cup caramelized onion.

The only list that matters is yours, Foundation of the World. Amen.

To the one who conquers I will give a place with me on my throne, just as I myself conquered and sat down with my Father on his throne. Revelation 3:21 NRSV

Chinese Carrots
¼ c. vegetable oil
½ c. white vinegar
¾ c. sugar or honey
1 can condensed tomato soup, undiluted
2 lbs. carrots
2 large green peppers, thinly sliced
1 large onion, thinly sliced

In medium saucepan combine oil, vinegar, honey and tomato soup. Mix thoroughly. Pare carrots, slice into "coins" and boil 25 minutes or until tender. Drain and place in large bowl. Add green peppers and onion. Mix well. Pour tomato sauce over vegetables and mix well. Refrigerate at least 24 hours before serving, stirring occasionally. Keeps up to 2 weeks in refrigerator.

My heart overflows because you, God of Forgiveness, have a place for me. Amen.

And all the angels stood around the throne and around the elders and the four living creatures, and they fell on their faces before the throne and worshiped God, singing,
> "Amen! Blessing and glory and wisdom
> and thanksgiving and honor
> and power and might
> be to our God forever and ever! Amen."
>
> Revelation 7:11,12 NRSV

Corn Pudding

20 oz. frozen kernel corn, about 4¼ c.
4 eggs, beaten
2 c. milk or light cream
⅓ c. finely chopped onion
¾ tsp. salt
⅛ tsp. pepper
2 tsp. sugar

Preheat oven to 350 degrees. Butter large casserole dish. In large bowl combine all ingredients. Mix thoroughly. Pour into prepared dish. Bake 1 hour or until set.

Human end is only godly beginning, and I long to begin forever with you, Yahweh. Amen.

"They will hunger no more, and thirst no more;
 the sun will not strike them,
 nor any scorching heat;
 for the Lamb at the center of the throne will be their shepherd,
  and he will guide them to springs of the water of life,
 and God will wipe away every tear from their eyes."
Revelation 7:16,17 NRSV

Danish Limas

20 oz. frozen lima beans
½ c. chopped celery
¼ c. chopped onion
1 c. dairy sour cream
½ c. crumbled blue cheese (2 oz.)
¼ c. chopped pimiento
4 slices bacon, cooked crisp, drained, crumbled

In medium saucepan cook beans, celery and onion in boiling salted water 10 minutes or until tender. Drain well. Stir in sour cream and blue cheese. Cook and stir over low heat until mixture is heated through and cheese is melted. Do not boil. Stir in pimiento. Pour into serving dish. Sprinkle with crumbled bacon.

No more sorrow, no more tears, no more worry, no more trials—I claim your promise as I struggle with mortal matters, God Who Prevails. Amen.

Then God's temple in heaven was opened, and the ark of his covenant was seen within his temple, and there were flashes of lightning, rumblings, peals of thunder, an earthquake, and heavy hail. Revelation 11:19 NRSV

Fried Cucumbers
2 T. butter
2 T. chopped onion
4 large cucumbers, sliced
¼ c. cold water
½ c. sour cream
1 egg yolk, beaten
2 T. sugar
3 T. cider vinegar
1½ tsp. salt
⅛ tsp. pepper
⅛ tsp. paprika

Melt butter in saucepan. Add onion and saute until delicate brown. Add sliced cucumbers and water. Cook until water is absorbed and cucumbers are browned. In small bowl mix sour cream, egg yolk, sugar, vinegar, salt, pepper and paprika. Add to cucumbers and cook slowly until mixture begins to boil.

Elohim, I acknowledge that you command the universe. Amen.

Then I looked, and there was a white cloud, and seated on the cloud was one like the Son of Man, with a golden crown on his head, and a sharp sickle in his hand!

Revelation 15:14 NRSV

Fried Eggplant

1 large eggplant
Salt
Pepper
2 eggs
Garlic powder
½ c. vegetable oil

Wash and pare eggplant. Cut into crosswise slices ⅜ inch thick. Season with salt and pepper. In small bowl beat eggs and garlic powder. Heat oil in skillet. Dip each eggplant slice into egg mixture and fry in skillet, adding oil as needed, until golden brown. May be served with mozzarella cheese, tomato and onion slices on rye toast.

Thank you, Alpha and Omega, for granting us a glimpse of your great glory. Amen.

Then I heard what seemed to be the voice of a great multitude, like the sound of many waters and like the sound of mighty thunderpeals, crying out,
"Hallelujah!
For the Lord our God the almighty reigns."

Revelation 19:6 NRSV

Fried Green Tomatoes

6 to 8 slices bacon
2 or 3 medium green tomatoes
1 egg
1 tsp. water
¼ c. flour
¼ c. light cream or coffee cream
¼ c. sliced green onions, including tops

In skillet fry bacon until crisp. Remove bacon from skillet and crush. Slice tomatoes ¼ inch thick. In small bowl beat egg lightly with water. Place flour in small dish. Dip tomato slices in egg mixture, then in flour. Using fat from bacon, fry tomatoes in skillet until golden brown. Drain well and place in serving dish. Pour off bacon fat. Pour cream into skillet and stir well. Heat cream gently. Spoon over tomatoes. Top with crushed bacon and green onions.

You reign, Mighty One—not kings, princes, premiers, presidents, tyrants, dictators, generals or political parties. Amen.

And the angel said to me, "Write this: Blessed are those who are invited to the marriage supper of the Lamb."

Revelation 19:9a NRSV

Frisky Granny
1 strip bacon, chopped, or 1 tsp. bacon fat
1 tsp. olive oil
1 small yellow onion, chopped
1 head red cabbage (about 2 lb.), trimmed, cored, thinly sliced
2 Granny Smith apples, peeled, cored, chopped
½ c. vegetable or chicken broth, plus more for moisture
¼ tsp. caraway seeds
2 T. red wine vinegar or rice vinegar
Black pepper

In a large nonstick saucepan heat bacon pieces in olive oil over medium heat until bacon crisps. If bacon fat is used, heat fat and oil in saucepan until shimmery. Add onion and saute until soft, about 5 minutes. Stir in cabbage, apples, ½ cup broth and caraway seeds. Increase heat to medium-high, cover and bring to boil. Reduce heat to low, cover and simmer, stirring occasionally, until cabbage is tender, about 20 minutes. If liquid evaporates before cabbage is done, stir in more broth 2 to 4 tablespoons at a time as needed. Add vinegar and pepper. Serve hot. Good with sausage or ham.

Christ the Lamb, I saw your marriage banquet in a dream one night, but I don't have words wonderful enough to describe it. Amen.

He seized the dragon, that ancient serpent, who is the Devil and Satan, and bound him for a thousand years, and threw him into the pit, and locked and sealed it over him, so that he would deceive the nations no more, until the thousand years were ended. Revelation 20:2,3 NRSV

Garlic Lemon Roasted Vegetables

1 lb. tiny new potatoes, halved
1 red bell pepper, cut into large strips or squares
1 green bell pepper, cut into large strips or squares
2 yellow squash, peeled and cubed
2 zucchini, cubed
3 stalks celery, sliced
6 cloves garlic, minced
1 tsp. lemon zest or dried lemon rind
¼ c. lemon juice
3 T. olive oil
1 tsp. sugar
½ tsp. salt
½ tsp. lemon pepper
½ tsp. oregano
¼ tsp. pepper

Preheat oven to 450 degrees. Coat large shallow baking dish. In large bowl combine potatoes, pepper, squash, zucchini, celery and garlic. Mix well. Pour evenly into prepared dish. In small bowl mix lemon zest, lemon juice, olive oil, sugar, salt, lemon pepper, oregano and pepper. Drizzle over vegetables. Bake 450 minutes or until vegetables are tender.

Your power over Satan is absolute, Elah Sh'maya. Amen.

And the devil who had deceived them was thrown into the lake of fire and sulfur, where the beast and the false prophet were, and they will be tormented day and night forever and ever.
Revelation 20:10 NRSV

Green Beans and Cream
2 T. flour
3 T. butter, divided
1 tsp. salt
1 tsp. sugar
¼ tsp. pepper
¼ c. onion, grated
1 c. sour cream
24 oz. cooked green beans
8 oz. grated cheese
½ c. cornflake crumbs

Preheat oven to 350 degrees. In large saucepan combine flour and 2 tablespoons of the butter. Cook gently until paste forms. Remove from heat. Stir in salt, sugar, pepper, onion and sour cream. Fold in cooked beans. Place in 9 by 13-inch baking dish and cover with cheese. In small bowl combine cornflake crumbs and remaining 1 tablespoon butter. Sprinkle on top of beans. Bake about 30 minutes.

Deception will not win in the end because of your power, El Yeshuati. Amen.

And I saw the dead, great and small, standing before the throne, and books were opened. Revelation 20:12a NRSV

Italian Zucchini Bake
3 c. zucchini, sliced thin
1 c. baking mix
½ c. chopped onion
½ c. Parmesan cheese
2 T. dried parsley or ½ c. chopped fresh parsley
½ tsp. salt
½ tsp. pepper
¼ tsp. garlic powder
¼ tsp. dried basil
¼ tsp. dried oregano
½ c. canola oil
4 eggs, beaten
¼ lb. pepperoni, sliced thin
2 c. shredded mozzarella cheese

Preheat oven to 350 degrees. Butter 8 by 12-inch baking dish, large pie pan or casserole dish. In large bowl combine all ingredients. Pour mixture into prepared pan. Bake 40 minutes or until firm. Let stand 10 minutes before serving.

When I stand before your throne, God of Truth, will I be worthy? Amen.

And the dead were judged according to their works, as recorded in the books. Revelation 20:12b NRSV

Marinated Cucumbers
1 c. sour cream
2 T. lemon juice
¼ c. white vinegar
1 tsp. salt
Dash pepper
2 large cucumbers, peeled or unpeeled, sliced thin
1 onion, sliced thin

In medium bowl mix sour cream, lemon juice, vinegar, salt and pepper. In separate bowl mix cucumbers and onion. Combine both mixtures. Cover. Refrigerate several hours before serving.

I heard that you hear our prayers for the dead, God of Knowledge, and ask you to remember.... Amen.

~~~

This is the second death, the lake of fire, and anyone whose name was not found written in the book of life was thrown into the lake of fire. Revelation 20:14b,15 NRSV

Onion Jam
2 T. butter
4 large red onions, thinly sliced
¼ c. balsamic vinegar
¼ c. firmly packed brown sugar
Salt and pepper

Melt butter in large heavy saucepan over medium heat. Add onions. Cover and cook until onions are limp, 10 to 15 minutes. Uncover and cook until all liquid evaporates. Add vinegar and brown sugar. Cook until onions turn deep golden brown and mixture is syrupy, stirring constantly, about 10 minutes.

Jesus, you are the Living Water that quenches the lake of fire before it is too late. Amen.

And I heard a loud voice from the throne saying,
"See, the home of God is among mortals.
He will dwell with them;
they will be his peoples,
and God himself will be with them."

Revelation 20:3 NRSV

Onion Roasted Potatoes

1 envelope onion soup mix
2 lbs. potatoes, cut in large chunks
⅓ c. olive oil or vegetable oil

Preheat oven to 450 degrees. Combine all ingredients in large plastic bag. Close bag securely and shake until potatoes are evenly coated. Pour potatoes into shallow baking dish. Bake, stirring occasionally, 40 minutes or until tender and golden.

Creation awaits your coming, Designer of the World. Amen.

~~~

Then I saw a new heaven and a new earth; for the first heaven and the first earth had passed away, and the sea was no more.

Revelation 21:1 NRSV

Oven Roasted Green Beans

1 lb. fresh green beans, trimmed
4 cloves garlic, thinly sliced
1 T. olive oil
Salt and pepper

Preheat oven to 400 degrees. Coat rimmed baking sheet with cooking spray. Arrange green beans and garlic in single layer on baking sheet. Drizzle with olive oil. Season with salt and pepper. Roast 30 minutes or until tender, stirring every 10 minutes. Transfer beans to bowl. Adjust seasoning if necessary.

We have not cherished the earth enough, Lord of Glory, and we repent. Are we too late? Amen.

He will wipe away every tear from their eyes.
Death will be no more;
mourning and crying and pain will be no more;
for the first things have passed away.
                              Revelation 21:4 NRSV

Picnic Beans

2 oz. sliced Canadian bacon, chopped
⅔ c. chopped onion
1 can black beans, drained, rinsed, about 16 oz.
1 can light red beans, drained, rinsed, about 16 oz.
1 can pinto beans, drained, rinsed, about 16 oz.
1 can great northern beans, drained, rinsed, about 16 oz.
1 can no-salt-added tomato sauce, about 16 oz.
¼ c. cider vinegar
3 T. molasses
¼ c. firmly packed brown sugar
1 tsp. chili powder

Preheat oven to 350 degrees. Place Canadian bacon and onion in nonstick skillet. Cook over medium-low heat, stirring frequently, until onion is tender and edges of bacon are lightly browned. Place beans in large bowl. Add bacon mixture. In separate bowl combine tomato sauce, vinegar, molasses, brown sugar and chili powder. Pour mixture over beans and stir to blend. Spoon into 2-quart baking dish. Bake 45 to 60 minutes.

My pains leave my body when I remember your promise of life eternal, God Who Hears. Amen.

And the one who was seated on the throne said, "See, I am making all things new." Revelation 21:5a NRSV

Roasted Garlic Spread

4 whole garlic heads
⅓ c. water
¼ c. olive or vegetable oil
Sliced French or Italian bread

Preheat oven to 350 degrees. Cut top off each garlic head (pointed end) so that each clove is exposed. Place with cut side up in small ungreased baking dish. Pour water around garlic. Cover and bake 1 hour or until garlic is very soft. Cool 5 minutes. Slowly drizzle oil into center of and over each garlic head. Remove soft garlic from skins. Spread on bread or over cooked meats or vegetables.

For additional herb flavor, place sprig of fresh thyme on cut surface of garlic before roasting.

Roasted garlic can also flavor cream of potato soup. Roast garlic as directed. When cool, squeeze garlic from skin into soup and puree mixture. One whole head flavors 6 to 8 quarts of soup.

I was five years old when I began learning of you, God of Justice, and every day brings another surprise of your goodness. Amen.

Then he said to me, "It is done! I am the Alpha and the Omega, the beginning and the end. To the thirsty I will give water as a gift from the spring of the water of life."

Revelation 21:6 NRSV

Stuffed Red Peppers

6 red bell peppers, seeded and cored
1 T. olive oil
¾ c. chopped onions
1½ c. sliced mushrooms
3 c. cooked rice
1 T. dried parsley flakes, crushed
½ tsp. dried basil
2 c. vegetable juice
1 T. ketchup

Preheat oven to 350 degrees. Boil peppers 5 minutes in boiling salted water. Cool and place in large baking pan. Heat oil in skillet. Saute onions and mushrooms until soft. Add rice, parsley and basil. Cook and mix well. Add vegetable juice and ketchup and mix well. Stuff peppers with mixture. Bake 50 to 60 minutes until tender.

Forgive me, God of My Salvation, for wondering when your kingdom will come, for it is enough to know that it will. Amen.

And there will be no more night; they need no light of lamp or sun, for the Lord God will be their light, and they will reign forever and ever. Revelation 22:8 NRSV

Stuffed Zucchini
3 medium zucchini, unpeeled
Salt and pepper
1 T. butter
½ lb. lean ground beef
⅓ c. chopped celery
¼ c. chopped onion
8 oz. tomato sauce
½ c. soft bread crumbs
¼ c. grated Parmesan cheese

Preheat oven to 375 degrees. Cook zucchini 5 minutes in boiling salted water. Cut in half lengthwise. Scoop out and discard seeds. Sprinkle salt and pepper on zucchini shells and set aside. Melt butter in medium skillet. Add ground beef, celery and onion. Cook and stir until beef turns brown. Add tomato sauce and bread crumbs. Stir well. Spoon mixture evenly into zucchini shells. Place in shallow baking dish. Sprinkle with cheese. Bake uncovered 30 minutes or until zucchini is tender.

My hands will be free on your great day, Emmanuel, to lift praises to you. Amen.

Blessed are those who wash their robes, so that they will have the right to the tree of life and may enter the city by the gates.
Revelation 22:14 NRSV

Sweet and Sour Cabbage

¼ c. butter
½ chopped onion
2 medium tart apples, peeled and coarsely chopped
5 c. shredded red cabbage
½ tsp. ground allspice
¼ c. granulated sugar
¼ c. plus 2 T. cider vinegar or red wine vinegar
1 c. plus 2 T. brown sugar
½ tsp. salt
¼ tsp. pepper
½ tsp. caraway seeds

Melt butter in large skillet. Add onion, apples and cabbage. Stir over medium heat until crisp and tender. In small bowl combine allspice, granulated sugar, vinegar, brown sugar, salt, pepper and caraway seeds. Mix well. Combine with cabbage mixture. Cook and stir until heated through.

Variation: Add ½ teaspoon ground cinnamon.

One True God, we have spent thousands of years making laws that you will erase in the twinkling of an eye. Forgive us for wasting the time and gifts you gave us. Amen.

The Spirit and the bride say, "Come."
And let everyone who hears say, "Come."
And let everyone who is thirsty come.
Let anyone who wishes take the water of life as a gift.

> Revelation 22:17 NRSV

Sweet and Sour Green Beans

3 strips bacon
⅔ c. chopped onions
3 T. flour
1 tsp. prepared mustard
2 tsp. cider vinegar
½ c. sugar
1 tsp. salt
¼ tsp. black pepper
2 cans green beans, drained, about 16 oz. each
½ c. juice from green beans

Brown bacon in skillet until crisp. Remove from pan and crumble. Saute onions in bacon fat until golden brown. Stir in flour, mustard, vinegar, sugar, salt, pepper, beans and juice. Bring to boil. Add more bean juice if needed. Sprinkle bacon pieces over top before serving.

I kneel, I touch the water, I drink the water, and I humbly thank you for receiving me as your own, Great God. Amen.

Amen. Come, Lord Jesus!   Revelation 22:20b NRSV

Zucchini Rounds
⅓ c. baking mix
¼ c. grated Parmesan cheese
⅛ tsp. pepper
2 eggs, lightly beaten
2 c. shredded unpared zucchini
2 T. butter

Combine baking mix, cheese and pepper. Add eggs and fold in zucchini. Melt butter in skillet and drop batter into 6 large rounds. Brown about 3 minutes on each side. Serve with butter.

Yes, Lord Jesus, we wait for you! Amen.

-0-

INDEX

APPETIZERS AND DIPS

ABC Dip	1
Bagelettes	2
Barbecued Mini Franks	2
Cheese and Spinach Puffs	3
Cheese Ball	4
Chip Dip	4
Girlfriend Friendly Dip	5
Gooey Bean Dip	5
Hanky Panky	6
Oriental Wings	6
Pizza Butter	7
Pocket Bread/Tomato Topping	8
Poor Folks' Caviar	8
Roberta's Shrimp Dip	9
Sausage Balls	10
Spicy Taco Dip	10
Spinach Bars	11
Spinach Dip	12
Stuffed Mushrooms	12
Sweet and Tangy Meatballs	13
Swiss Cheese Spread	13
Taco Chips	14
Tortilla Bean Dip	14
Veggie Dip	15
Water Chestnuts with Sauce	15

BEEF AND PORK

Barbecued Beef	17
Basic Barbecue Sauce	18
Beef Stroganoff	19
Big Burger	20
Braised Steak	21
Cheesy Barbecued Meatballs	22
Cola Pot Roast	23
Enchiladas	24
Gone All Day Stew	24
Ham Barbecue	25
Ham Cassoulet	26
Ham Loaf	26
Hawaiian Kielbasa	27
Honey Glazed Baked Ham	28
Hungarian Pork Chops	28
Mock Cabbage Rolls	29
Norwegian Meatballs	30
Poor People's Steak	30
Roast Beef	31
Shish Kebab Formula	32
Smothered Pork Chops	34
Sukiyaki	35
Sweet and Sour Meatballs	36
Teriyaki Steak	37
Unstuffed Peppers	37

BEVERAGES

Berry Banana Smoothie	39
Berry Smoothie	40
"Champagne" Punch	40

Cocoa Mix	41
Cranberry Punch	41
Double Lime Punch	42
Egg Nog	42
Flavored Coffees	43
Friendship Tea	44
Fruit Punch for 75 People	44
Hymn Book Punch	45
Kool Fruit Punch	46
Mock Champagne	46
Orange Crush Punch	47
Orange Julie	47
Orange Julius	48
Orange Smoothie	48
Party Punch	49
Presbyterian Punch	49
Punch from Gelatin	50
Russian Tea	50
Slush	51
Spiced Tea Mix	51
Wassail	52
Wedding Punch	52

BREAD, ROLLS AND BISCUITS

Angel Biscuits	53
Baking Mix	54
Baking Powder Biscuits	54
Breakfast Sticky Buns	55
Bride's Bread or Rolls	56
Buttermilk Cornbread	57
Butterscotch Rolls	58
Cheese Boereg	59
Cinnamon Raisin Biscuits	60
Cream of Tartar Biscuits	61
English Muffins	62
Garlic Biscuits	62
Garlic Pizza Crust	63
Garlic Toast	64
Hoagie Buns	65
Honey Cornbread	66
Hush Puppies	67
Kentucky Spoon Bread	67
Never Fail Bread	68
Oatmeal Bread	69
Raisin Bread	70
Sixty Minute Rolls	70
Smoky Mountain Cornbread	71
Sour Milk Biscuits	72
Spoon Bread	72

BROWNIES AND BARS

Blondies	73
Bunny Delights	74
Caramel Chocolate Bars	75
Caramel Oatmeal Squares	76
Chocolate Revel Bars	77
Colonial Pumpkin Bars	78
Date Bars	79
Date Chews	80
Dirt Bars	80
English Toffee	81
Fig Newsomes	82

Fruit and Chocolate Dreams	82
Fudge Nut Orange Bars	84
Happy Squares	85
Kate's Brownies	86
Lemon Bars	87
Lemon Chiffon Dessert	88
Minty Refrigerator Brownies	89
Oatmeal Toffee Bars	90
O-Henriettas	91
Peanut Butter Brownies	92
Peanut Butter Fudgy Bars	92
Pecan Turtle Bars	93
Seven Layer Bars	94
Valentine Fudge Brownies	95

CAKES AND FROSTINGS

Apple Dapple Cake	97
Banana Cake with Olive Oil	98
Blackberry Cake	99
Brownie Cheesecake	100
Caramel Pecan Coffee Cake	101
Caramel White Chocolate Cheesecake	102
Carrot Cake	103
Chocolate Skinny Cake	104
Cinnamon Crunch Coffee Cake	105
Coconut Cake	106
Cola Cake	107
Dark Applesauce Cake	108
Maude's Fudge Butter Pudding Cake	110
Overnight Coffee Cake	111
Pineapple Orange Sunshine Cake	112
Pumpkin Pie Cake	113
Quick Pineapple Coffee Cake	114
Ring of Coconut Fudge Cake	114
Spanish Bar Cake	116
Texax Sheetcake	118
Turtle Cake	120
Twinkles	121
Unfrosted Oatmeal Cake	122
Upside Down German Chocolate Cake	123
Vanilla Texas Sheetcake	124

CANDY

Butterscotch Fudge	126
Caramels	127
Caramel Fudge	127
Caramel Turtles	128
Chocolate Big Batch Fudge	128
Chocolate Covered Cherries	129
Chocolate Fantasy Fudge	130
Chocolate Yummies	131
Clark Larks	132
Coconut Cremes	132
Fanny Farmer Fudge	133
Honey Nut White Fudge	134
Martha's Fudge	135
Microwave Caramels	136
Molasses Fudge	136
Never Fail Chocolate Fudge	137

Old Time Peanut Butter Fudge	138
Pastel Butter Mints	138
Pecan Logs	139
Penuche	140
Seafoam Fudge	140
Soda Cracker Candy	141
Sweetened Condensed Milk	142
Vanilla Caramels	142
Vanilla Fudge	143
White Candy Fantasy Clusters	144

CASSEROLES

Armenian Pizza	145
Baked Potato Skin Casserole	146
Big Deal Mexican Dish	146
Block Party Beans	147
Cabbage Casserole	148
Cavatini	148
Cheeseburger Casserole	149
Cheese Potato Casserole	150
Cheesy Chicken and Rice	150
Chicken Casserole	151
Chicken Noodle Casserole	152
Creamy Mushroom Chicken	152
Easy Potato Casserole	153
Houseboat Chicken	154
Hungarian Goulash	154
Meatloaf Casserole	155
One Dish Casserole	156
Oven Baked Beef Stew	157
Pizza Casserole	158
Pork Chop Supper	159
Spinach Meat Roll	160
Stuffed Spaghetti Squash	161
Various Veggie Lasagna	162
Veggie Casserole	164
Yum-A-Setta	164

CHICKEN AND TURKEY

Baked Chicken	165
Barbecued Turkey Meatballs	166
Basic Stuffing for Birds	167
Brined Turkey	168
Chicken and Chestnuts	170
Chicken and Rice	171
Chicken Bake	171
Chicken Mozzarella	172
Chicken Noodles in the Slow Cooker	172
Chicken Parmesan	173
Chicken Pilau	174
Chicken Quicken	174
Chicken Rollups	175
Chicken Spaghetti	176
Chicken and Cashews	177
Church Supper Chicken Sandwiches	178
Company Chicken	178
Country Style Chicken	179
Feta Chicken Bake	180
Meatloaf Sensation	180
Shredded Chicken Sandwiches	181
So Speedy Chicken	181

Sour Cream Chicken	182
Sweet and Sour Chicken	183
Turkey Meatloaf	184

COOKIES

Applesauce Raisin Cookies	185
Best Oatmeal Cookies	186
Butterscotch Refrigerator Cookies	186
Cake Mix Cookies	187
Cranberry Sugar Cookies	188
Crunch Drop Cookies	188
Date Pinwheels	189
Date Surprises	190
Everyday Cookies	191
Favorite Oatmeal Cookies	192
Forgotten Cookies	193
Gingerbread Cookies	194
Grandma's Soft Sugar Cookies	195
Lemon Whippersnaps	196
Neverland Cookies	196
Outrageous Chocolate Chip Cookies	197
Peanut Butter Cutouts	198
Shortbread Cookies	199
Slice and Bake Lemon Crisps	200
Soft Sugar Cutouts	200
Special Cookies	202
Stone Jar Cookies	202
Sugar-Free Oatmeal Cookies	203
Texas-Size Almond Church Cookies	204
Thick and Chewy Chocolate Chip Cookies	205

EGGS AND QUICHES

Arlington Brunch	207
Bacon and Egg Pizza	208
Breadless Egg Casserole	208
Breakfast Casserole	209
Breakfast Pizza	210
Creamed Eggs	210
Egg and Cheese Bake	211
Frittata with Veggies	212
Eggs Creole with Sausage	213
Egg Souffle	214
Holiday Breakfast Casserole	214
Make Ahead Breakfast Casserole	215
Mediterranean Frittata	216
Omelet Sandwiches	216
Poached Eggs	217
Potato Egg Casserole	218
Potato Omelet	218
Potluck Casserole	219
Quiche Lorraine	220
Sausage and Sun-Dried Tomato Strata	221
Skinny Spinach Cheddar Squares	222
Sour Cream Quiche	223
Springtime Egg Skillet	224
Super Easy Quiche	224
Tomato Egg Scramble	225

FISH AND SEAFOOD

Baked Fish	227
Baked Tuna and Cheese Swirls	228
Broiled Lake Trout	229
Chinese Egg Lobster	230
Cod Sandwiches	230
Fish and Chips	231
Fish Batter for Frying	232
Fish with Butter Sauce	233
Hearty Nicoise Salad	234
Hot Tuna Sandwiches	235
Poached Italian Cod	236
Salmon Baked in Potato Shells	237
Salmon Cakes with Creamed Peas	238
Salmon Croquettes	239
Salmon Loaf	240
Salmon Easy Patties	240
Shrimp and Rice	241
Shrimp Salad	242
Shrimp Scampi Four Ways	243
South Pacific Filets	244
Stuffed Filet of Sole	245
Sweet and Sour Shrimp	246
Tuna Burgers	246
Tuna Noodle Casserole	247
Tuna-Potato Chip Casserole	248

FROZEN TREATS AND TOPPINGS

Blender Peach Sherbet	249
Butter Pecan Topping	250
Butterscotch Topping	250
Chocolate Marble Freeze	251
Cocoa Syrup	252
Freezer Ice Cream	252
Frozen Pineapple Dessert	253
Frozen Pumpkin Dessert	254
Frozen Strawberry Dessert	254
Fruit Slush	255
Hot Fudge Topping	255
Ice Cream Pie	256
Italian Sorbet	256
Lemon Freeze	257
Lemon Milk Sherbet	258
Lemon Topping	258
Lime Delight	259
Milky Way Dessert	260
Orange Ice	260
Orangy Chocolate Pops	261
Pineapple Delight	261
Pistachio Ice Cream Dessert	262
Pumpkin Ice Cream Squares	262
Three Fruit Sherbet	263
Strawberry Ice	264

PASTA AND RICE

Baked Macaroni and Cheese	265
Cajun Chicken Fettucine	266
Cheesy Rice	266
Chicken Noodle Stew	267
Deluxe Macaroni Salad	268
Easy Baked Manicotti	269

Fettucine Alfredo	270
Fried Rice with Ham, Onion and Peas	271
Lasagna	272
Macaroni Salad	273
Mexican Rice	274
Nutty Vegetable Pilaf	274
One Skillet Spaghetti	275
Orzo Salad	276
Pasta Salad	276
Pasta Salad with Sweet Vinaigrette	277
Rice and Mushroom Bake	278
Rice Creole	279
Rice Pilaf	280
Sesame Noodles	281
Skillet Spaghetti	282
Souper Macaroni	283
Stir Fried Rice Confetti	284
Tuna and Bowtie Salad	285
Vegetable Lasagna	286

PIES, COBBLERS AND DUMPLINGS

Apple Dumplings	287
Banana Cream Pie	288
Blini	288
Butterscotch Pie	289
Caramel Crunch Peach Pie	290
Caramel Pecan Pie	290
Carrot Pie	291
Cherry Pie	291
Chocolate Pie	292
Chuck's Never Fail Meringue	293
Coconut Creme Pie	294
Decadent Peanut Butter Pie	295
Easy Fruit Cobbler	296
Frozen Lime Pie	296
Key Lime Pie	297
Lemon Velvet Pie	298
No-Crust Pecan Pie	299
Oatmeal Pie	300
Old Fashioned Cobbler	300
Perfect Pumpkin Pie	301
Pie Crust for Prebaking	302
Pie Crust with Buttery Shortening	302
Pie Crust with Egg	303
Pie Crust with Graham Crumbs	303
Pie Crust with Lard and Shortening	304
Pie Crust with Oatmeal	304
Pie Crust with Puffed Rice	305
Pie Crust with Shortening	305
Pie Crust with Vegetable Oil	306
Pie Crust with Vegetable Oil and Sugar	306
Pie Crust with Whole Wheat Flour	307
Pineapple Sour Cream Pie	307
Raisin Pie	308
Russian Apple Pie	308
Shoo Fly Pie	309
Slow Cooker Cobbler	310
Sour Cream Apple Pie	311
Walnut Cream Pie	312

POTATOES

Baked Sliced Potatoes	313
Breakfast Potatoes	314
Candied Sweet Potatoes	314
Caramel Sweet Potatoes	315
Company Potatoes	316
Crumb Topped Potatoes	316
Decadent Mashed Potatoes	317
Golden Parmesan Potatoes	318
Gourmet Cheese Potatoes	318
Grated Potatoes	319
Hash Brown Cheese Potato Casserole	320
Honey Mustard Potato Salad	320
Hot German Potato Salad with Bacon	321
No-Fry Spicy Potato Skins	322
Old Fashioned Potato Salad	323
Orange Pecan Sweet Potatoes	324
Oven Fries	325
Potato Stuffing	326
Refrigerator Mashed Potatoes	327
Scalloped Potatoes	328
Supper Potatoes	328
Sweet Potato Balls	329
Sweet Potato Casserole	330
Twice Baked Potatoes	331
Zesty Sweet Potato Sticks	332

SALADS AND DRESSINGS

Amish Cole Slaw	333
Bacon Dressing	334
Bean Salad Dressing	334
Blue Cheese Dressing	335
Caesar Dressing	335
Chicken Salad	336
Cucumber Freezer Salad	336
Foo Yung Toss	337
Frosted Cranberry Salad	338
Fruit Salad Dressing	338
Green Salad	339
Hot Bacon Dressing	340
Italian Dressing	341
Kathy's Shower Salad	342
Macaroni Vegetable Salad	343
Navy Bean Salad	344
Romaine Orange Salad	345
Spicy Sweet Ham Salad	346
Spinach Salad	347
Strawberry Pretzel Salad	348
Sweet Balsamic Mayonnaise	348
Taco Salad	349
Thousand Island Dressing	349
Three Bean Wacky Salad	350
Western Dressing	350

SOUPS AND STEWS

Baked Potato Soup	351
Campfire Chicken Noodle Stew	352
Cheese Soup	352
Cheesy Baked Potato Soup	353
Chicken Chowder with Cheese	354
Clam Chowder	355

Country Clam Chowder	356
Cream of Celery Soup	357
Cream of Pea Soup	357
Cream of Potato Soup	358
Cream of Tomato Soup	358
French Onion Soup	359
Ham Stew	360
Healthy Chicken Chowder	360
Hearty Bean and Frank Soup	361
High Fiber Chili	362
Lentil Soup	363
One Nation Chicken Stew	364
Onion Soup	365
Potato Bean Soup	366
Quick Minestrone Soup	367
Quick Tortellini Bean Soup	368
Sausage and Bean Chowder	368
Split Pea and Ham Soup	369
Wild Rice Soup	370

SWEET BREADS AND MUFFINS

Apple Muffins	371
Banana Muffins	372
Becky's Banana Bread	373
Blueberry Muffins	374
Bran Cereal Muffins	374
Bran Muffins	375
Carrot Raisin Muffins	376
Cranberry Bread	377
Easy Drop Danish	378
Fresh Apple Loaves	378
Great Gingerbread Muffins	379
Holiday Pumpkin Bread	380
Lemon Bread	381
Monkey Bread	382
Morning Muffins	382
Peach Muffins	383
Peanut Butter Bread	384
Pineapple Bread	384
Prune Bread	385
Raisin Nut Bread	386
Rhubarb Bread	387
Ripe Banana Bread	388
Sweet Cornbread	388
Whole Wheat Banana Bread	389
Zucchini Bread	390

VEGGIES AND BEANS

Baked Stuffed Tomato	391
Belgian Carrots	392
Black Bean Chili	392
Caramelized Onions	393
Chinese Carrots	394
Corn Pudding	395
Danish Limas	396
Fried Cucumbers	397
Fried Eggplant	398
Fried Green Tomatoes	399
Frisky Granny	400
Garlic Lemon Roasted Vegetables	401
Green Beans and Cream	402

Italian Zucchini Bake	403
Marinated Cucumbers	404
Onion Jam	404
Onion Roasted Potatoes	405
Oven Roasted Green Beans	405
Picnic Beans	406
Roasted Garlic Spread	407
Stuffed Red Peppers	408
Stuffed Zucchini	409
Sweet and Sour Cabbage	410
Sweet and Sour Green Beans	411
Zucchini Rounds	412

www.ingramcontent.com/pod-product-compliance
Lightning Source LLC
Chambersburg PA
CBHW070715160426
43192CB00009B/1192